99

WITHDR

THE STRUGGLE FOR
WOMEN'S RIGHTS

THE STRUGGLE FOR
WOMEN'S RIGHTS

THEORETICAL AND HISTORICAL SOURCES

GEORGE KLOSKO   MARGARET G. KLOSKO

 Prentice Hall Upper Saddle River, New Jersey 07458

Library of Congress Cataloging-in-Publication Data
The Struggle for women's rights / [edited by] George Klosko, Margaret
   G. Klosko
       p.   cm.
   Includes bibliographical references (p.   ) and index.
   ISBN 0-13-676552-1
       1. Women—Suffrage—United States—History. 2. Women—Suffrage—
   Great Britain—History.   3. Suffragists—United States.
   4. Suffragists—Great Britain.   I. Klosko, Margaret G.
   JK1896.S85   1999
   324.6′23′0973—dc21   98-8552
                                                                       CIP

Editorial Director: *Charlyce Jones Owen*
Editor in chief: *Nancy Roberts*
Sr. acquisitions editor: *Beth Gillett*
Associate editor: *Nicole Conforti*
Marketing manager: *Christopher DeJohn*
Production liaison: *Fran Russello*
Editorial/production supervision: *Kerry Reardon*
Prepress and manufacturing buyer: *Mary Ann Gloriande*
Cover director: *Jayne Conte*

This book was set in 10/12 Palatino by KR Publishing Services
andwas printed and bound by Courier Companies, Inc.
The cover was printed by Phoenix Color Corp.

©1999 Prentice-Hall, Inc.
Simon & Schuster/A Viacom Company
Upper Saddle River, New Jersey 07458

Printed in the United States of America

10 9 8 7 6 5 4 3 2 1

ISBN 0-13-676552-1

Prentice-Hall International (UK) Limited, *London*
Prentice-Hall of Australia Pty. Limited, *Sydney*
Prentice-Hall of Canada Inc., *Toronto*
Prentice-Hall Hispanoamericana, S.A., *Mexico*
Prentice-Hall of India Private Limited, *New Delhi*
Prentice-Hall of Japan, *Tokyo*
Simon & Schuster Asia Pte. Ltd., *Singapore*
Editora Prentice-Hall do Brasil, Ltda., *Rio de Janeiro*

To Caroline, Susanna, and Deborah Klosko
and Roberta Gutman

CONTENTS

PREFACE

In the Introduction to *A Vindication of the Rights of Women*, Mary Wollstonecraft begs women's indulgence if she should "treat them like rational creatures, instead of flattering their *fascinating graces* ... as if they were in a state of perpetual childhood." Until her time, women had been viewed "as a kind of subordinate beings, and not as part of the human species." In her great work, Wollstonecraft makes important strides toward permanently altering this conception of women throughout the Western world. As we see in this volume, the struggle to define women's essential nature was the theoretical plane on which concrete political issues concerning women's rights and their place in society were fought out.

In this volume, we present both theoretical and historical sources bearing on the struggle for women's rights in the United States and Great Britain. We focus on the right to vote, though earlier sources are less tightly bound to this. Because the two greatest theoretical discussions of women's rights were by British authors, Wollstonecraft and John Stuart Mill, we concentrate on the theoretical side of the conflict in Britain and present a greater volume of historical sources for the United States in which the political struggle was more protracted. But for each side of the Atlantic, we present both theoretical and historical sources, thus allowing the reader to see exactly how abstract ideas were applied to practical political issues by figures on different sides of the issues.

It may seem that discussion of women's right to vote is of little con-temporary relevance. Women have had the vote since the early decades of this century, and few people now contest this. But the material we present has implications concerning not only the status of women but wider politi-cal issues as well. The debates over women's suffrage presented in this vol-ume demonstrate how conceptualizations of women's nature worked them-selves out politically, and how attempts to alter the political status of women required theoretical redefinition of their nature. Ideas have conse-quences. Debates over women's suffrage allow the reader to trace out spe-cific implications of specific abstract ideas.

By concentrating on women's right to vote, we are able to trace the development of ideas in detail. Arguments were advanced against women's suffrage as well as for it, and central issues cannot be understood without proper attention to both. Inclusion of substantial antisuffrage material is this volume's most distinctive feature. Although these arguments may seem to have passed into the dustbin of history, full equality for women has not been achieved in either the United States or Britain. Arguments similar to those employed by opponents of women's suffrage are still used to justi-fy women's subordinate status in different areas of contemporary societies.

Connections between conceptions of women's nature and views of their rightful place in society have important implications for other areas of political life. But many of our sources go beyond the theoretical plane. The struggle for women's suffrage was a political struggle. We include pro-nouncements by central political actors and attempt to capture discussion of the issues in popular publications. We also present a selection of argu-ments from expediency that were employed in the United States, to give a fuller picture of the political debate. In order to provide some idea of how the debate was carried on in British society, we present two important pub-lications against woman's suffrage and their replies.

We would like to thank a number of people who have helped make this a better book. First are Richard Holway, Debra Morris, and, especially, the many scholars who have preceded us in this area. We are also grateful to Beth Gillett, our editor at Prentice Hall, for valuable suggestions. We wish to thank Gregg Stelmach, Jannea Prescott, Maureen Morrison, and Ann Witkowski for research assistance, and our reviewers for Prentice Hall: Virginia Curry, *Southern Methodist University;* Lynn H. Leverty, *University of Florida;* and Jeffrey L. Bernstein, *Eastern Michigan University.* Above all we are grateful to the professional staff at Alderman Library at the University of Virginia, especially Interlibrary Loan, Library Express on Grounds, and the Microfilm Room, without whose assistance this work would not have been possible.

George Klosko
Margaret G. Klosko

THE STRUGGLE FOR
WOMEN'S RIGHTS

INTRODUCTION

In the eighteenth century, women in the colonial United States and Britain had few legal and political rights. Their social standing, inferior to that of men, was held to be justified according to distinctive ideas of women's nature. In this volume, we trace the process through which women gained the right to vote—and other political rights. But this was more than a political struggle. In the realm of ideas, woman's nature had to be reconceived as substantially equal to men's, if not identical in all respects. Though success on this level has been less than complete, it has been an integral part of the struggle for women's rights.

I WOMEN IN THE EIGHTEENTH CENTURY

In the eighteenth century, in both social and legal terms, the position of women was decidedly inferior to that of men. The legal systems of most American colonies were based on English Common Law which denied women important rights. They were excluded from juries, not allowed to vote, or to sue in court. While single women, needing a certain degree of independence, were able to hold property, the legal status of married women was akin to that of children and the mentally deficient. They were not allowed to own property; legally, all of a woman's property belonged to her husband. This included whatever she inherited or brought into the marriage, her wages, if she worked outside the home, and even the clothes on her back. An American woman enjoyed certain rights denied an English woman. She was granted the right to share her husband's home and bed, to be supported by her husband, even if he abandoned her, and to be protected from physical violence.[1] But on the whole women in both countries were legally second-class citizens.

In both the colonies and Britain, women's status was supported on religious and philosophical grounds and deeply grounded in Common Law. Under Common Law, a married woman was held not to require legal rights of her own, because her rights were "covered" by her husband. This doctrine of *coverture* was supported by the Common Law notion that husband and wife are one person. This is signified by the fact that, at marriage, the wife takes the husband's name, to be known henceforth as Mrs. John Smith. Coverture is explicated in the important *Commentaries on the Laws of England,* written by William Blackstone in 1765–1769:

> By marriage the husband and wife are one person in law; that is, the very being or legal existence of the woman is suspended during the marriage, or at least incorporated and consolidated into that of the husband; under whose wing, protection and cover, she performs everything.[2]

The conception of coverture is consistent with and no doubt strongly influenced by Biblical teaching. Christianity arose against a background of ancient social practices and teachings. Throughout the ancient world, women were relegated to an inferior position. This is justified in the story of Eve in Genesis. The opening chapter of Genesis describes the simultaneous creation of man and woman: "So God created man in his own image, in the image of God he created him; male and female" (Gen. 1:27). However, in the following chapter, a second creation is described, according to which man was created alone (Gen. 2:7) and placed in the Garden of Eden. Because it was not good for man to be alone, God made woman as a helper for him:

> So the Lord God caused a deep sleep to fall upon the man, and while he slept took one of his ribs and closed up its place with flesh; and the rib which the Lord God had taken from the man he made into a women and brought her to the man. (Gen. 2:21–2)

And she was called "Woman, because she was taken out of man" (Gen. 2:23). It was of course woman who was seduced by the serpent, as a result of which Adam and Eve, man and woman, were expelled from the Garden of Eden. As further consequences of Eve's transgression, women were to be afflicted with pain during childbirth and were to be ruled over by their husbands (Gen. 3).

Detailed discussion of women's position in society was given by St. Paul. Although he declared that all people are equal in the eyes of God, whether slave or free, male or female (Gal. 3:38), Paul meant this in regard to spiritual equality, or equality in the sight of God. He emphatically supported the social distinctions of his time—in regard to existing subordination of women and preserving the institution of slavery.[3]

In non-Christian philosophy as well, women's inferior status was justified. For instance, Aristotle claims females are imperfect. They are in effect incomplete males.[4] In the *Politics*, he argues that their souls are inferior to those of men. As slaves justly occupy inferior status because of deficiencies in the reasoning parts of their souls, something similar is true of women: "The deliberative faculty in the soul is not present at all in a slave; in a female it is present but without authority, in a child present but undeveloped."[5] It is therefore natural for men to rule over women. Rule over women is similar to rule over children, but while the latter is a temporary condition because (male) children grow to be like and equal to their parents, rule over women is permanent.[6]

Throughout most of the world and the bulk of human history, the realities of women's lives were consistent with accounts of their natural inferiority. This was true in Britain and the colonial United States. To focus on the latter, women's activities were largely confined to the home and family. Women had virtually no public life and few educational opportunities. No college in the United States would admit women before 1834 (Oberlin College). It was unheard of for women to speak in public outside the sphere of religious activity. They were debarred from participation in the political process. In an era before modern, labor-saving devices, providing for basic necessities was enormously laborious. While men worked in the fields, or for wages, women were engaged in endless rounds of preparing food, cooking, sewing, childbearing, and childrearing. Though the legal position of a married woman was actually inferior to that of a single woman, for most women life centered on marriage and family. Securing the best possible husband was essential for a woman's future happiness, and so, not surprisingly, a central theme of women's education was how they could be most appealing to men.

In sum, then, the upshot of women's position in the eighteenth century in both Britain and the colonial United States was that women were held to be by nature different from men. Naturally suited to the activities of home and family, they should live out their lives in this domain, leaving the public realm for men in regard to business, politics, and economics. The characteristics and activities of the two sexes were naturally distinct and the differences should be respected. It was not until the end of the eighteenth century, with the American and French revolutions and their doctrines of natural rights, that this entire structure was seriously challenged.

In England at the close of the eighteenth century, traditional ideas of women's nature were criticized and a new view given classic expression in Mary Wollstonecraft's *Vindication of the Rights of Women* (1792). Earlier writers, such as John Fordyce, John Gregory, and Jean-Jacques Rousseau, had presented a view of women as by nature delicate, sensual creatures, lacking fully developed reasoning capacities. According to Wollstonecraft, such views "have contributed to render women more artificial, weak characters, than they would otherwise have been, and consequently, more useless members of society." Their works "tend ... to degrade one-half of the human species and render women pleasing at the expense of every solid virtue."[7] The presence of Rousseau on Wollstonecraft's list is at first sight surprising since he was a radical democrat and proponent of equality in his major political work *The Social Contract* (1762). In his celebrated *Discourse on the Origin of Inequality* (1755), he had depicted women's nature as essentially equal to that of men. But Rousseau clearly presents women as inferior and frivolous creatures in Book V of his classic work on education, *Emile* (1762). In *Vindication*, Wollstonecraft excoriates Rousseau and other writers who had propounded similar views. Upholding the equality and rationality of women, she argues for women's education and women's rights.[8]

II WOMEN'S SUFFRAGE IN THE UNITED STATES

In the United States in the nineteenth century, demands for women's rights first emerged within the struggle against slavery. The Abolition movement was fed by Enlightenment ideas of natural rights and political equality of all men, regardless of wealth, and Protestant Christian ideas of individualism (especially as espoused in certain Quaker circles). In the 1830s women such as Sarah and Angelina Grimké, Sojourner Truth, Lucretia Mott, and Elizabeth Cady Stanton formed anti-slavery societies and worked tirelessly to secure the abolition of slavery. It was through their efforts to secure freedom for slaves, and subsequently to gain political rights for freed black men, that these women came to embrace the notion of political equality—with special emphasis on universal suffrage—for all people regardless of color or gender.

These women learned to organize politically in defiance of conservative public opinion that women's proper sphere was the home, not the political arena. Although bred in a culture that denied women political rights and did not permit women any degree of political expression, these particular women gained limited access to the political arena in their abolitionist work. Along with other delegates, American women attended the World's Anti-Slavery Convention in London in 1840. When the assembled delegates voted to deny the women in the American delegation participation in the conference, relegating them to a curtained balcony above the convention floor, Elizabeth Cady Stanton and Lucretia Mott saw the need for a movement to work for the political rights of women. Using the parlance of twentieth-century political activism, one might say that American women at the London convention were "radicalized."

Deeply disappointed by their treatment at the hands of the most politically enlightened men in Britain, Stanton and Mott vowed to fight for rights for American women. In her memoirs, Stanton recalls walking about London arm-in-arm with Lucretia Mott. Speaking of their disappointment, they "resolved to hold a convention as soon as we returned home, and form a society to advance the rights of women."[9]

Eight years after the demoralizing English Abolitionist convention, Stanton and Mott convened a woman's rights convention in Seneca Falls, New York, which was attended by more than 300 people. From this meeting issued one of the earliest and most famous documents of American feminism—the Declaration of Sentiments (see pages 99–103). This manifesto, written the same year as Karl Marx' and Friedrich Engels' *Communist Manifesto*, self-consciously echoed the Declaration of Independence: "We hold these truths to be self-evident; that all men and women are created equal." Accordingly, Stanton and the delegates at the first woman's rights convention equated the rights of America's unenfranchised, politically unendowed female population with the inalienable and God-given rights that Thomas Jefferson had claimed for white, male citizens of the newly sovereign United States of America. The Seneca Falls Declaration also enumerated a long list of grievances and specific resolutions calling for granting various rights to women. These included rights to free speech and to own property; the Declaration went so far as to call for women's "equal participation with men in the various trades, professions and commerce." But the resolution that caused the most controversy was the one calling for enfranchisement of women. Henry Stanton, Elizabeth Cady Stanton's husband, who had been a staunch supporter of women's rights, found the demand for enfranchisement so outrageous that he left town to avoid seeing his wife humiliated when she publicly claimed woman's right to vote. Indeed, the 11 other resolutions in the Declaration passed unanimously, while the resolution demanding suffrage for women passed by a close margin. Curiously, 60 years later, when women's rights workers were gearing up for a final push to achieve the vote for women, demands for economic equality and equal access to professions were set aside as too radical in favor of the more politically acceptable demand for suffrage.

In the years intervening between the Seneca Falls Convention and the Civil War, women worked for all manner of rights for women. In 1854, Susan B. Anthony, guided by the campaign in New York that led to the achievement of property rights for women in the Married Woman's

Property Act of 1848, collected six thousand signatures for a petition demanding women's control over their own earnings, their children in the event of divorce, and for the vote.

These issues were largely set aside because of the Civil War, which absorbed the attention and energy of most Americans. The public-spirited women who had fought for abolition and who had recently focused on women's rights now turned their attention to the war effort, especially to emancipating slaves. Stanton (who had not invited any black women to the Seneca Falls convention) passionately reengaged in the fight for the emancipation, and after emancipation, the enfranchisement of African-Americans.

After the war, Congress ratified the Thirteenth Amendment (1865), which abolished slavery. After achieving the long sought freedom for enslaved Africans, abolitionist suffragists set their sights on constitutional remedies for women's disenfranchisement. They viewed the Fourteenth Amendment, which was to include voting rights provisions, as the means by which women might finally achieve the vote. Republican framers of the legislation, however, had a different purpose. Hoping to consolidate power in the South, they wanted to swell Southern voting rolls with new Republican voters. Not inclined to have passage of the Amendment crippled by contentious debate, they mandated federally protected citizenship rights for all men "born or naturalized in the United States." Under this amendment, black men were assured citizenship and accompanying rights. Suffrage became a federally guaranteed right. This right, which heretofore had been under the jurisdiction of individual states, was now under federal jurisdiction; the federal government protected the right of black men to vote. Unfortunately for women, for the first time in the Constitution, the Fourteenth Amendment attached the word, "male," to citizenship and suffrage rights, thus introducing gender discrimination into the right to vote. Ratification of the amendment, in 1868, was a bitter blow to women who had worked for Emancipation and had hoped to gain voting rights for women along with those for freed slaves. Suffragists watched black men gain the right to vote, while their own right to vote, along with full citizenship status, was constitutionally denied.

After the ratification of the Fourteenth Amendment, suffragists attached their hopes for achieving the vote for women to the Fifteenth Amendment. This amendment, ratified in 1870, sought further to ensure the right to vote for formerly enslaved Africans by prohibiting the denial of suffrage on the basis of "race, color, or previous condition of servitude." Suffragists argued that the word, "sex," should be included in the list of protected conditions, but Republicans could not be swayed from their intention to grant suffrage only to black men. Because of Republican intransigence on this issue, Northern feminists who had passionately aligned themselves with the Republican party before and during the war became resolutely non-partisan (with occasional political demonstrations against the party in power) throughout the 50 years it took to gain the franchise for women.

In addition to congressional Republicans' refusal to support women's suffrage, abolitionists would not help in this effort either. They argued that efforts to gain the vote for women would undermine the campaign to gain political rights for black men. White female suffragists, never free of the racism of their time, broke with their former allies in the abolition movement. They adopted racist arguments in their increasingly desperate fight to achieve political equity with men. They claimed that educated white women were degraded by the granting of the vote to uneducated black men. They argued that they were more deserving than uneducated former slaves and recent immigrants, who voted only by right of their sex.[10]

In part because their efforts to gain the vote were frustrated, suffragists became focused on this issue to the exclusion of other political and personal rights. The cause of women's suffrage took on added importance in women's rights organizations and in the general political sphere. Discussions about suffrage became more tendentious. Anti-suffrage organizations sprang up over the political landscape, with writers and speakers producing anti-suffrage arguments for an alarmed male electorate and their unenfranchised wives. The telescoping of the woman's rights agenda into the singular demand for suffrage energized suffrage opponents along with proponents. Controversy over the relationship between rights for former slaves and rights for women broke the woman suffrage movement into two opposing camps. When abolitionists refused to support the enfranchisement of women along with the enfranchisement of freed slaves, Elizabeth Cady Stanton pointed out that freed slaves included women also. Frederick Douglass, who had supported Stanton's call for woman suffrage at Seneca Falls, now argued that the oppression of and violence committed against black men in the South during the Reconstruction period was so serious that acquisition of voting rights for black men was more urgent than for black women. Only Sojourner Truth among black political activists supported the enfranchisement of women. She said that "if coloured men get their rights and not coloured women theirs, you see, coloured men will be masters over the women."[11]

Boston-based suffragists such as Lucy Stone and Julia Ward Howe would not break from the Abolitionist movement and acceded to its demands that women wait for the vote until a politically more opportune moment. In 1869, New York feminists, who refused to wait, withdrew from the Equal Rights Association, the umbrella organization for women's rights activists, and formed the National Woman Suffrage Association (NWSA). In response, in 1870 Boston suffragists formed a second organization, the American Woman Suffrage Association (AWSA). The narrowly focused names of these organizations, compared to their mother organization

(Equal Rights Association), underline the emerging new emphases of women's rights activists. But under the leadership of Elizabeth Cady Stanton, the NWSA argued for more far-ranging rights for women as well. Stanton saw women's oppression as deep rooted in Western culture, originating in biblical attitudes toward women. Stanton and Susan Anthony regarded the enfranchisement of women as attaining only the first political tool women would need to gain full human rights. This larger perspective also led NWSA to focus on a constitutional amendment to achieve suffrage for women.

Further exacerbating the split in the suffrage movement was the case of Victoria Woodhull, a New York stockbroker and woman-about-town. Woodhull was an anomalous suffragist. One of ten children of a former tavern maid and spiritualist mother and a father who ran a traveling medicine show, she did not fit the suffragist profile—middle class, liberal, and devoutly Protestant. Therefore, in January 1871, the suffragist community was shocked to hear that a woman unknown to them would be addressing the House Judiciary Committee on the subject of woman suffrage—the first woman in the history of Congress to appear in such a role. Woodhull's speeches in front of the committee were impressive—assured and argued like a lawyer with citations of recent Supreme Court cases and state and constitutional law (see Victoria Woodhull's Address to the Judiciary Committee on pages 112–116). According to Woodhull, even without a new constitutional amendment, women were guaranteed suffrage by virtue of constitutional guarantees in the Fourteenth and Fifteenth Amendments that ensured political rights to all citizens. Because women are citizens, her argument went, women already had the franchise. She urged Congress to enforce this guarantee with legislation that would prevent abridgement of this right. Although members of the Judiciary Committee were impressed with the force of Woodhull's argument, they voted to table the proposal, never to revisit it.

Delegates of NWSA present at the hearing were also impressed with Woodhull's presentation, but although unwilling to dismiss her with the alacrity of the men of the committee, they found her background and unusual domestic arrangements troubling. In addition to living with her colorful parents in a New York City mansion, she shared quarters with various relatives who assumed phony ranks and professional titles and with her first and second husbands. Susan B. Anthony, Elizabeth Cady Stanton, and the NWSA supported Woodhull, even after she began calling marriage legalized prostitution and advocating free love. Although her views, stated vigorously without regard for Victorian sensibilities, did not differ greatly from those of the more radical wing of the suffrage movement, Lucy Stone and the conservative AWSA called for suffragists to disassociate themselves from both the message and the messenger. Anthony and Stanton did so only after Woodhull became enmeshed in scandal over her shocking ideas and unconventional living arrangements, ruining her career and damaging the credibility of her supporters. The Woodhull episode helped drive the woman's rights movement in more conservative directions, including fierce and exclusive focus on achieving the vote for women.

Lucy Stone as leader of AWSA, always more conservative than Stanton and Anthony in her view of women's rights, helped take charge of this new approach. She and Julia Ward Howe believed the most practical strategy was to work to amend individual state constitutions. In 1869 the territory of Wyoming granted women the vote, but it wasn't until after 1890 when AWSA and NWSA merged into the new National American Woman Suffrage Association (NAWSA) that the piecemeal fashion envisioned by Stone and Howe achieved significant results. In 1890 Wyoming entered the Union as the first state that provided suffrage for women in its constitution. Colorado granted the vote to women in 1893; Utah and Idaho did the same in 1896. After a 14-year hiatus, Washington gave women suffrage in 1910, followed by California in 1911, Arizona, Kansas, and Oregon in 1912, the Alaska territory in 1913, Montana and Nevada in 1914, New York in 1917, and Michigan, Oklahoma, and South Dakota in 1918. Women were granted suffrage in presidential elections in Illinois in 1913, Nebraska, North Dakota, and Rhode Island in 1917, and in Indiana, Iowa, Maine, Minnesota, Missouri, Ohio, Tennessee, and Wisconsin in 1919.

After the brief NAWSA presidencies of Stanton and Anthony, Stone's conservative vision prevailed in the leadership of Carrie Chapman Catt. Catt and other spokeswomen for the movement employed arguments formerly eschewed by women's rights activists. While earlier in the nineteenth century, the argument for expanding women's political rights had been based on the idea of natural rights, especially as enunciated in the Declaration of Independence, at the end of the century, suffragists argued for women's suffrage on more instrumental grounds. Especially important was an argument based on perceived dangers from enfranchising illiterate former slaves in the South and hordes of immigrants in the North. Suffragists argued that the influence of such undesirable voters could be countered by enfranchising educated women. Although they did not propose to take the vote away from people who already had it, they wished to institute education requirements for the future enfranchisement of men as well as women. In this way, suffragists began to appeal to nativist sentiments in the North and racist ones in the South. Arguments along these lines were made by Stanton, Catt, and other suffragists, including Henry Blackwell and Belle Kearney. (see Henry Blackwell, "A Solution to the Southern Question" on pages 157–161 and Belle Kearney, "The South and Woman Suffrage" on pages 162–169).

Suffragists also responded to anti-suffrage writers who claimed that women were by nature unsuited to participate in the political process. Anti-suffrage authors argued that women's emotional nature and divinely ordained role as keeper of the children and home made them incapable of operating in the political sphere. Antis argued that women were too good, too morally pure, to vote. They claimed that the political process would taint and corrupt womanly virtue. To counter these arguments, suffragists claimed that womanly virtue when applied to the political process would morally elevate the electorate, the government, and the entire body politic. Claims of female moral superiority inspired claims that led suffragists to depart from the original Enlightenment assumption of the equality of all human beings. Suffragists resorted to anti-democratic claims of moral superiority of women in order to address Victorian sentiments about the sacredness of hearth and home.

A more radical tack was taken by Stanton, who directly assailed the religious foundation of anti-suffragist views. As Stanton noted:

> When in the early part of the Nineteenth Century, women began to protest against their civil and political degradation, they were referred to the Bible for an answer. When they protested against their unequal position in the church, they were referred to the Bible for an answer.[12]

Stanton therefore organized a revising committee to assess and criticize what were traditionally understood to be anti-woman elements of the Bible.

But more important than such radical criticisms were political events and the role the woman's movement played in them. By the second decade of the Twentieth Century NAWSA had about two million members. Around the year 1910, it was joined by women who had worked in Britain with "suffragettes" in their campaign for the vote. American suffragists were tutored in the more radical, militant tactics of their British counterparts and returned to the United States determined to energize the American woman suffrage movement. While their organization, the Women's Party, could claim only 50,000 members, it became highly visible on the political scene. The Women's Party led by Alice Paul (1885–1977) worked to defeat Woodrow Wilson in the 1916 presidential campaign. The party targeted woman suffrage states, and its members crisscrossed the country holding rallies and railing against an administration that had kept women from exercising their citizenship rights. While Wilson carried 10 of the 12 equal suffrage states, it was apparent that women had voted against him. Women voters in Illinois, the only state where votes were tallied by sex, voted against Wilson by a ratio of two to one.

The Women's Party's tactics became more militant after the United States' entry into the First World War. Its members picketed the White House 24 hours a day for weeks on end. They derided the Wilson government's claims that the United States was fighting for democracy abroad when, according to them, democratic principles were egregiously violated at home. For several months, the government tolerated raucous vigils outside the White House, but it was eventually emboldened by editorials that condemned the picketers, calling them militant and unpatriotic. Police began arresting picketers, who were imprisoned in the brutal Occaquan workhouse in Virginia. Emulating previously imprisoned British suffragettes, Alice Paul and others of her party demanded to be treated as political prisoners and went on hunger strikes. Their ill-treatment captured the public's attention and created sympathy for their cause. Several months after their imprisonment, the women were released and immediately returned to their picketing.

NAWSA never joined the Women's Party pickets, and its members condemned the latter's antiwar stand. American women in general and members of NAWSA specifically were active in support of war efforts, and their support was noted by the public and by politicians. In 1914, at the beginning of the war, a proposed amendment to the Constitution granting women suffrage was reintroduced. This amendment, known as the "Anthony Amendment," had first been introduced in Congress in 1878 and defeated in 1887. Reintroduced, it was defeated by a vote of 34 in favor, 35 against, a good deal short of the two-thirds majority required for an amendment to the United States Constitution. At the end of the war, on January 10, 1918, the amendment was passed by the House of Representatives, 274 to 136; in the Senate it was passed on June 4, 1919, 66 to 30. An extensive ratification campaign was carried out during the next year. Because the antis generally controlled the Southern states, suffragists had to carry almost all the other states to achieve ratification. On August 18, 1920, the state of Tennessee became the twenty-sixth state to ratify the Nineteenth Amendment. American women had at last won the right to vote. The text of the Amendment is as follows:

> Sect. 1. The rights of citizens of the United States to vote, shall not be denied or abridged by the United States or by any State on account of sex.
>
> Sect. 2. Congress shall have power to enforce this article by appropriate legislation.

III THE BRITISH EXPERIENCE

In Britain, philosophical discussions about women's rights began earlier than in the United States, but political action began later. The struggle for women's rights in the United States produced no theoretical work comparable to Wollstonecraft's *Vindication of the Rights of Women* or John Stuart Mill's *The Subjection of Women* (1869) (see Mary Wollstonecraft, *Vindication of the Rights of Women* on pages 32–51 and John Stuart Mills, *Subjection of Women* on pages 57–74). Mill, who is a major figure in the history of philosophy and the history of political thought, was unusual among great theorists in the liberal tradition in defending women's rights. As a member of Parliament, he attempted to amend the second Reform Act of 1867, which increased suffrage in Britain to include women's suffrage (see John Stuart Mill, "Suffrage for Women" on pages 173–176). This was the first time the question of women's right to vote was debated in the legislature of a modern country. Although Mill's attempt failed, it attracted 73 votes.[13]

Mill's father, James Mill, also a noted theorist, had developed an important argument for democracy in his "Essay on Government" (1820). James Mill argued that only a democratic government, in which public officials were elected and subject to dismissal by the people, could be trusted to safeguard the people's interest. But according to Mill, this did not require that women be allowed to vote, because their interests were encompassed in those of their fathers and husbands. The flaws in this reasoning were sharply pointed out by Thomas Macaulay, among others, who noted circumstances in which women's interests could diverge from those of the men in their households (see Thomas Macaulay, "Mill On Government" on pages 55–56).

In *Subjection of Women,* Mill presents a detailed account of the treatment of women in existing societies, how this stifles their ability to develop to their full potential, and detracts from the happiness of their husbands as well as their own. Addressing the central question of women's nature, Mill argues that, because of the subordinate position in which they have been kept, women's nature cannot be known in existing society. Far from being justified by distinctive qualities in their nature, women's subordination to men is simply a residue of the slavery and tyranny that had been pervasive in earlier forms of society.

On the plane of practical politics, the British movement for woman suffrage had origins quite different from those in the United States. As we have noted, in the United States, the movement originated in the Abolitionist movement. In Britain, slavery, abolished in 1833, did not have a deep hold on the non-colonial economy and did not have the power to inspire efforts to democratize the electoral process. Instead, the woman suffrage movement originated in general efforts to expand political rights to a larger proportion of the British citizenry.

The first great reform of voting rights statutes came with the Reform Act of 1832, which extended the narrowly held franchise to a wider range of English citizens. But even with this reform, five out of six British men were left unenfranchised. In addition, this act formally disenfranchised women by the addition of the words "male person" to the requirements for voting. But as in the United States, a parliamentary flourish that was meant to put an end to talk of female enfranchisement energized the beginnings of a movement.

Subsequent extensions of the franchise did not help women's cause. The Reform Acts of 1867 and 1884 further extended the vote to some working-class voters, leaving the electorate at about 16.5 percent of the British citizenry. In Britain, the dilemma for suffragists (called "suffragettes") was somewhat similar to that of American suffragists. The suffragists fought for the franchise for themselves, although possibly at the expense of the enfranchisement of formerly enslaved African men. In Britain, most early discussions of extending the franchise to women focused on property-holding women. Thus suffragettes had to worry about gaining the vote for upper-class women at the expense of unenfranchised working-class men.

In Britain, the issue of woman suffrage became entangled in political competition between the Conservative and Liberal parties. The Liberal party was more reformist than the Conservative, and the suffragettes at first saw it as the political engine for achieving their goals. But in 1866, the Conservative party seemed to offer some hope when Benjamin Disraeli, the Tory prime minister, made a speech in Parliament arguing that if women were allowed to own land and to be peeresses, they should be allowed to vote. This endorsement led women to think they were assured the vote, since they had support in Parliament from both parties. As time went by, however, suffragettes discovered that they had no support at all among lawmakers. Through four ministries, the Liberal Prime Minister William Gladstone resisted Parliamentary efforts to enfranchise women, while the Conservative party, in spite of Disraeli's early endorsement, voted against all measures to extend parliamentary voting rights to women. Much as in the United States, women in Britain were kept from voting because of a variety of motives—genuine belief that women were not morally and emotionally suited to participate in government, conservative adherence to the status quo, and political expedience. It was argued by the Liberal party, and later by the Labor party, that agitation for suffrage for British women would undermine the chances of extending the franchise to unenfranchised British men. But widespread opposition was a spur to political action.

In 1865 John Stuart Mill was elected to Parliament from Westminster after an election campaign in which he did not spend any money toward his election, or actively campaign for the office. Before the election, he had clearly expressed his support for the enfranchisement of women and treated a scandalized electorate to the spectacle of women speaking out in public in support of his election. Not even his friends expected him to be elected.

In 1866, Barbara Bodichon approached Mill about presenting an as yet uncanvassed petition for woman suffrage in the House of Commons. He agreed to do so with the condition that at least 100 signatures be on the document. Within three weeks, 1499 signatures were gathered, and the British woman suffrage movement was born. As noted above, in 1867 Mill presented the first amendment on woman suffrage to the House of Commons. The 73 votes his amendment received gave suffragettes reason to foresee future progress. Further increasing their hopes, an amendment granting women the vote in municipal elections was successful. The argument was advanced that women had been granted the vote by the parliamentary Act of 1850 which stated that "all Acts importing the masculine gender shall be deemed to include females unless the contrary be expressly provided." But as in the United States, with the Woodhull argument, this maneuver was repulsed. In 1868, the decision of a British Court went against woman suffrage.

Faced with such defeats, activists in the newly mobilized British movement developed arguments much the same as those of their American counterparts. They did not demand the vote on the basis of natural rights that implied similarity between their natures and those of men. Rather, women were owed the vote because of unique qualities of the female sex. In 1878 Millicent Fawcett explained that she advocated suffrage for women "because I wish to strengthen true womanliness in women, and because I want to see the womanly and domestic side of things weigh more and count for more in all public concerns."[14] Having seen resistance to the idea that women's nature is the same as men's, suffragettes began to fight fire with fire. Fawcett and other moderates argued that women were different and declared that this difference made women's vote valuable.

Radical suffragettes pursued different tactics. Emmeline Pankhurst and her cohort were radicalized by Parliamentary failures to gain suffrage for women. Pankhurst led the Women's Social and Political Union (WSPU), an organization whose ideology and tactics were in stark contrast to the rival National Union of Women's Suffrage Societies (NUWSS) led by Millicent Fawcett. Fawcett had faith that a gradualist approach would eventually yield parliamentary results; Faith, Perseverance, Patience was the motto of the NUWSS. Pankhurst, on the other hand, declared that "the argument of the broken pane of glass is the most valuable argument in modern politics."[15] And panes of glass she, her daughter Christabel, and the women of the WSPU did break. A campaign of window breaking in the streets of West London in 1912 was accompanied by demonstrations, arrests, hunger strikes, forced feeding of hunger strikers, vandalization of art, and the interruption of Derby Day in 1913 when a leader of the movement, Emily Wilding, threw herself in front of the king's horse, bringing down the horse, the jockey, and ending her life.

Wilding's sacrifice drove the militants to a frenzy of activity. By 1913, one thousand suffragettes had been jailed, with many further challenging authority in jail with hunger strikes. To avoid furnishing more martyrs to the cause, Parliament passed the so-called "Cat and Mouse Act" that permitted authorities to release hunger-striking prisoners and then rearrest them after they had regained their health to serve the rest of their sentences. Emmeline Pankhurst, jailed 12 times in 1913, became ever more cantankerous in her views, expelling many members, including her daughters Sylvia and Adela Pankhurst, from the WSPU for insufficient dedication to the movement. Very few beside Emmeline, her daughter Christabel, and a few devotees of Pankhurst remained in the WSPU. Men were now vilified as oppressors of women—because they opposed woman suffrage and because, the claim went, they promoted venereal disease and prostitution. Though emotions had reached a fevered pitch, when World War I broke out in 1914, Emmeline and Christabel Pankhurst abruptly gave up their fanatic suffrage activity to devote themselves to the war effort. Germans replaced British men as the enemy in the Pankhurst rhetoric, and the government granted amnesty to all imprisoned suffragettes. Millicent Fawcett also abandoned suffrage activity, devoting the NUWSS to supporting the war effort.

As in the United States, the wartime dedication of suffrage activists in Great Britain swayed public opinion in their favor. In 1918, British women over 30 were granted the vote. Women between the age of 21, the age when men could vote, and 30 were not granted the vote until 1928. Partial measures extending the franchise were typical in Great Britain. However, hesitancy at granting women under 30 full voting rights was indicative of the refusal to see women's nature as on a par with men's. The moral, political, and emotional reliability of women has continued to be a subject of widespread debate, both in Britain and the United States.

NOTES

1. Carol Hymowitz and Michaele Weissman, *A History of Women in America* (New York, 1978), p. 23.
2. William Blackstone, *Commentaries on the Laws of England*, 4 vols., Vol. I; *Of the Rights of Persons* (1765; rpt. Chicago, 1979), p. 430.
3. 1 Cor. 12:13; Gal. 3:28; Ephes. 5:22–4; 1 Cor. 11:3, 14:34–5; 1 Tim. 2:11–14.
4. *Generation of Animals* 729a21–b25, 775a15–16, 776a30–1.
5. Aristotle, *Politics* 1260a12–4; Aristotle, *The Politics*, rev. ed., T. Sinclair and T. Saunders, eds. and trans. (Harmondsworth, 1981).
6. Aristotle, *Politics*, 1259b9–10.
7. M. Wollstonecraft, *A Vindication of the Rights of Women* (1792; rpt. New York, 1891), p. 38. See also below, pp. 32–51..
8. Material from *Emile* is found below, pp. 19–25.
9. Elizabeth Cady Stanton, *Eighty Years and More* (1898; rpt. New York, 1971), pp. 82–3.
10. See Elizabeth Cady Stanton et al., eds., *History of Woman Suffrage*, 6 vols. (New York and Rochester, 1881–1922), Vol. II, Chap. 19.
11. Ibid., pp. 193–4.
12. Elizabeth Cady Stanton, *The Woman's Bible*, 2 parts (New York, 1895 and 1898) Part I, p. 8. See also below, pp. 125–130.
13. M. S. Packe, *The Life of John Stuart Mill* (London, 1954), p. 492.
14. Quoted in Bonnie Anderson and Judith Zinsser, *A History of Their Own* (New York, 1988), Vol. II, p. 361.
15. Ibid., p. 364.

Part I

Theoretical Contributions

JEAN-JACQUES ROUSSEAU

J ean-Jacques Rousseau (1712–1778) is one of the great figures in the history of political thought. Author of classic works such as *Discourse on the Origins of Inequality* (1755) and *The Social Contract* (1762), he had a profound effect on political and social thought in the eighteenth century; his ideas were perhaps the most important intellectual influence on the French Revolution. Rousseau was a master of many genres; he wrote plays, operas, a dictionary of music, and devised a new system of musical notation. His epistolary novel, *The New Heloise*, was the most popular novel of the eighteenth century. Rousseau's autobiography, *Confessions*, helped launch the Romantic movement which stressed emotion and man's closeness to nature over reason and its accomplishments. In *Emile*, he made profound and long-lasting contributions to educational theory. *Emile*, from which the selections here are taken, contains Rousseau's best known reflections on women's nature and potential.

EMILE (SELECTIONS)

Although Rousseau was generally a radical critic of existing social and political structures, his views on women were deeply problematic. In the *Discourse on the Origins of Inequality*, Rousseau describes women's nature as essentially the same as men's, with the implication that existing subordination of women is part of the overall process of corruption and decay that accounts for the basic features of modern society. However, in *Emile*, published in 1762, Rousseau presents an account of women as naturally different from men. In the excerpt reproduced here from Book 5 of *Emile*, he moves from the need for women to cultivate the virtues necessary to ensure the legitimacy of their children to far-reaching claims concerning their nature, which is different from that of men, and so requires different education. "Even the tiniest little girls love finery." Girls are naturally interested in adornment, because of their concern for what people think of them. They are incapable of difficult intellectual pursuits: "The search for abstract truths ... is beyond a woman's grasp; their studies should be thoroughly practical." *Emile* provides a veritable catalog of eighteenth-century sexual stereotypes. Because Rousseau was a vivid, popular, and enormously influential writer, it is not surprising that Mary Wollstonecraft assails his views, in *A Vindication of the Rights of Women*, granting him pride of place as the first of her targets.

EMILE*

BOOK V

We have reached the last act of youth's drama; we are approaching its closing scene.

It is not good that man should be alone. Emile is now a man, and we must give him his promised helpmeet. That helpmeet is Sophy. Where is her dwelling-place, where shall she be found? We must know beforehand what she is, and then we can decide where to look for her. And when she is found, our task is not ended. "Since our young gentleman," says Locke, "is about to marry, it is time to leave him with his mistress." And with these words he ends his book. As I have not the honour of educating "A young gentleman," I shall take care not to follow his example.

SOPHY, OR WOMAN

Sophy should be as truly a woman as Emile is a man, *i.e.*, she must possess all those characters of her sex which are required to enable her to play her part in the physical and moral order. Let us inquire to begin with what respects her sex differs from our own....

The consequences of sex are wholly unlike for man and woman. The male is only a male now and again, the female is always a female, or at least all her youth; everything reminds her of her sex; the performance of her functions requires a special constitution. She needs care during pregnancy and freedom from work when her child is born; she must have a quiet, easy life while she nurses her children; their education calls for patience and gentleness, for a zeal and love which nothing can dismay; she forms a bond

*Selections from the Barbara Foxley translation of *Emile* are reprinted with permission from David Cambell Publishers, Ltd.

between father and child, she alone can win the father's love for his children and convince him that they are indeed his own. What loving care is required to preserve a united family! And there should be no question of virtue in all this, it must be a labour of love, without which the human race would be doomed to extinction.

The mutual duties of the two sexes are not, and cannot be, equally binding on both. Women do wrong to complain of the inequality of man-made laws; this inequality is not of man's making, or at any rate it is not the result of mere prejudice, but of reason. She to whom nature has entrusted the care of the children must hold herself responsible for them to their father. No doubt every breach of faith is wrong, and every faithless husband, who robs his wife of the sole reward of the stern duties of her sex, is cruel and unjust; but the faithless wife is worse; she destroys the family and breaks the bonds of nature; when she gives her husband children who are not his own, she is false both to him and them, her crime is not infidelity but treason. To my mind, it is the source of dissension and of crime of every kind. Can any position be more wretched than that of the unhappy father who, when he clasps his child to his breast, is haunted by the suspicion that this is the child of another, the badge of his own dishonour, a thief who is robbing his own children of their inheritance. Under such circumstances the family is little more than a group of secret enemies, armed against each other by a guilty woman, who compels them to pretend to love one another.

Thus it is not enough that a wife should be faithful; her husband, along with his friends and neighbours, must believe in her fidelity; she must be modest, devoted, retiring; she should have the witness not only of a good conscience, but of a good reputation. In a word, if a father must love his children, he must be able to respect their mother. For these reasons it is not enough that the woman should be chaste, she must preserve her reputation and her good name....

When once it is proved that men and women are and ought to be unlike in constitution and in temperament, it follows that their education must be different. Nature teaches us that they should work together, but that each has its own share of the work; the end is the same, but the means are different, as are also the feelings which direct them. We have attempted to paint a natural man, let us try to paint a helpmeet for him.

You must follow nature's guidance if you would walk aright. The native characters of sex should be respected as nature's handiwork. You are always saying, "Women have such and such faults, from which we are free." You are misled by your vanity; what would be faults in you are virtues in them; and things would go worse, if they were without these so-called faults. Take care that they do not degenerate into evil, but beware of destroying them.

On the other hand, women are always exclaiming that we educate them for nothing but vanity and coquetry, that we keep them amused with trifles that we may be their masters; we are responsible, so they say, for the faults we attribute to them. How silly! What have men to do with the education of girls? What is there to hinder their mothers educating them as they please? There are no colleges for girls; so much the better for them! Would God there were none for the boys, their education would be more sensible and more wholesome. Who is it that compels a girl to waste her time on foolish trifles? Are they forced, against their will, to spend half their time over their toilet, following the example set them by you? Who prevents you teaching them, or having them taught, whatever seems good in your eyes? Is it our fault that we are charmed by their beauty and delighted by their airs and graces, if we are attracted and flattered by the arts they learn from you, if we love to see them prettily dressed, if we let them display at leisure the weapons by which we are subjugated? Well then, educate them like men. The more women are like men, the less influence they will have over men, and then men will be masters indeed.

All the faculties common to both sexes are not equally shared between them, but taken as a whole they are fairly divided. Woman is worth more as a woman and less as a man; when she makes a good use of her own rights, she has the best of it; when she tries to usurp our rights, she is our inferior. It is impossible to controvert this, except by quoting exceptions after the usual fashion of the partisans of the fair sex....

When I consider the special purpose of woman, when I observe her inclinations or reckon up her duties, everything combines to indicate the mode of education she requires. Men and women are made for each other, but their mutual dependence differs in degree; man is dependent on woman through his desires; woman is dependent on man through her desires and also through her needs; he could do without her better than she can do without him. She cannot fulfill her purpose in life without his aid, without his goodwill, without his respect; she is dependent on our feelings, on the price we put upon her virtue, and the opinion we have of her charms and her deserts. Nature herself has decreed that woman, both for herself and her children, should be at the mercy of man's judgment.

Worth alone will not suffice, a woman must be thought worthy; nor beauty, she must be admired; nor virtue, she must be respected. A woman's honour does not depend on her conduct alone, but on her reputation, and no woman who permits herself to be considered vile is really virtuous. A man has no one but himself to consider, and so long as he does right he may defy public opinion; but when a woman does right her task is only half finished, and what people think of her matters as much as what she really is. Hence her education must, in this respect, be different from man's education. "What will people think" is the grave of a man's virtue and the throne of a woman's....

Even the tiniest little girls love finery; they are not content to be pretty, they must be admired; their little airs and graces show that their heads are full of this idea, and as soon as they can understand they are controlled by "What will people think of you?" If you are foolish enough to try this way with little boys, it will not have the same effect; give them their freedom and their sports, and they care very little what people think; it is a work of time to bring them under the control of this law.

However acquired, this early education of little girls is an excellent thing in itself. As the birth of the body must precede the birth of the mind, so the training of the body must precede the cultivation of the mind. This is true of both sexes; but the aim of physical training for boys and girls is not the same; in the one case it is the development of strength, in the other of grace; not that these qualities should be peculiar to either sex, but that their relative values should be different. Women should be strong enough to do anything gracefully; men should be skillful enough to do anything easily.

The exaggeration of femine delicacy leads to effeminacy in men. Women should not be strong like men but for them, so that their sons may be strong. Convents and boarding-schools, with their plain food and ample opportunities for amusements, races, and games in the open air and in the garden, are better in this respect than the home, where the little girl is fed on delicacies, continually encouraged or reproved, where she is kept sitting in a stuffy room, always under her mother's eye, afraid to stand or walk or speak or breathe, without a moment's freedom to play or jump or run or shout, or to be her natural, lively, little self; there is either harmful indulgence or misguided severity, and no trace of reason. In this fashion heart and body are alike destroyed....

Boys and girls have many games in common, and this is as it should be; do they not play together when they are grown up? They have also special tastes of their own. Boys want movement and noise, drums, tops, toy-carts; girls prefer things which appeal to the eye, and can be used for dressing up—mirrors, jewellery, finery, and specially dolls. The doll is the girl's special plaything; this shows her instinctive bent towards her life's work. The art of pleasing finds its physical basis in personal adornment, and this physical side of the art is the only one which the child can cultivate.

Here is a little girl busy all day with her doll; she is always changing its clothes, dressing and undressing it, trying new combinations of trimmings well or ill matched; her fingers are clumsy, her taste is crude, but there is no mistaking her bent; in this endless occupation time flies unheeded, the hours slip away unnoticed, even meals are forgotten. She is more eager for adornment than for food. "But she is dressing her doll, not herself," you will say. Just so; she sees her doll, she cannot see herself; she cannot do anything for herself, she has neither the training, nor the talent, nor the strength; as yet she herself is nothing, she is engrossed in her doll and all her coquetry is devoted to it. This will not always be so; in due time she will be her own doll.

We have here a very early and clearly-marked bent; you have only to follow it and train it. What the little girl most clearly desires is to dress her doll, to make its bows, its tippets, its sashes, and its tuckers; she is dependent on other people's kindness in all this, and it would be much pleasanter to be able to do it herself. Here is a motive for her earliest lessons, they are not tasks prescribed, but favours bestowed. Little girls always dislike learning to read and write, but they are always ready to learn to sew. They think they are grown up, and in imagination they are using their knowledge for their own adornment.

The way is open and it is easy to follow it; cutting out, embroidery, lace-making follow naturally. Tapestry is not popular; furniture is too remote from the child's interests, it has nothing to do with the person, it depends on conventional tastes. Tapestry is a woman's amusement; young girls never care for it.

This voluntary course is easily extended to include drawing, and art which is closely connected with taste in dress; but I would not have them taught landscape and still less figure painting. Leaves, fruit, flowers, draperies, anything that will make an elegant trimming for the accessories of the toilet, and enable the girl to design her own embroidery if she cannot find a pattern to her taste; that will be quite enough. Speaking generally, if it is desirable to restrict a man's studies to what is useful, this is even more necessary for women, whose life, though less laborious, should be even more industrious and more uniformly employed in a variety of duties, so that one talent should not be encouraged at the expense of others....

I would not altogether blame those who would restrict a woman to the labours of her sex and would leave her in profound ignorance of everything else; but that would require a standard of morality at once very simple and very healthy, or a life withdrawn from the world. In great towns, among immoral men, such a woman would be too easily led astray; her virtue would too often be at the mercy of circumstances; in this age of philosophy, virtue must be able to resist temptation; she must know beforehand what she may hear and what she should think of it.

Moreover, in submission to man's judgment she should deserve his esteem; above all she should obtain the esteem of her husband; she should not only make him love her person, she should make him approve her conduct; she should justify his choice before the world, and do honour to her husband through the honour given to the wife. But how can she set about this task if she is ignorant of our institutions, our customs, our notions of propriety, if she knows nothing of the source of man's judgment, not the passions by which it is swayed? Since she depends both on her own conscience and on public opinion, she must learn to know and reconcile these two laws, and to put her own conscience first only when the two are opposed to each other. She becomes the judge of her own judges, she decides when she should obey and when she should refuse her obedience. She weights their prejudices before she accepts or rejects them; she learns to trace them to their source, to foresee what they will be, and to turn them in her own favour; she is careful never to give cause for blame if duty allows her to avoid it. This cannot be properly done without cultivating her mind and reason....

The search for abstract and speculative truths, for principles and axioms in science, for all that tends to wide generalisation, is beyond a woman's grasp; their studies should be thoroughly practical. It is their business to apply the principles discovered by men, it is their place to make the observations which lead men to discover those principles. A woman's thoughts, beyond the range of her immediate duties, should be directed to the study of men, or the acquirement of the agreeable learning whose sole end is the formation of taste; for the works of genius are beyond her reach, and she has neither the accuracy nor the attention for success in the exact sciences; as for the physical sciences, to decide the relations between living creatures and the laws of nature is the task of that sex which is more active and enterprising, which sees more things, that sex which is possessed of greater strength and is more accustomed to the exercise of that strength. Woman, weak as she is and limited in her range of observation, perceives and judges the forces at her disposal to supplement her weakness, and those forces are the passions of man. Her own mechanism is more powerful than ours; she has many levers which may set the human heart in motion. She must find a way to make us desire what she cannot achieve unaided and what she considers necessary or pleasing; therefore she must have a thorough knowledge of the mind of man in general, but the mind of those men who are about her, the mind of those men who have authority over her, either by law or custom. She must learn to divine their feelings from speech and action, look and gestures. By her own speech and action, look and gesture, she must be able to inspire them with the feelings she desires, without seeming to have any such purpose. The men will have a better philosophy of the human heart, but she will read more accurately in the heart of men. Woman should discover, so to speak, an experimental morality, man should reduce it to a system. Woman has more wit, man more genius; woman observes, man reasons; together they provide the clearest light and the profoundest knowledge which is possible to the unaided human mind; in a word, the surest knowledge of self and of others of which the human race is capable. In this way art may constantly tend to the perfection of the instrument which nature has given us.

JAMES FORDYCE

J ames Fordyce (1720–1796), a Scottish Presbyterian divine, received a doc-
torate in divinity from the University of Glasgow and served in different
posts, eventually at Monkwell Street, in London. He is best remembered
for his *Sermons to Young Women,* published in 1766 and often reprinted,
excerpts of which are reproduced here.

SERMONS TO YOUNG WOMEN (SELECTIONS)

Fordyce's *Sermons* presents a sentimental and idealized view of woman's
nature. Addressing men, he writes: "Behold these smiling innocents, whom I
have graced with my fairest gifts, and committed to your protection; behold
them with tenderness and honour. They are timid and want to be defended.
They are frail; O do not take advantage of their weakness" ("Sermon III").
One of Fordyce's central themes is how Nature has created men and women
differently and endowed them with different gifts. Women are incapable of
"reasoning and accuracy." Their "empire" is that which "has the heart as its
object." Their principal goal is to make themselves attractive to men.
Although Fordyce encourages women to read books in order to help attain
their ends, their chief business is to read men."

Fordyce's views are not only criticized by Mary Wollstonecraft in *A
Vindication of the Rights of Women,* but also in *Pride and Prejudice,* Jane Austen
has the tedious Mr. Collins read these sermons to the Bennett sisters. The
selections reproduced here are from "Sermon VII," in which Fordyce discusses the education of young women.

SERMONS TO YOUNG WOMEN

SERMON VII

The degree of those Intellectual Accomplishments which your sex should aim at, I pretend not to determine. That must depend on the capacities, opportunities, and encouragements, which you severally enjoy. With regard to all these however, this may be said in general, that they are better, and more than many of you seem solicitous to improve.

As to the first indeed, I scruple not to declare my opinion, that Nature appears to have formed the faculties of your sex for the most part with less vigour than those of ours; observing the same distinction here, as in the more delicate frame of your bodies. Exceptions we readily admit, and such as do the individuals great honour in those particular walks of excellence, wherein they have been distinguished. But you yourselves, I think, will allow that war, commerce, politics, exercises of strength and dexterity, abstract philosophy, and all the abstruser sciences, are most properly the province of men. I am sure those masculine women, that would plead for your sharing any part of this province equally with us, do not understand your true interests. There is an influence, there is an empire which belongs to you, and which I wish you ever to possess: I mean that which has the heart for its object, and is secured by meekness and modesty, by soft attraction and virtuous love.

But now I must add, that your power in this way will receive a large accession from the culture of your minds, in the more elegant and polished branches of knowledge. When I say so, I would by no means insinuate, that you are not capable of the judicious and the solid, in such proportion as is suited to your destination in life. This, I apprehend, does not require reasoning or accuracy, so much as observation and discernment. Your business chiefly is to read Men, in order to make yourselves agreeable and useful. It is not the argumentative but the sentimental talents, which give you that insight and those openings into the human heart, that leads to your principal ends as Women. Nevertheless, in this study you may derive great assistance from books. Without them in effect, your progress here will be partial and confined. Neither are you to attach yourselves wholly to this study, important as it is, and grateful as you may find it. Whatever kinds of reading may contribute to your general improvement and satisfaction, as reasonable beings designed for society, virtue and religion, will deserve your attentive regard....

Permit me to ask, whence it proceeds that studies like these are neglected by the generality of your sex? Is it because they are not calculated to inflame the fancy, and flatter the passions; or because to relish them to purpose, requires some degree of solidity and judgment?—But did not the preacher say, that there were women who are no way deficient in these latter qualities? He did, and therefore pleases himself with the hope, that the hints now offered may imprint conviction on such, where there has been an omission, and encourage perseverance where there has not....

I should not on this occasion do justice to your sex, if I did not say, that such books as those last mentioned are, in a particular degree, proportioned to the scope of your capacities. Of this I am certain, that amongst women of sense I have discovered an uncommon penetration in what relates to characters, an uncommon dexterity in hitting them off through their several specific distinctions, and even nicer discriminations, together with a race of fancy, and a fund of what may be strictly termed Sentiment, or a pathetic manner of thinking, which I have not so frequently met with in men. It should seem that Nature, by her liberality to the female mind in these respects, has seen fit to compensate what has been judged a defect in point of depth and force; and a real defect, I believe it is, if estimated absolutely. If estimated with a due regard to the design and formation of the sex, it ought to be considered as no defect at all.…

In the last place, your complaints of want of Encouragement to that pursuit. Who are they then that seek to discourage you? I have read of foolish mothers, that would not suffer their daughters to read, lest they should dim the lustre of their eyes, or spoil the bloom of their complexions. But I have never met with one, that seriously carried her folly so far. On the other hand, I have known parents not a few, who, though they had no taste for knowledge themselves, would yet speak with the utmost satisfaction of a girl that was fond of her books.

But perhaps my little friend is afraid, lest the men should suspect her of being what the world styles in derision a Learned Lady. Indeed? Is this then a character so very easily acquired, that you are in danger of it the moment you emerge from the depth of ignorance, and begin to think and speak like a reasonable being? You are over hasty in your apprehension. A Learned Lady is by no means a creature that we run the risk of being often shocked with. For my own part, I have never strictly speaking seen such a one; and when at any time I have met with what approached to that character, I must profess, I found nothing to excite terror. But possibly you mean a smatterer in learning. There, indeed, I join with you in wishing you may never incur the imputation.

JOHN GREGORY

John Gregory (1724–1773) received medical training before becoming professor of philosophy at the University of Aberdeen, where he lectured on mathematics and moral and natural philosophy. In 1749, he resigned in order to practice medicine and was eventually appointed professor of medicine at the University of Edinburgh where he was a close friend of David Hume and other figures in the Scottish Enlightenment. Excerpts reproduced here are from *A Father's Legacy to His Daughters* (1774), his most popular work.

A FATHER'S LEGACY TO HIS DAUGHTERS

A Father's Legacy to His Daughters is an example of a "conduct book." In the passages presented here, Gregory advises women on proper modes of behavior to make themselves attractive to men. They are advised to cultivate "modest reserve" and "extreme sensibility," to be silent in company, conversing through expressive countenances, while wit is a dangerous talent. "[I]f you happen to have any learning, keep it a profound secret, especially from the men, who generally look with a jealous and malignant eye on a woman of great parts, and a cultivated understanding."

In Chapter 5 of *A Vindication of the Rights of Women*, Wollstonecraft criticizes the "mode of dissimulation" Gregory recommends: "Women are always to *seem* to be this and that...." She commends "the paternal solicitude" that pervades his book but "cannot silently pass over arguments that so speciously support opinions which ... have had the most baneful effect on the morals and manners of the female world."

A FATHER'S LEGACY TO HIS DAUGHTERS

CONDUCT AND BEHAVIOR

One of the chief beauties in a female character is that modest reserve, that retiring delicacy, which avoids the public eye, and is disconcerted even at the gaze of admiration.—I do not wish you to be insensible to applause. If you were, you must become, if not worse, at least less amiable women. But you may be dazzled by that admiration, which yet rejoices your hearts.

When a girl ceases to blush, she has lost the most powerful charm of beauty. That extreme sensibility which it indicates, may be a weakness and incumbrance in our sex, as I have too often felt; but in yours it is peculiarly engaging. Pedants, who think themselves philosophers, ask why a woman should blush when she is conscious of no crime. It is a sufficient answer, that Nature has made you to blush when you are guilty of no fault, and has forced us to love you because you do so.—Blushing is so far from being necessarily an attendant on guilt, that it is the usual companion of innocence.

This modesty, which I think so essential in your sex, will naturally dispose you to be rather silent in company, especially in a large one.— People of sense and discernment will never mistake such silence for dullness. One may take a share in conversation without uttering a syllable. The expression in the countenance shews it, and this never escapes an observing eye.

I should be glad that you had an easy dignity in your behaviour at public places, but not that confident ease, that unabashed countenance, which seems to set the company at defiance.—If, while a gentleman is speaking to you, one of superior rank addresses you, do not let your eager attention and visible preference betray the flutter of your heart. Let your pride on this occasion preserve you from that meanness into which your vanity would sink you. Consider that you expose yourselves to the ridicule of the company, and affront one gentleman, only to swell the triumph of another, who perhaps thinks he does you honour in speaking to you.

Converse with men even of the first rank with that dignified modesty, which may prevent the approach of the most distant familiarity, and consequently prevent them from feeling themselves your superiors.

Wit is the most dangerous talent you can possess. It must be guarded with great discretion and good-nature, otherwise it will create you many enemies. Wit is perfectly consistent with softness and delicacy; yet they are seldom found united. Wit is so flattering to vanity, that they who possess it become intoxicated, and lose all self-command.

Humour is a different quality. It will make your company much solicited; but be cautious how you indulge it.—It is often a great enemy to delicacy, and a still greater one to dignity of character. It may sometimes gain you applause, but will never procure you respect.

Be even cautious in displaying your good sense. It will be thought you assume a superiority over the rest of the company.—But if you happen to have any learning, keep it a profound secret, especially from the men, who generally look with a jealous and malignant eye on a woman of great parts, and a cultivated understanding.

A man of real genius and candour is far superior to this meanness. But such a one will seldom fall in your way; and if by accident he should, do not be anxious to shew the full extent of your knowledge. If he has any opportunities of seeing you, he will soon discover it himself; and if you have any advantages of person or manner, and keep your own secret, he will probably give you credit for a great deal more than you possess.—The great art of pleasing in conversation consists in making the company pleased with themselves. You will more readily hear than talk yourselves into their good graces....

Virgin purity is of that delicate nature, that it cannot hear certain things without contamination. It is always in your power to avoid these. No man, but a brute or a fool, will insult a woman with conversation which he sees gives her pain; nor will he dare to do it, if she resent the injury with a becoming spirit.—There is a dignity in conscious virtue which is able to awe the most shameless and abandoned of men.

You will be reproached perhaps with prudery. By prudery is usually meant an affectation of delicacy. Now I do not wish you to affect delicacy; I wish you to possess it. At any rate, it is better to run the risk of being thought ridiculous than disgusting.

The men will complain of your reserve. They will assure you that a franker behaviour would make you more amiable. But trust me, they are not sincere when they tell you so.—I acknowledge, that on some occasions it might render you more agreeable as companions, but it would make you less amiable as women: An important distinction, which many of your sex are not aware of.—After all, I wish you to have great ease and openness in your conversation. I only point out some considerations which ought to regulate your behaviour in that respect.

MARY WOLLSTONECRAFT

M ary Wollstonecraft's *A Vindication of the Rights of Women* is often
viewed as the first great classic work of the modern women's movement. Wollstonecraft (1759–1797) was in many ways an unlikely
candidate for so important a contribution. Born into a poor family, she had to
support herself as a governess, by sewing, and other similar occupations. In
spite of these hardships, she managed to become a successful writer, publishing novels as well as nonfiction works. Her *A Vindication of the Rights of Men*,
published anonymously in 1790, was a response to Edmund Burke's conservative critique of the French Revolution, *Reflections on the Revolution in France*
(1790). Wollstonecraft married the philosopher William Godwin in 1797 but
died later that year of an infection contracted giving birth to their daughter,
Mary (the future wife of Percy Shelley and author of *Frankenstein*). She was 38
years old.

A VINDICATION OF THE RIGHTS OF WOMEN (SELECTIONS)

A Vindication of the Rights of Women (1792) provides a classic account of society's deforming effects on women's nature and the potential of improved education to remedy this situation. Though conceding men's natural superiority
in regard to physical strength, Wollstonecraft argues for what is in effect a single human nature beyond that, common to both sexes. Although women's
"minds are not in a healthy state," this is the fault of social forces, a false conception of women's essence, supported by a false system of education.

Wollstonecraft argues that, according to the prevailing view, women are created for the sake of men, to be objects of pleasure and desire. Their education has been intended to render them "alluring objects for a moment," rather than rational and virtuous beings.

Wollstonecraft recognizes that her proposals constitute "a REVOLUTION in female manners." But the force of her assault is limited. Wollstonecraft does not argue against women's traditional role but claims instead that allowing their natural potential to unfold will make them better suited to it, to serve as "affectionate wives and rational mothers." Throughout *Vindication,* her goal for women is clear: "The end, the grand end, of their exertions should be to unfold their own faculties, and acquire the dignity of conscious virtue."

The importance of Wollstonecraft's arguments is well established. In her introduction to the edition used here, the British women's suffrage leader Millicient Garrett Fawcett says that the women's rights movement in England and America owes as much to Wollstonecraft as political economy owes to "her famous contemporary" Adam Smith. The substantial selections included here are from the introduction and Chapters 2, 3, 4, 5, and 13 and present the work's central arguments.

A VINDICATION OF THE RIGHTS OF WOMEN

INTRODUCTION TO THE FIRST EDITION.

After considering the historic page, and viewing the living world with anxious solicitude, the most melancholy emotions of sorrowful indignation have depressed my spirits, and I have sighed when obliged to confess that either nature has made a great difference between man and man, or that the civilization which has hitherto taken place in the world has been very partial. I have turned over various books written on the subject of education, and patiently observed the conduct of parents and the management of schools; but what has been the result?—a profound conviction that the neglected education of my fellow-creatures is the grand source of the misery I deplore; and that women, in particular, are rendered weak and wretched by a variety of concurring causes, originating from one hasty conclusion. The conduct and manners of women, in fact, evidently prove that their minds are not in a healthy state; for, like the flowers which are planted in too rich a soil, strength and usefulness are sacrificed to beauty; and the flaunting leaves, after having pleased a fastidious eye, fade, disregarded, on the stalk, long before the season when they ought to have arrived at maturity. One cause of this barren blooming I attribute to a false system of education, gathered from the books written on this subject by men who, considering females rather as women than human creatures, have been more anxious to make them alluring mistresses than affectionate wives and rational mothers; and the understanding of the sex has been so bubbled by this specious homage, that the civilized women of the present century, with a few exceptions, are only anxious to inspire love, when they ought to cherish a nobler ambition, and, by their abilities and virtues, exact respect.

In a treatise, therefore, on female rights and manners, the works which have been particularly written for their improvement must not be overlooked; especially when it is asserted, in direct terms, that the minds of women are enfeebled by false refinement; that the books of instruction, written by men of genius, have had the same tendency as more frivolous productions; and that, in the true style of Mahometanism, they are treated as a kind of subordinate beings, and not as a part of the human species, when improvable reason is allowed to be the dignified distinction which raises men above the brute creation, and puts a natural sceptre in a feeble hand.

Yet, because I am a woman, I would not lead my readers to suppose that I mean violently to agitate the contested question respecting the quality or inferiority of the sex; but as the subject lies in my way, and I cannot pass it over without subjecting the main tendency of my reasoning to misconstruction, I shall stop a moment to deliver, in a few words, my opinion. In the government of the physical world it is observable that the female in point of strength is, in general, inferior to the male. This is the law of nature; and it does not appear to be suspended or abrogated in favor of woman. A degree of physical superiority cannot, therefore, be denied—and it is a noble prerogative! But not content with this natural pre-eminence, men endeavor to sink us still lower, merely to render us alluring objects for a moment; and women, intoxicated by the adoration which men, under the influence of their senses, pay them, do not seek to obtain a durable interest in their hearts, or to become the friends of the fellow-creatures who find amusement in their society.

I am aware of an obvious inference—from every quarter have I heard exclamations against masculine women; but where are they to be found? If by this appellation men mean to inveigh against their ardor in hunting, shooting, and gaming, I shall most cordially join in the cry; but if it be against the imitation of manly virtues, or, more properly speaking, the attainment of those talents and virtues the exercise of which ennobles the human character, and which raise females in the scale of animal being, when they are comprehensively termed mankind, all those who view them with a philosophic eye must, I should think, wish with me that they may every day grow more and more masculine.

This discussion naturally divides the subject. I shall first consider women in the grand light of human creatures, who, in common with men, are placed on this earth to unfold their faculties; and afterwards I shall more particularly point out their peculiar designation.

I wish also to steer clear of an error which many respectable writers have fallen into; for the instruction which has hitherto been addressed to women has rather been applicable to *ladies*, if the little indirect advice that is scattered through "Sandford and Merton" be accepted; but, addressing my sex in a firmer tone, I pay particular attention to those in the middle class, because they appear to be in the most natural state. Perhaps the seeds of false refinement, immorality, and vanity have ever been shed by the great. Weak, artificial beings, raised above the common wants and affections of their race, in a premature, unnatural manner, undermine the very foundation of virtue, and spread corruption through the whole mass of society! As a class of mankind they have the strongest claim to pity; the education of the rich tends to render them vain and helpless, and the unfolding mind is not strengthened by the practice of those duties which dignify the human character. They only live to amuse themselves, and by the same law which in Nature invariably produces certain effects, they soon only afford barren amusement.

But as I purpose taking a separate view of the different ranks of society, and of the moral character of women in each, this hint is for the present sufficient; and I have only alluded to the subject because it appears to me to be the very essence of an introduction, to give a cursory account of the contents of the work it introduces.

My own sex, I hope, will excuse me if I treat them like rational creatures, instead of flattering their *fascinating* graces, and viewing them as if they were in a state of perpetual childhood, unable to stand alone. I earnestly wish to point out in what true dignity and human happiness consist; I wish to persuade women to endeavor to acquire strength, both of mind and body, and to convince them that the soft phrases, "susceptibility of heart," "delicacy of sentiment," and "refinement of taste" are almost synonymous with epithets of weakness, and that those beings who are only the objects of pity and that kind of love which has been termed its sister, will soon become objects of contempt.

Dismissing, then, those pretty feminine phrases which the men condescendingly use to soften our slavish dependence, and despising that weak elegancy of mind, exquisite sensibility, and sweet docility of manners supposed to be the sexual characteristics of the weaker vessel, I wish to show that elegance is inferior to virtue, that the first object of laudable ambition is to obtain a character as a human being, regardless of the distinction of sex; and that secondary views should be brought to this simple touchstone.

This is a rough sketch of my plan; and should I express my conviction with the energetic emotions that I feel whenever I think of the subject, the dictates of experience and reflection will be felt by some of my readers. Animated by this important object, I shall disdain to cull my phrases or polish my style; I aim at being useful, and sincerity will render me unaffected; for, wishing rather to persuade by the force of my arguments than dazzle by the elegance of my language, I shall not waste my time in rounding periods, or in fabricating the turgid bombast of artificial feelings, which, coming from the head, never reach the heart. I shall be employed about things, not words! and, anxious to render my sex more respectable members of society, I shall try to avoid that flowery diction which has slided from essays into novels, and from novels into familiar letters and conversation.

These pretty superlatives, dropping glibly from the tongue, vitiate the taste, and create a kind of sickly delicacy that turns away from simple, unadorned truth; and a deluge of false sentiments and overstretched feelings, stifling the natural emotions of the heart, render the domestic pleasures insipid, that ought to sweeten the exercise of those severe duties which educated a rational and immortal being for a nobler field of action.

The education of women has, of late, been more attended to than formerly; yet they are still reckoned a frivolous sex, and ridiculed or pitied by the writers who endeavor by satire or instruction to improve them. It is acknowledged that they spend many of the first years of their lives in acquiring a smattering of accomplishments; meanwhile strength of body and mind are sacrificed to libertine notions of beauty, to the desire of establishing themselves—the only way women can rise in the world—by marriage. And this desire making mere animals of them, when they marry they act as such children may be expected to act—they dress, they paint, and nickname God's creatures. Surely these weak beings are only fit for a seraglio! Can they be expected to govern a family with judgment, or take care of the poor babes whom they bring into the world?

If, then, it can be fairly deduced from the present conduct of the sex, from the prevalent fondness for pleasure which takes place of ambition and those nobler passions that open and enlarge the soul, that the instruction which women have hitherto received has only tended, with the constitution of civil society, to render them insignificant objects of desire—mere propagators of fools!—if it can be proved that in aiming to accomplish them without cultivating their understandings, they are taken out of their sphere of duties, and made ridiculous and useless when the short-lived bloom of beauty is over, I presume that *rational* men will excuse me for endeavoring to persuade them to become more masculine and respectable.

Indeed, the word "masculine" is only a bugbear; there is little reason to fear that women will acquire too much courage or fortitude; for their apparent inferiority with respect to bodily strength must render them, in some degree, dependent on men in the various relations of life; but why should it be increased by prejudices that give a sex to virtue, and confound simple truths with sensual reveries?

Women are, in fact, so much degraded by mistaken notions of female excellence, that I do not mean to add a paradox when I assert that this artificial weakness produces a propensity to tyrannize, and gives birth to cunning, the natural opponent of strength, which leads them to play off those contemptible infantine airs that undermine esteem even while they excite desire. Let men become more chaste and modest, and if women do not grow wiser in the same ratio it will be clear that they have weaker understandings. It seems scarcely necessary to say that I now speak of the sex in general. Many individuals have more sense than their male relatives; and, as nothing preponderates where there is a constant struggle for an equilibrium without it has naturally more gravity, some women govern their husbands without degrading themselves, because intellect will always govern.

CHAPTER II.
THE PREVAILING OPINION
OF A SEXUAL CHARACTER DISCUSSED.

To account for and excuse the tyranny of man, many ingenious arguments have been brought forward to prove that the two sexes, in the acquirement of virtue, ought to aim at attaining a very different character; or, to speak explicitly, women are not allowed to have sufficient strength of mind to acquire what really deserves the name of virtue. Yet it should seem, allowing them to have souls, that there is but one way appointed by Providence to lead *mankind* to either virtue or happiness.

If, then, women are not a swarm of ephemeron triflers, why should they be kept in ignorance under the specious name of innocence? Men complain, and with reason, of the follies and caprices of our sex, when they do not keenly satirize our headstrong passions and groveling vices. Behold, I should answer, the natural effect of ignorance! The mind will ever be unstable that has only prejudices to rest on, and the current will run with destructive fury when there are no barriers to break its force. Women are told from their infancy, and taught by the example of their mothers, that a little knowledge of human weakness, justly termed cunning, softness of temper, *outward* obedience, and a scrupulous attention to a puerile kind of propriety, will obtain for them the protection of man; and should they be beautiful, everything else is needless, for, at least, twenty years of their lives.

Thus Milton describes our first frail mother; though when he tells us that women are formed for softness and sweet attractive grace, I cannot comprehend his meaning, unless, in the true Mahometan strain, he meant to deprive us of souls, and insinuate that we were beings only designed, by sweet, attractive grace and docile, blind obedience, to gratify the senses of man when he can no longer soar on the wing of contemplation.

How grossly do they insult us who thus advise us only to render ourselves gentle, domestic brutes! For instance, the winning softness so warmly and frequently recommended, that governs by obeying. What childish expressions, and how insignificant is the being—can it be an immortal one?—who will condescend to govern by such sinister methods! "Certainly," says Lord Bacon, "man is of kin to the beast by his body; and if he be not of kin to God by his spirit, he is a base and ignoble creature!" Men, indeed appear to me to act in a very unphilosophical manner when they try to secure the good conduct of women by attempting to keep them always in a state of childhood. Rousseau was more consistent when he wished to stop the progress of reason in both sexes, for if men eat of the tree of knowledge, women will come in for a taste; but, from the imperfect cultivation which their understandings now receive, they only attain a knowledge of evil.

Children, I grant, should be innocent; but when the epithet is applied to men or women it is but a civil term for weakness. For if it be allowed that women were destined by Providence to acquire human virtues, and by the exercise of their understandings that stability of character which is the firmest ground to rest our future hopes upon, they must be permitted to turn to the Fountain of Light, and not forced to shape their course by the twinkling of a mere satellite....

In treating, therefore, of the manners of women, let us, disregarding sensual arguments, trace what we should endeavor to make them in order to co-operate, if the expression be not too bold, with the Supreme Being.

By individual education I mean—for the sense of the word is not precisely defined—such an attention to a child as will slowly sharpen the senses, form the temper, regulate the passions as they begin to ferment, and set the understanding to work before the body arrives at maturity; so that the man may only have to proceed with, not to begin, the important task of learning to think and reason.

To prevent any misconstruction, I must add, that I do not believe that a private education can work the wonders which some sanguine writers have attributed to it. Men and women must be educated, in a great degree, by the opinions and manners of the society they live in. In every age there has been a stream of popular opinion that has carried all before it, and given a family character, as it were, to the century. It may then fairly be inferred, that, till society be differently constituted, much cannot be expected from education. It is, however, sufficient for my present purpose to assert, that, whatever effect circumstances have on the abilities, every being may become virtuous by the exercise of its own reason; for if but one being was created with vicious inclinations, that is, positively bad, what can save us from atheism? Or, if we worship a God, is not that God a devil?

Consequently, the most perfect education, in my opinion, is such an exercise of the understanding as is best calculated to strengthen the body and form the heart—or, in other words, to enable the individual to attain such habits of virtue as will render it independent. In fact, it is a farce to call any being virtuous whose virtues do not result from the exercise of its own reason. This was Rousseau's opinion respecting men; I extend it to women, and confidently assert that they have been drawn out of their sphere by false refinement, and not by an endeavor to acquire masculine qualities. Still, the regal homage which they receive is so intoxicating, that till the manners of the times are changed, and formed on more reasonable principles, it may be impossible to convince them that the illegitimate power which they obtain by degrading themselves, is a curse, and that they must return to Nature and equality if they wish to secure the placid satisfaction that unsophisticated affections impart. But for this epoch we must wait— wait, perhaps, till kings and nobles, enlightened by reason, and preferring the real dignity of man to childish state, throw off their gaudy hereditary trappings; and if then women do not resign the arbitrary power of beauty, they will prove that they have *less* mind than man.

I may be accused of arrogance; still I must declare what I firmly believe, that all the writers who have written on the subject of female education and manners, from Rousseau to Dr. Gregory, have contributed to render women more artificial, weak characters than they would otherwise have been, and, consequently, more useless members of society. I might have expressed this conviction in a lower key; but I am afraid it would have been the whine of affectation, and not the faithful expression of my feelings, of the clear result which experience and reflection have led me to draw. When I come to that division of the subject, I shall advert to the passages that I more particularly disapprove of in the works of the authors I have just alluded to; but it is first necessary to observe, that my objection extends to the whole purport of those books, which tend, in my opinion, to degrade one half of the human species, and render women pleasing at the expense of every solid virtue.

Though, to reason on Rousseau's ground, if man did attain a degree of perfection of mind when his body arrived at maturity, it might be proper, in order to make a man and his wife *one*, that she should rely entirely on his understanding; and the graceful ivy, clasping the oak that supported it, would form a whole in which strength and beauty would be equally conspicuous. But, alas! husbands, as well as their helpmates, are often only overgrown children; nay, thanks to early debauchery, scarcely men in their outward form—and if the blind lead the blind, one need not come from heaven to tell us the consequence....

Strengthen the female mind by enlarging it, and there will be an end to blind obedience; but, as blind obedience is ever fought for by power, tyrants and sensualists are in the right when they endeavor to keep women in the dark, because the former only want slaves, and the latter a plaything. The sensualist, indeed, has been the most dangerous of tyrants, and women have been duped by their lovers, as princes by their ministers, while dreaming that they reigned over them.

I now principally allude to Rousseau, for his character of *Sophia* is, undoubtedly, a captivating one, though it appears to me grossly unnatural;

however, it is not the superstructure, but the foundation, of her character, the principles on which her education was built, that I mean to attack; nay, warmly as I admire the genius of that able writer, whose opinions I shall often have occasion to cite, indignation always takes place of admiration, and the rigid frown of insulted virtue effaces the smile of complacency, which his eloquent periods are wont to raise, when I read his voluptuous reveries. Is this the man, who, in his ardor for virtue, would banish all the soft arts of peace, and almost carry us back to Spartan discipline? Is this the man who delights to paint the useful struggles of passion, the triumphs of good dispositions, and the heroic flights which carry the glowing soul out of itself? How are these mighty sentiments lowered when he describes the pretty foot and enticing airs of his little favorite! But, for the present, I waive the subject, and, instead of severely reprehending the transient effusions of overweening sensibility, I shall only observe, that whoever has cast a benevolent eye on society must often have been gratified by the sight of humble, mutual love, not dignified by sentiment nor strengthened by a union in intellectual pursuits. The domestic trifles of the day have afforded matters for cheerful converse, and innocent caresses have softened toils which did not require great exercise of mind or stretch of thought: yet, has not the sight of this moderate felicity excited more tenderness than respect?—an emotion similar to what we feel when children are playing, or animals sporting—whilst the contemplation of the noble struggles of suffering merit has raised admiration, and carried our thoughts to that world where sensation will give place to reason.

Women are, therefore, to be considered either as moral beings, or so weak that they must be entirely subjected to the superior faculties of men.

Let us examine this question. Rousseau declares that a woman should never, for a moment, feel herself independent; that she should be governed by fear to exercise her *natural* cunning, and made a coquettish slave in order to render her a more alluring object of desire, a *sweeter* companion to man, whenever he chooses to relax himself. He carries the arguments, which he pretends to draw from the indications of Nature, still further, and insinuates that truth and fortitude, the corner-stones of all human virtue, should be cultivated with certain restrictions, because, with respect to the female character, obedience is the grand lesson which ought to be impressed with unrelenting rigor.

What nonsense! When will a great man arise with sufficient strength of mind to puff away the fumes which pride and sensuality have thus spread over this subject? If women are by nature inferior to men, their virtues must be the same in quality, if not in degree, or virtue is a relative idea; consequently, their conduct should be founded on the same principles, and have the same aim.

Connected with man as daughters, wives and mothers, their moral character may be estimated by their manner of fulfilling those simple duties; but the end, the grand end, of their exertions should be to unfold their own faculties, and acquire the dignity of conscious virtue. They may try to render their road pleasant; but ought never to forget, in common with man, that life yields not the felicity which can satisfy an immortal soul. I do not mean to insinuate that either sex should be so lost in abstract reflections, or distant views, as to forget the affections and duties that lie before them, and are, in truth, the means appointed to produce the fruit of life; on the contrary, I would warmly recommend them, even while I assert, that they afford most satisfaction when they are considered in their true, sober light.

Probably, the prevailing opinion that woman was created for man may have taken its rise from Moses' poetical story; yet, as very few, it is presumed who have bestowed any serious thought on the subject, ever supposed that Eve was, literally speaking, one of Adam's ribs, the deduction must be allowed to fall to the ground; or only be so far admitted as it proves that man, from the remotest antiquity, found it convenient to exert his strength to subjugate his companion; and his invention, to show that she ought to have her neck bent under the yoke, because the whole creation was only created for his convenience or pleasure.

Let it not be concluded that I wish to invert the order of things; I have already granted that, from the constitution of their bodies, men seem to be designed by Providence to attain a greater degree of virtue. I speak, collectively, of the whole sex; but I see not the shadow of a reason to conclude that their virtues should differ in respect to their nature. In fact, how can they, if virtue has only one eternal standard? I must, therefore, if I reason consequentially, as strenuously maintain that they have the same simple direction, as that there is a God.

It follows, then, that cunning should not be opposed to wisdom, little cares to great exertions, or insipid softness, varnished over with the name of gentleness, to that fortitude which grand views alone can inspire.

I shall be told that woman would then lose many of her peculiar graces, and the opinion of a well-known poet might be quoted to refute my unqualified assertion. For Pope has said, in the name of the whole male sex,

"Yet ne'er so sure our passion to create
As when she touch'd the brink of all we hate."

In what light this sally places men and women I shall leave to the judicious to determine; meanwhile I shall content myself with observing that I cannot discover why, unless they are mortal, females should always be degraded by being made subservient to love or lust.

To speak disrespectfully of love is, I know, high treason against sentiment and fine feelings; but I wish to speak the simple language of truth, and rather to address the head than the heart. To endeavor to reason love out of the world would be to out-Quixote Cervantes, and equally offend against common sense; but an endeavor to restrain this tumultuous passion, and to prove that it should not be allowed to dethrone superior powers, or to usurp the sceptre which the understanding should ever coolly wield, appears less wild.

Youth is the season for love in both sexes; but in those days of thoughtless enjoyment provision should be made for the more important years of life, when reflection takes the place of sensation. But Rousseau, and most of the male writers who have followed his steps, have warmly inculcated that the whole tendency of female education ought to be directed to one point—to render them pleasing.

Let me reason with the supporters of this opinion who have any knowledge of human nature. Do they imagine that marriage can eradicate the habitude of life? The woman who has only been taught to please will soon find that her charms are oblique sunbeams, and that they cannot have much effect on her husband's heart when they are seen every day, when the summer is passed and gone. Will she then have sufficient native energy to look into herself for comfort, and cultivate her dormant faculties? Or is it not more rational to expect that she will try to please other men; and, in the emotions raised by the expectation of new conquests, endeavor to forget the mortification her love or pride has received? When the husband ceases to be a lover—and the time will inevitably come—her desire of pleasing will then grow languid, or become a spring of bitterness; and love, perhaps the most evanescent of all passions, gives place to jealousy or vanity.

I now speak of women who are restrained by principle or prejudice; such women, though they would shrink from an intrigue with real abhorrence, yet, nevertheless, wish to be convinced by the homage of gallantry that they are cruelly neglected by their husbands; or days and weeks are spent in dreaming of the happiness enjoyed by congenial souls, till their health is undermined and their spirits broken by discontent. How, then, can the great art of pleasing be such a necessary study? It is only useful to a mistress; the chaste wife and serious mother should only consider her power to please as the polish of her virtues, and the affection of her husband as one of the comforts that render her task less difficult and her life happier. But, whether she be loved or neglected, her first wish should be to make herself respectable, and not to rely for all her happiness on a being subject to like infirmities with herself....

CHAPTER III.
THE SAME SUBJECT CONTINUED.

Bodily strength, from being the distinction of heroes, is now sunk into such unmerited contempt that men, as well as women, seem to think it unnecessary: the latter as it takes from their feminine graces, and from that lovely weakness the source of their undue power; and the former, because it appears inimical to the character of a gentleman.

That they have both, by departing from one extreme, run into another, may easily be proved; but first it may be proper to observe, that a vulgar error has obtained a degree of credit, which has given force to a false conclusion, in which an effect has been mistaken for a cause.

People of genius have, very frequently, impaired their constitutions by study or careless inattention to their health, and the violence of their passions bearing a proportion to the vigor of their intellects, the sword's destroying the scabbard has become almost proverbial, and superficial observers have inferred from thence, that men of genius have commonly weak, or, to use a more fashionable phrase, delicate, constitutions. Yet the contrary, I believe, will appear to be the fact; for, on diligent inquiry, I find that strength of mind has, in most cases, been accompanied by superior strength of body—natural soundness of constitutions—not that robust tone of nerves and vigor of muscles, which arise from bodily labor, when the mind is quiescent, or only directs the hands.

Dr. Priestley has remarked, in the preface to his biographical chart, that the majority of great men have lived beyond forty-five. And, considering the thoughtless manner in which they have lavished their strength—when, investigating a favorite science, they have wasted the lamp of life, forgetful of the midnight hour; or, when, lost in poetic dreams, fancy has peopled the scene, and the soul has been disturbed, till it shook the constitution, by the passions that meditation had raised; whose objects, the baseless fabric of a vision, faced before the exhausted eye—they must have had iron frames. Shakespeare never grasped the airy dagger with a nerveless hand, nor did Milton tremble when he led Satan far from the confines of his dreary prison. These were not the ravings of imbecility, the sickly effusions of distempered brains; but the exuberance of fancy that, "in a fine phrenzy" wandering, was not continually reminded of its material shackles.

I am aware that this argument would carry me further than it may be supposed I wish to go; but I follow truth, and, still adhering to my first position, I will allow that bodily strength seems to give man a natural superiority over women; and this is the only solid basis on which the superiority of the sex can be built. But I still insist that not only the virtue, but the *knowledge* of the two sexes should be the same in nature, if not in degree, and that women, considered not only as moral, but rational, creatures, ought to endeavor to acquire human virtues (or perfections) by the *same* means as men, instead of being educated like a fanciful kind of *half* being—one of Rousseau's wild chimeras.

But if strength of body be, with some show of reason, the boast of men, why are women so infatuated as to be proud of a defect? Rousseau has furnished them with a plausible excuse, which could only have occurred to a man whose imagination had been allowed to run wild, and refine on the impressions made by exquisite senses; that they might, forsooth, have a pretext for yielding to a natural appetite without violating a romantic species of modesty, which gratifies the pride and libertinism of man. Women, deluded by these sentiments, sometimes boast of their weakness, cunningly obtaining power by playing on the *weakness* of men; and they may well glory in their illicit sway, for, like Turkish bashaws, they have more real power than their masters; but virtue is sacrificed to temporary gratifications, and the respectability of life to the triumph of an hour.

Women, as well as despots, have now, perhaps, more power than they would have if the world, divided and subdivided into kingdoms and families, were governed by laws deduced from the exercise of reason; but in obtaining it (to carry on the comparison) their character is degraded, and licentiousness spread through the whole aggregate of society. The many become pedestal to the few. I, therefore, will venture to assert, that till women are more rationally educated, the progress of human virtue and improvement in knowledge must receive continual checks. And if it be granted that woman was not created merely to gratify the appetite of man, or to be the upper servant, who provides his meals and takes care of his linen, it must follow that the first care of those mothers, or fathers, who really attend to the education of females, should be, if not to strengthen the body, at least not to destroy the constitution by mistaken notions of beauty and female excellence; nor should girls ever be allowed to imbibe the pernicious notion that a defect can, by any chemical process of reasoning, become an excellence....

But should it be proved that woman is naturally weaker than man, whence does it follow that it is natural for her to labor to become still weaker than Nature intended her to be? Arguments of this cast are an insult to common sense, and savor of passion. The *divine right* of husbands, like the divine right of kings, may, it is to be hoped, in this enlightened age, be contested without danger; and though conviction may not silence many boisterous disputants, yet, when any prevailing prejudice is attacked, the wife will consider, and leave the narrow-minded to rail with thoughtless vehemence at innovation.

The mother who wishes to give true dignity of character to her daughter must, regardless of the sneers of ignorance, proceed on a plan diametrically opposite to that which Rousseau has recommended with all the deluding charms of eloquence and philosophical sophistry; for his eloquence renders absurdities plausible, and his dogmatic conclusions puzzle, without convincing, those who have not ability to refute them.

Throughout the whole animal kingdom every young creature requires almost continual exercise, and the infancy of children, conformable to this intimation, should be passed in harmless gambols, that exercise the feet and hands, without requiring very minute direction from the head or the constant attention of a nurse. In fact, the care necessary for self-preservation is the first natural exercise of the understanding, as little inventions to amuse the present moment unfold the imagination. But these wise designs of Nature are counteracted by mistaken fondness or blind zeal. The child is not left a moment to its own direction, particularly a girl, and thus rendered dependent—dependence is called natural.

To preserve personal beauty—woman's glory!—the limbs and faculties are cramped with worse than Chinese bands, and the sedentary life which they are condemned to live, while boys frolic in the open air, weakens the muscles and relaxes the nerves. As for Rousseau's remarks, which have since been echoed by several writers, that they have naturally (that is from their birth, independent of education) a fondness for dolls, dressing and talking, they are so puerile as not to merit a serious refutation. That a girl, condemned to sit for hours together listening to the idle chat of weak nurses, or to attend at her mother's toilet, will endeavor to join the conversation, is, indeed, very natural; and that she will imitate her mother or aunts, and amuse herself by adorning her lifeless doll as they do in dressing her, poor, innocent babe! is undoubtedly a most natural consequence. For men of the greatest abilities have seldom had sufficient strength to rise above the surrounding atmosphere; and if the pages of genius have always been blurred by the prejudices of the age, some allowance should be made for a sex who, like kings, always see things through a false medium.

Pursuing these reflections, the fondness for dress, conspicuous in women, may be easily accounted for, without supposing it the result of a desire to please the sex on which they are dependent. The absurdity, in short, of supposing that a girl is naturally a coquette, and that a desire, connected with the impulse of Nature, to propagate the species, should appear even before an improper education has, by heating the imagination, called it forth prematurely, is so unphilosophical, that such a sagacious observer as Rousseau would not have adopted it if he had not been accustomed to make reason give way to his desire of singularity, and truth to a favorite paradox....

CHAPTER IV.
OBSERVATIONS ON THE STATE OF DEGRADATION
TO WHICH WOMAN IS REDUCED BY VARIOUS CAUSES.

It would be an endless task to trace the variety of meannesses, cares and sorrows into which women are plunged by the prevailing opinion that they were created rather to feel than reason, and that all the power they obtain must be obtained by their charms and weakness:

"Fine by defect, and amiably weak!"

And, made by this amiable weakness entirely dependent, excepting what they gain by illicit sway, on man, not only for protection, but advice, is it surprising that, neglecting the duties that reason alone points out, and shrinking from trials calculated to strengthen their minds, they only exert themselves to give their defects a graceful covering, which may serve to heighten their charms in the eye of the voluptuary, though it sink them below the scale of moral excellence?

Fragile in every sense of the word, they are obliged to look up to man for every comfort. In the most trifling dangers they cling to their support with parasitical tenacity, piteously demanding succour; and their *natural* protector extends his arm, or lifts up his voice, to guard the lovely trembler—from what? Perhaps the frown of an old cow, or the jump of a mouse; a rat would be serious danger. In the name of reason, and even common sense, what can save such beings from contempt, even though they be soft and fair?

These fears, when not affected, may produce some pretty attitudes, but they show a degree of imbecility which degrades a rational creature in a way women are not aware of—for love and esteem are very distinct things.

I am fully persuaded that we should hear of none of these infantine airs if girls were allowed to take sufficient exercise, and not confined in close rooms till their muscles are relaxed and their powers of digestion destroyed. To carry the remark still further—if fear in girls, instead of being cherished, perhaps, created, were treated in the same manner as cowardice in boys, we should quickly see women with more dignified aspects. It is true that they could not then, with equal propriety, be termed the sweet flowers that smile in the walk of man; but they would be more respectable members of society, and discharge the important duties of life by the light of their own reason. "Educate women like men," says Rousseau, "and the more they resemble our sex the less power will they have over us." This is the very point I aim at. I do not wish them to have power over men but over themselves.

In the same strain have I heard men argue against instructing the poor, for many are the forms that aristocracy assumes. "Teach them to read and write," say they, "and you take them out of the station assigned them by Nature." An eloquent Frenchman has answered them; I will borrow his sentiments: "But they know not, when they make man a brute, that they may expect every instant to see him transformed into a ferocious beast. Without knowledge there can be no morality!"

Ignorance is a frail base for virtue! Yet, that it is the condition for which woman was organized, has been insisted upon by the writers who have most vehemently argued in favor of the superiority of man—a superiority not in degree but essence—though, to soften the argument, they have labored to prove, with chivalrous generosity, that the sexes ought not to be compared; man was made to reason, woman to feel; and that together, flesh and spirit, they make the most perfect whole, by blending happily reason and sensibility into one character....

CHAPTER V.
ANIMADVERSIONS ON SOME OF THE WRITERS WHO HAVE RENDERED WOMEN OBJECTS OF PITY, BORDERING ON CONTEMPT.

The opinions, speciously supported in some modern publications, on the female character and education, which have given the tone to most of the observations made, in a more cursory manner, on the sex, remain now to be examined.

SECTION I.

I shall begin with Rousseau, and give a sketch of his character of woman, in his own words, interspersing comments and reflections. My comments, it is true, will all spring from a few simple principles, and might have been deduced from what I have already said; but the artificial structure has been raised with so much ingenuity that it seems necessary to attack it in a more circumstantial manner, and make the application myself.

"Sophia," says Rousseau, "should be as perfect a woman as Emilius is a man, and to render her so it is necessary to examine the character which Nature has given to the sex."

He then proceeds to prove that woman ought to be weak and passive, because she has less bodily strength than man, and hence infers that she was formed to please and to be subject to him, and that it is her duty to render herself *agreeable* to her master—this being the grand end of her existence. Still, however, to give a little mock dignity to lust, he insists that man should not exert his strength, but depend on the will of the woman when he seeks for pleasure with her.

"Hence we deduce a third consequence from the different constitutions of the sexes; which is, that the strongest should be master in appearance, and be dependent, in fact, on the weakest; and that not from any frivolous practice of gallantry or vanity of protectorship, but from an invariable law of Nature, which, furnishing woman with a greater facility to excite desires than she has given man to satisfy them, makes the latter dependent on the good pleasure of the former, and compels him to endeavor to please in his turn, *in order to obtain her consent that he should be strongest.* On these occasions the most delightful circumstance a man finds in his victory is, to doubt whether it was the woman's weakness that yielded to his superior strength, or whether her inclinations spoke in his favor; the females are also generally artful enough to leave this matter in doubt. The understanding of women answers in this respect perfectly to their constitutions: so far from being ashamed of their weakness, they glory in it; their tender muscles make no resistance; they affect to be incapable of lifting the smallest burdens, and would blush to be thought robust and strong. To what purpose is all this? Not merely for the sake of appearing delicate, but through an artful precaution: it is thus they provide an excuse beforehand, and a right to be feeble when they think it expedient."

I have quoted this passage lest my readers should suspect that I warped the author's reasoning to support my own arguments. I have already asserted that in educating women these fundamental principles lead to a system of cunning and lasciviousness....

I now appeal from the reveries of fancy and refined licentiousness to the good sense of mankind, whether, if the object of education be to prepare women to become chaste wives and sensible mothers, the method so plausibly recommended in the foregoing sketch be the one best calculated to produce those ends? Will it be allowed that the surest way to make a wife chaste is to teach her to practice the wanton arts of a mistress, termed virtuous coquetry, by the sensualist who can no longer relish the artless charms of sincerity, or taste the pleasure arising from a tender intimacy, when confidence is unchecked by suspicion, and rendered interesting by sense?

The man who can be contented to live with a pretty, useful companion, without a mind, has lost in voluptuous gratifications a taste for more refined enjoyments; he has never felt the calm satisfaction that refreshes the parched heart, like the silent dew of heaven, of being beloved by one who could understand him. In the society of his wife he is still alone, unless when the man is sunk in the brute. "The charm of life," says a grave philosophical reasoner, is "sympathy; nothing pleases us more than to observe in other men a fellow-feeling with all the emotions of our own breast."

But, according to the tenor of reasoning by which women are kept from the tree of knowledge, the important years of youth, the usefulness of age, and the rational hopes of futurity, are all to be sacrificed to render women an object of desire for a *short* time. Besides, how could Rousseau expect them to be virtuous and constant when reason is neither allowed to be the foundation of their virtue, nor truth the object of their inquiries?

But all Rousseau's errors in reasoning arose from sensibility, and sensibility to their charms women are very ready to forgive! When he should have reasoned he became impassioned, and reflection inflamed his imagination instead of enlightening his understanding. Even his virtues also led him farther astray; for, born with a warm constitution and lively fancy, Nature carried him toward the other sex with such eager fondness, that he soon became lascivious. Had he given way to these desires, the fire would have extinguished itself in a natural manner; but virtue, and a romantic kind of delicacy, made him practice self-denial; yet, when fear, delicacy, or virtue restrained him he debauched his imagination, and, reflecting on the sensations to which fancy gave force, he traced them in the most glowing colors, and sunk them deep into his soul....

The pernicious tendency of those books, in which the writers insidiously degrade the sex while they are prostrate before their personal charms, cannot be too often or two severely exposed.

Let us, my dear contemporaries, rise above such narrow prejudices! If wisdom be desirable on its own account; if virtue, to deserve the name, must be founded on knowledge; let us endeavor to strengthen our minds by reflection, till our heads become a balance for our hearts; let us not confine all our thoughts to the petty occurrences of the day, or our knowledge to an acquaintance with our lovers' or husbands' hearts; but let the practice of every duty be subordinate to the grand one of improving our minds and preparing our affections for a more exalted state!

Beware then, my friends, of suffering the heart to be moved by every trivial incident: the reed is shaken by a breeze, and annually dies; but the oak stands firm, and for ages braves the storm!...

CHAPTER XIII.
SOME INSTANCE OF THE FOLLY WHICH THE IGNORANCE
OF WOMEN GENERATES

It is not necessary to inform the sagacious reader (now I enter on my concluding reflections) that the discussion of this subject merely consists in opening a few simple principles and clearing away the rubbish which obscured them. But, as all readers are not sagacious, I must be allowed to add some explanatory remarks to bring the subject home to reason—to that sluggish reason which supinely takes opinions on trust, and obstinately supports them to spare itself the labor of thinking.

Moralists have unanimously agreed that unless virtue be nursed by liberty it will never attain due strength—and what they say of man I extend to mankind, insisting that in all cases morals must be fixed on immutable principles—and that the being cannot be termed rational or virtuous who obeys any authority but that of reason.

To render women truly useful members of society, I argue that they should be led, by having their understandings cultivated on a large scale, to acquire a rational affection for their country, founded on knowledge, because it is obvious that we are little interested about what we do not understand. And to render this general knowledge of due importance, I have endeavored to show that private duties are never properly fulfilled unless the understanding enlarges the heart, and that public virtue is only an aggregate of private. But the distinctions established in society undermine both, by beating out the solid gold of virtue, till it becomes only the tinsel-covering of vice; for, while wealth renders a man more respectable than virtue, wealth will be sought before virtue; and while women's persons are caressed when a childish simper shows an absence of mind, the mind will lie fallow. Yet true voluptuousness must proceed from the mind; for what can equal the sensations produced by mutual affection supported by mutual respect? What are the cold or feverish caresses of appetite, but sin embracing death, compared with the modest overflowings of a pure heart and exalted imagination? Yes, let me tell the libertine of fancy when he despises understanding in woman, that the mind, which he disregards, gives life to the enthusiastic affection from which rapture, short-lived as it is, alone can flow! And that without virtue a sexual attachment must expire, like a tallow candle in the socket, creating intolerable disgust. To prove this I need only observe that men, who have wasted great part of their lives with women, and with whom they have sought for pleasure with eager thirst, entertain the meanest opinion of the sex. Virtue, true refiner of joy! if foolish men were to fritter thee from earth in order to give loose to all their appetites without a check, some sensual wight of taste would scale the heavens to invite thee back to give a zest to pleasure!

That women at present are by ignorance rendered foolish or vicious is, I think, not to be disputed; and that the most salutary effects tending to improve mankind might be expected from a REVOLUTION in female manners, appears, at least with a face of probability, to rise out of the observation. For, as marriage has been termed the parent of those endearing charities which draw men from the brutal herd, the corrupting intercourse that wealth, idleness and folly produce between the sexes is more universally injurious to morality than all the other vices of mankind collectively considered. To adulterous lust the most sacred duties are sacrificed, because, before marriage, men, by a promiscuous intimacy with women, learned to consider love as a selfish gratification—learned to separate it not only from esteem, but from the affection merely built on habit which mixes a little humility with it. Justice and friendship are also set at defiance, and that purity of taste is vitiated which would naturally lead a man to relish an artless display of affection rather than affected airs. But that noble simplicity of affection which dares to appear unadorned, has few attractions for the libertine, though it be the charm which, by cementing the matrimonial tie, secures to the pledges of a warmer passion the necessary parental attention; for children will never be properly educated till friendship subsists between parents. Virtue flies from a house divided against itself, and a whole legion of devils take up their residence there.

The affection of husbands and wives cannot be pure when they have so few sentiments in common, and when so little confidence is established at home, as must be the case when their pursuits are so different. That intimacy from which tenderness should flow, will not, can not, subsist between the vicious.

Contending, therefore, that the sexual distinction which men have so warmly insisted upon is arbitrary, I have dwelt on an observation that several sensible men, with whom I have conversed on the subject, allowed to be well founded, and it is simply this—that the little chastity to be found amongst men and consequent disregard of modesty tend to degrade both sexes; and, further, that the modesty of women, characterized as such, will often be only the artful veil of wantonness, instead of being the natural reflection of purity, till modesty be universally respected.

From the tyranny of man, I firmly believe, the greater number of female follies proceed; and the cunning, which I allow makes at present a part of their character, I likewise have repeatedly endeavored to prove is produced by oppression....

Asserting the rights which women, in common with men, ought to contend for, I have not attempted to extenuate their faults, but to prove them to be the natural consequence of their education and station in society. If so, it is reasonable to suppose that they will change their character and correct their vices and follies when they are allowed to be free in physical, moral and civil sense.

Let women share the rights, and she will emulate the virtues, of man; for she must grow more perfect when emancipated, or justify the authority that chains such a weak being to her duty. If the latter, it will be expedient to open a fresh trade with Russia for whips: a present which a father should always make to his son-in-law on his wedding-day, that a husband may keep his whole family in order by the same means; and, without any violation of justice, reign, wielding his sceptre, sole master of his house, because he is the only being in it who has reason:—the Divine, indefeasible, earthly sovereignty breathed into man by the Master of the Universe. Allowing this position, women have not any inherent rights to claim; and by the same rule their duties vanish, for rights and duties are inseparable.

Be just then, O ye men of understanding! and mark not more severely what women do amiss than the vicious tricks of the horse or the ass for whom ye provide provender—and allow her the privileges of ignorance to whom ye deny the rights of reason, or ye will be worse than Egyptian taskmasters, expecting virtue where Nature has not given understanding!

JAMES MILL

James Mill (1773–1836) was born in Scotland. After working as a journalist and writer, he met the utilitarian philosopher and reformer, Jeremy Bentham, and became his follower. For many years Mill and his family lived in a house owned by Bentham and spent long periods of time at Bentham's country house. Though he achieved literary success with the publication of his *History of British India* in 1817, Mill is better known today as a popularizer of Bentham's ideas. Possessing a highly logical mind, and a prose style clearer than Bentham's, Mill communicated Bentham's ideas on politics, economics, and law to a wider public. His *Essay on Government* (1820) provides a powerful argument for democratic government.

ESSAY ON GOVERNMENT (SELECTIONS)

In his *Essay on Government*, Mill begins by assuming that people, including those who are given positions of power over others, are self-interested. They will act to promote their own interests, even at the expense of other people, unless they are prevented from doing so. Accordingly, if one wants a government that will pursue the interests of the people rather than of the rulers, it must be made accountable to the people. A representative system is necessary, in which the representatives are regularly elected by the people. However, Mill did not carry this line of argument to its logical conclusion in regard to political rights for women. Whereas his logic would seem to imply that women too should have the right to elect their representatives, to make sure their interests are protected, Mill argues instead that their interests are encompassed by those of their fathers or husbands and so can be represented by them. The excerpt presented here is from Chapter 8 of the work.

ESSAY ON GOVERNMENT

CHAPTER 8

We have seen already, that if one man has power over others placed in his hands, he will make use of it for an evil purpose; for the purpose of rendering those other men the abject instruments of his will. If we, then, suppose, that one man has the power of choosing the Representatives of the people, it follows, that he will choose men who will use their power as Representatives for the promotion of this his sinister interest.

We have likewise seen, that when a few men have power given them over others, they will make use of it exactly for the same ends, and to the same extent, as the one man. It equally follows, that, if a small number of men have the choice of the Representatives, such Representatives will be chosen as will promote the interests of that small number, by reducing, if possible, the rest of the community to be the abject and helpless slaves of their will. ...

The general conclusion, therefore, which is evidently established is this; that the benefits of the Representative system are lost, in all cases in which the interests of the choosing body are not the same with those of the community.

It is very evident, that if the community itself were choosing the body, the interest of the community and that of the choosing body would be the same. The question is, whether that of any portion of the community, if erected into the choosing body, would remain the same?

One thing is pretty clear, that all those individuals whose interests are indisputably included in those of other individuals, may be struck off without inconvenience. In this light may be viewed all children, up to a certain age, whose interests are involved in those of their parents. In this light, also, women may be regarded, the interest of almost all of whom is involved either in that of their fathers or in that of their husbands.

Having ascertained that an interest identical with that of the whole community, is to be found in the aggregate males, of an age to be regarded as *sui juris*, who may be regarded as the natural Representatives of the whole population, we have to go on, and inquire, whether this requisite quality may not be found in some less number, some aliquot part of that body.

THOMAS BABINGTON MACAULAY

Thomas Babington Macaulay (1800–1859) was an English historian and political figure. He sat in Parliament and served as secretary of war. Macaulay's best known work was the five-volume *History of England from the Accession of James the Second* (1859–1861). The selection here is from his essay, "Mill on Government," published in 1829.

"MILL ON GOVERNMENT" (SELECTIONS)

In this selection, Macaulay harshly criticizes Mill. He has little trouble finding flaws in Mill's assumption that women's interests are "indisputably included" in those of their husbands or fathers. Although Mill assumes that it is part of human nature for people to wish to have power over others, this assumption unaccountably does not hold for men's desires in regard to women, although, as Macaulay says, throughout history "women have always been, and still are, over the greatest part of the globe, humble companions, playthings, captives, menials, beasts of burden."

MILL ON GOVERNMENT

We have seen how Mr. Mill proposes to render the interest of the representative body identical with that of the constituent body. The next question is, in what manner the interest of the constituent body is to be rendered identical with that of the community. Mr. Mill shows that a minority of the community, consisting even of many thousands, would be a bad constituent body, and, indeed, merely a numerous aristocracy.

"The benefits of the representative system," says he, "are lost, in all cases in which the interests of the choosing body are not the same with those of the community. It is very evident, that if the community itself were the choosing body, the interest of the community and that of the choosing body would be the same."

On these grounds, Mr. Mill recommends that all males of mature age, rich and poor, educated and ignorant, shall have votes. But why not the women too? This question has often been asked in parliamentary debate, and has never, to our knowledge, received a plausible answer. Mr. Mill escapes from it as fast as he can. But we shall take the liberty to dwell a little on the words of the oracle. "One thing," he says, "is pretty clear, that all those individuals whose interests are involved in those of other individuals, may be struck off without inconvenience.... In this light women may be regarded, the interest of almost all of whom is involved either in that of their fathers, or in that of their husbands."

If we were to content ourselves with saying, in answer to all the arguments in Mr. Mill's essay, that the interest of a king is involved in that of the community, we should be accused, and justly, of talking nonsense. Yet such an assertion would not, as far as we can perceive, be more unreasonable than that which Mr. Mill has here ventured to make. Without adducing one fact, without taking the trouble to perplex the question by one sophism, he placidly dogmatises away the interest of one half of the human race. If there be a word of truth in history, women have always been, and still are, over the greater part of the globe, humble companions, playthings, captives, menials, beasts of burden. Except in a few happy and highly civilised communities, they are strictly in a state of personal slavery. Even in those countries where they are best treated, the laws are generally unfavourable to them, with respect to almost all the points in which they are most deeply interested.

Mr. Mill is not legislating for England or the United States; but for mankind. Is then the interest of a Turk the same with that of the girls who compose his haram? Is the interest of a Chinese the same with that of the women whom he harnesses to his plough? Is the interest of an Italian the same with that of the daughter whom he devotes to God? The interest of a respectable Englishman may be said, without any impropriety, to be identical with that of his wife. But why is it so? Because human nature is *not* what Mr. Mill conceives it to be; because civilised men, pursuing their own happiness in a social state, are not Yahoos fighting for carrion; because there is a pleasure in being loved and esteemed, as well as in being feared and servilely obeyed. Why does not a gentleman restrict his wife to the bare maintenance which the law would compel him to allow her, that he may have more to spend on his personal pleasures? Because, if he loves her, he has pleasure in seeing her pleased; and because, even if he dislikes her, he is unwilling that the whole neighbourhood should cry shame on his meanness and ill-nature. Why does not the legislature, altogether composed of males, pass a law to deprive women of all civil privileges whatever, and reduce them to the state of slaves? By passing such a law they would gratify what Mr. Mill tells us is an inseparable part of human nature, the desire to possess unlimited power of inflicting pain upon others. That they do not pass such a law, though they have the power to pass it, and that no man in England wishes to see such a law passed, proves that the desire to possess unlimited power of inflicting pain is not inseparable from human nature.

If there be in this country an identity of interest between the two sexes, it cannot possibly arise from any thing but the pleasure of being loved, and of communicating happiness. For, that it does not spring from the mere instinct of sex, the treatment which women experience over the greater part of the world abundantly proves. And, if it be said that our laws of marriage have produced it, this only removes the argument a step further; for those laws have been made by males. Now, if the kind feelings of one half of the species be a sufficient security for the happiness of the other, why may not the kind feelings of a monarch or an aristocracy be sufficient at least to prevent them from grinding the people to the very utmost of power?

JOHN STUART MILL

ohn Stuart Mill (1806–1873) is a great figure in the history of Western political theory. Educated by his father, James Mill, who was a follower of the
utilitarian philosopher, Jeremy Bentham, John Stuart was remarkably pre-
cocious, studying Greek at age three and doing involved work in political
economy in his teens. The nervous breakdown he suffered as a result of being
turned into a "reasoning machine" is described in Mill's Autobiography
(1873).

Becoming increasingly dissatisfied with the strictures of Bentham's utili-
tarianism, Mill studied Romantic literature and philosophy, and in effect
attempted to synthesize elements of the utilitarian and Romantic traditions in
his own philosophy. Mill's *On Liberty* (1859) is perhaps the greatest defense of
individual liberty in our tradition. His other important works include *A
System of Logic* (1843), *Principles of Political Economy* (1848), and *Considerations
on Representative Government* (1861).

THE SUBJECTION OF WOMEN (SELECTIONS)

The *Subjection of Women* (1869) reflects Mill's longstanding interest in the situation of women in English society. An important factor in the work's genesis
was Mill's relationship with Harriet Taylor, "the most admirable person I had
ever known,"[1] whom he first met in 1830 and with whom he maintained a
close friendship until her husband died in 1849. Mill and Taylor married in
1851 and were intimate intellectual collaborators until her death in 1858. Mill

attributed a good part of *Subjection* and other works, notably *On Liberty*, to her inspiration and influence.

Subjection is a forceful piece of advocacy, especially notable for Mill's criticisms of attempts to justify women's subordination by appeal to their different and inferior natures.

Mill argues that women's "nature" cannot be discovered by observing women in existing society. For women have been molded by existing circumstances and a long history of oppressive subordination, dating back to earliest times: "I deny that any one knows, or can know, the nature of the two sexes, as long as they have only been seen in their present relation to one another." Until women are given opportunities to develop unhindered, their potential cannot be known.

According to Mill, women's situation in modern society originated in the rule of force. Because of men's superior physical strength, women have always been subordinate to men. In different areas, however, history has witnessed the abolition of superior force as a claim to rule. Slavery has been abolished and, in Western countries, the same is true of despotic political systems. But relations between men and women persist on that basis, "the primitive state of slavery lasting on."

Women's subordination to men is especially pernicious and difficult to dislodge because its benefits are so widespread. While political despotism benefited the tyrant himself and ruling circles, at the expense of the rest of the population, in every family, men profit at women's expense. And so it is not difficult to understand why men view the present system as "natural." The fact that women share this opinion is also easily understood in the light of powerful social forces inducing conformity.

In addition to criticizing the "naturalness" of existing relations, Mill argues for the benefits of an alternative system. This will not only free women from their subordinate status but also improve relationships between men and women and allow the family to inculcate virtue and the value of freedom in children more effectively. Mill presents the pragmatic argument for woman suffrage that his father had overlooked. Women require the vote for self-protection: "Women require the suffrage, as their guarantee of just and equal consideration." The contention that giving them the vote could create problems because their interests can clash with those of men clinches Mill's argument that women cannot rely on others to defend their interests but must be able to do so themselves. Mill argues that society will benefit from allowing women to exercise political rights and that they are qualified to do so.

Clear evidence of the influence of *The Subjection of Women* is frequent citation by later writers, including attempts by antisuffrage authors to refute Mill's arguments. The selections included here are from Chapters 1 and 3.

NOTE

1. John Stuart Mill, *Autobiography* (1873; rpt. Indianapolis, 1957), p. 119.

THE SUBJECTION OF WOMEN

CHAPTER 1

The generality of a practice is in some cases a strong presumption that it is, or at all events once was, conducive to laudable ends. This is the case, when the practice was first adopted, or afterwards kept up, as a means to such ends, and was grounded on experience of the mode in which they could be most effectually attained. If the authority of men over women, when first established, had been the result of a conscientious comparison between different modes of constituting the government of society; if, after trying various other modes of social organization—the government of women over men, equality between the two, and such mixed and divided modes of government as might be invented—it had been decided, on the testimony of experience, that the mode in which women are wholly under the rule of men, having no share at all in public concerns, and each in private, being under the legal obligation of obedience to the man with whom she has associated, her destiny, was the arrangement most conducive to the happiness and well being of both; its general adoption might then be fairly thought to be some evidence that, at the time when it was adopted, it was the best: though even then the considerations which recommended it may, like so many other primeval social facts of the greatest importance, have subsequently, in the course of ages, ceased to exist. But the state of the case is in every respect the reverse of this. In the first place, the opinion in favour of the present system, which entirely subordinates the weaker sex to the stronger, rests upon theory only; for there never has been trial made of any other: to that experience, in the sense in which it is vulgarly opposed to theory, cannot be pretended to have pronounced any verdict. And in the second place, the adoption of this system of inequality never was the result of deliberation, or forethought, or any social ideas, or any notion whatever of what conduced to the benefit of humanity or the good order of society. It arose simply from the fact that from the very earliest twilight of human society, every woman (owing to the value attached to her by men, combined with her inferiority in muscular strength) was found in a state of bondage to some man. Laws and systems of polity always begin by recognising the relations they find already existing between individuals. They convert what was a mere physical fact into a legal right, give it the sanction of society, and principally aim at the substitution of public and organized means of asserting and protecting these rights, instead of the irregular and lawless conflict of physical strength. Those who had already been compelled to obedience became in this manner legally bound to it. Slavery, from being a mere affair of force between the master and the slave, became regularized and a matter of compact among the masters, who, binding themselves to one another for common protection, guaranteed by their collective strength the private possessions of each, including his slaves. In early times, the great majority of the male sex were slaves, as well as the whole of the female. And many ages elapsed, some of them ages of high cultivation, before any thinker was bold enough to question the rightfulness, and the absolute social necessity, either of the one slavery or of the other. By degrees such thinkers did arise: and (the general progress of society assisting) the slavery of the male sex has, in all the countries of Christian Europe at least (though, in one of them, only within the last few years) been at length abolished, and that of the female sex has been gradually changed into a milder form of dependence. But this dependence, as it exists at present, is not an original institution, taking a fresh start from considerations of justice and social expediency—it is the primitive state of slavery lasting on, through successive mitigations and modifications occasioned by the same causes which have softened the general manners, and brought all human relations more under the control of justice and the influence of humanity. It has not lost the taint of its brutal origin. No presumption in its favour, therefore, can be drawn from the fact of its existence. The only such presumption which it could be supposed to have, must be grounded on its having lasted till now, when so many other things which came down from the same odious source have been done away with. And this, indeed, is what makes it strange to ordinary ears, to hear it asserted that the inequality of rights between men and women has no other source than the law of the strongest.

That this statement should have the effect of a paradox, is in some respects creditable to the progress of civilization, and the improvement of the moral sentiments of mankind. We now live—that is to say, one or two of the most advanced nations of the world now live—in a state in which the law of the strongest seems to be entirely abandoned as the regulating principle of the world's affairs: nobody professes it, and, as regards most of the relations between human beings, nobody is permitted to practise it. When any one succeeds in doing so, it is under cover of some pretext which gives him the semblance of having some general social interest on his side. This being the ostensible state of things, people flatter themselves that the rule of mere force is ended; that the law of the strongest cannot be the reason of existence of anything which has remained in full operation down to the present time. However any of our present institutions may have begun, it can only, they think, have been preserved to this period of advanced civilization by a well-grounded feeling of its adaptation to human nature, and conduciveness to the general good. They do not understand the great vitality and durability of institutions which place right on the side of might; how intensely they are clung to; how the good as well as the bad propensities and sentiments of those who have power in their hands, become identified with retaining it; how slowly these bad institutions give way, one at a time, the weakest first, beginning with those which are least interwoven with the daily habits of life; and how very rarely those who have obtained legal power because they first had physical, have ever lost their hold of it until the physical power had passed over to the other side. Such shifting of the physical force not having taken place in the case of women; this fact, combined with all the peculiar and characteristic features of the particular case, made it certain from the first that this branch of the system of right founded on might, though softened in its most atrocious features at an earlier period than several of the others, would be the very last to disappear. It was inevitable that this one case of a social relation grounded on force, would survive through generations of institutions grounded on equal justice, an almost solitary exception to the general character of their laws and customs; but which, so long as it does not proclaim its own origin, and as discussion has not brought out its true character, is not felt to jar with modern civilization, any more than domestic slavery among the Greeks jarred with their notion of themselves as a free people.

The truth is, that people of the present and the last two or three generations have lost all practical sense of the primitive condition of humanity; and only the few who have studied history accurately, or have much frequented the parts of the world occupied by the living representatives of ages long past, are able to form any mental picture of what society then was. People are not aware how entirely, in former ages, the law of superior strength was the rule of life; how publicly and openly it was avowed, I do not say cynically or shamelessly—for these words imply a feeling that there was something in it to be ashamed of, and no such notion could find a place in the faculties of any person in those ages, except a philosopher or a saint. History gives a cruel experience of human nature, in shewing how exactly the regard due to the life, possessions, and entire earthly happiness of any class of persons, was measured by what they had the power of enforcing; how all who made any resistance to authorities that had arms in their hands, however dreadful might be the provocation, had not only the law of force but all other laws, and all the notions of social obligation against them; and in the eyes of those whom they resisted, were not only guilty of crime, but of the worst of all crimes, deserving the most cruel chastisement which human beings could inflict. The first small vestige of a feeling of obligation in a superior to acknowledge any right in inferiors, began when he had been induced, for convenience, to make some promise to them. Though these promises, even when sanctioned by the most solemn oaths, were for many ages revoked or violated on the most trifling provocation or temptation, it is probable that this, except by persons of still worse than the average morality, was seldom done without some twinges of conscience. The ancient republics, being mostly grounded from the first upon some kind of mutual compact, or at any rate formed by an union of persons not very unequal in strength, afforded, in consequence, the first instance of a portion of human relations fenced around, and placed under the dominion of another law than that of force. And though the original law of force remained in full operation between them and their slaves, and also (except so far as limited by express compact) between a commonwealth and its subjects, or other independent commonwealths; the banishment of that primitive law even from so narrow a field, commenced the regeneration of human nature, by giving birth to sentiments of which experience soon demonstrated the immense value even for material interests, and which thenceforward only required to be enlarged, not created. Though slaves were no part of the commonwealth, it was in the free states that slaves were first felt to have rights as human beings. The Stoics were, I believe, the first (except so far as the Jewish law constitutes an exception) who taught as a part of morality that men were bound by moral obligations to their slaves. ...

If people are mostly so little aware how completely, during the greater parts of the duration of our species, the law of force was the avowed rule of general conduct, any other being only a special and exceptional consequence of peculiar ties—and from how very recent a date it is that the affairs of society in general have been even pretended to be regulated according to any moral law; as little do people remember or consider, how institutions and customs which never had any ground but the law of force, last on into ages and states of general opinion which never would have permitted their first establishment. Less than forty years ago, Englishmen might still by law hold human beings in bondage as saleable property: within the present century they might kidnap them and carry them off, and work them literally to death. This absolutely extreme case of the law of force, condemned by those who can tolerate almost every other form of arbitrary power, and which, of all others, presents features the most revolting to the feelings of all who look at it from an impartial position, was the law of civilized and Christian England within the memory of persons now living: and in one half of Anglo-Saxon America three or four years ago, not only did slavery exist, but the slave trade, and the breeding of slaves expressly for it, was a general practice between slave states. Yet not only was there a greater strength of sentiment against it, but, in England at least, a less amount either of feeling or of interest in favour of it, than of any other of the customary abuses of force: for its motive was the love of gain, unmixed and undisguised; and those who profited by it were a very small numerical fraction of the country, while the natural feeling of all who were not personally interested in it, was unmitigated abhorrence. So extreme an instance makes it almost superfluous to refer to any other: but consider the long duration of absolute monarchy. In England at present it is the almost universal conviction that military despotism is a case of the law of force, having no other origin or justification. Yet in all the great nations of Europe except England it either still exists, or has only just ceased to exist, and has even now a strong party favourable to it in all ranks of the people, especial-ly among persons of station and consequence. Such is the power of an established system, even when far from universal; when not only in almost every period of history there have been great and well-known examples of the contrary system, but these have almost invariably been afforded by the most illustrious and most prosperous communities. In this case, too, the possessor of the undue power, the person directly interested in it, is only one person, while those who are subject to it and suffer from it are literally all the rest. The yoke is naturally and necessarily humiliating to all persons, except the one who is on the throne, together with, at most, the one who expects to succeed to it. How different are these cases from that of the power of men over women! I am not now prejudging the question of its jus-tifiableness. I am showing how vastly more permanent it could not but be, even if not justifiable, than these other dominations which have neverthe-less lasted down to our own time. Whatever gratification of pride there is in the possession of power, and whatever personal interest in its exercise, is in this case not confined to a limited class, but common to the whole male sex. Instead of being, to most of its supporters, a thing desirable chiefly in the abstract, or, like the political ends usually contended for by factious, of little private importance to any but the leaders; it comes home to the person and hearth of every male head of a family, and of every one who looks forward to being so. The clodhopper exercises, or is to exercise, his share of the power equally with the highest nobleman. And the case is that in which the desire of power is the strongest: for every one who desires power, desires it most over those who are nearest to him, with whom his life is passed, with whom he has most concerns in common, and in whom any independence of his authority is oftenest likely to interfere with his individual prefer-ences. If, in the other cases specified, powers manifestly grounded only on force, and having so much less to support them, are so slowly and with so much difficulty got rid of, much more must it be so with this, even if it rests on no better foundation than those. We must consider, too, that the posses-sors of the power have facilities in this case, greater than in any other, to prevent any uprising against it. Every one of the subjects lives under the very eye, and almost, it may be said, in the hands, of one of the masters—in closer intimacy with him than with any of her fellow-subjects; with no means of combining against him, no power of even locally overmastering him, and, on the other hand, with the strongest motives for seeking his favour and avoiding to give him offence. In struggles for political emanci-pation, everybody knows how often its champions are bought off by bribes, or daunted by terrors. In the case of women, each individual of the subject-class is in a chronic state of bribery and intimidation combined. In setting up the standard of resistance, a large number of the leaders, and still more of the followers, must make an almost complete sacrifice of the pleasures or the alleviations of their own individual lot. If ever any system of privilege and enforced subjection had its yoke tightly riveted on the necks of those who are kept down by it, this has. I have not yet shown that it is a wrong system: but every one who is capable of thinking on the subject must see that even if it is, it was certain to outlast all other forms of unjust authority. And when some of the grossest of the other forms still exist in many civilized countries, and have only recently been got rid of in others, it would be strange if that which is so much the deepest-rooted had yet been perceptibly shaken anywhere. There is more reason to wonder that the protests and testimonies against it should have been so numerous and so weighty as they are.

Some will object, that a comparison cannot fairly be made between the government of the male sex and the forms of unjust power which I have adduced in illustrations of it, since these are arbitrary, and the effect of mere usurpation, while it on the contrary is natural. But was there ever any domination which did not appear natural to those who possessed it? There was a time when the division of mankind into two classes, a small one of masters and a numerous one of slaves, appeared, even to the most cultivated minds, to be a natural, and the only natural, condition of the human race. No less an intellect, and one which contributed not less to the progress of human thought, than Aristotle, held this opinion without doubt or misgiving; and rested it on the same premises on which the same assertion in regard to the dominion of men over women is usually based, namely that there are different natures among mankind, free natures, and slave natures; that the Greeks were of a free nature, the barbarian races of Thracians and Asiatics of a slave nature. But why need I go back to Aristotle? Did not the slaveowners of the Southern United States maintain the same doctrine, with all the fantacism with which men cling to the theories that justify their passions and legitimate their personal interests? Did they not call heaven and earth to witness that the dominion of white men over the black is natural, that the black race is by nature incapable of freedom, and marked out for slavery? some even going so far as to say that the freedom of manual labourers is an unnatural order of things anywhere. Again, the theorists of absolute monarchy have always affirmed it to be the only natural form of government; issuing from the patriarchal, which was the primitive and spontaneous form of society, framed on the model of the paternal, which is anterior to society itself, and, as they contend, the most natural authority of all. Nay, for that matter, the law of force itself, to those who could not plead any other, has always seemed the most natural of all grounds for the exercise of authority. Conquering races hold it to be Nature's own dictate that the conquered should obey the conquerors, or, as they euphoniously paraphrase it, that the feebler and more unwarlike races should submit to the braver and manlier. The smallest acquaintance with human life in the middle ages, shows how supremely natural the dominion of the feudal nobility over men of low condition appeared to the nobility themselves, and how unnatural the conception seemed, of a person of the inferior class claiming equality with them, or exercising authority over them. It hardly seemed less so to the class held in subjection. The emancipated serfs and burgesses, even in their most vigorous struggles, never made any pretension to a share of authority; they only demanded more or less of limitation to the power of tyrannizing over them. So true is it that unnatural generally means only uncustomary, and that everything which is usual appears natural. The subjection of women to men being a universal custom, any departure from it quite naturally appears unnatural. But how entirely, even in this case, the feeling is dependent on custom appears by ample experience. Nothing so much astonishes the people of distant parts of the world, when they first learn anything about England, as to be told that it is under a queen: the thing seems to them so unnatural as to be almost incredible. To Englishmen this does not seem in the least degree unnatural, because they are used to it; but they do feel it unnatural that women should be soldiers or members of parliament. In the feudal ages, on the contrary, war and politics were not thought unnatural to women, because not unusual; it seemed natural that women of the privileged classes should be of manly character, inferior in nothing but bodily strength to their husbands and fathers. The independence of women seemed rather less unnatural to the Greeks than to other ancients, on account of the fabulous Amazons (whom they believed to be historical), and the partial example afforded by the Spartan women; who, though no less subordinate by law than in other Greek states, were more free in fact, and being trained to bodily exercises in the same manner with men, gave ample proof that they were not naturally disqualified for them. There can be little doubt that Spartan experience suggested to Plato, among many other of his doctrines, that of the social and political equality of the two sexes.

But, it will be said, the rule of men over women differs from all these others in not being a rule of force: it is accepted voluntarily; women make no complaint, and are consenting parties to it. In the first place, a great number of women do not accept it. Ever since there have been women able to make their sentiments known by their writings (the only mode of publicity which society permits to them), an increasing number of them have recorded protests against their present social condition: and recently many thousands of them headed by the most eminent women known to the public, have petitioned Parliament for their admission to the Parliamentary Suffrage. The claim of women to be educated as solidly, and in the same branches of knowledge, as men, is urged with growing intensity, and with a great prospect of success; while the demand for their admission into professions and occupations hitherto closed against them, becomes every year more urgent. Though there are not in this country, as there are in the United States, periodical Conventions and an organized party to agitate for the Rights of Women, there is a numerous and active Society organized and managed by women, for the more limited object of obtaining the political franchise. Nor is it only in our own country and in America that women are beginning to protest, more or less collectively, against the disabilities under which they labour. France, and Italy, and Switzerland, and Russia now afford examples of the same thing. How many more women there are who silently cherish similar aspirations, no one can possibly know; but there are abundant tokens how many *would* cherish them, were they not so strenuously taught to repress them as contrary to the proprieties of their sex. It must be remembered, also, that no enslaved class ever asked for complete liberty at once. When Simon de Montfort called the deputies of the commons to sit for the first time in Parliament, did any of them dream of demanding that an assembly, elected by their constituents, should make and destroy ministries, and dictate to the king in affairs of state? No such thought entered into the imagination of the most ambitious of them. The nobility had already these pretensions; the commons pretended to nothing but to be exempt from arbitrary taxation, and from the gross individual oppression of the king's officers. It is a political law of nature that those who are under any power of ancient origin, never begin by complaining of the power itself, but only of its oppressive exercise. There is never any want of women who complain of ill usage by their husbands. There would be infinitely more, if complaint were not the greatest of all provocatives to a repetition and increase of the ill usage. It is this which frustrates all attempts to maintain the power but protect the woman against its abuses. In no other case (except that of a child) is the person who has been proved judicially to have suffered an injury, replaced under the physical power of the culprit who inflicted it. Accordingly wives, even in the most extreme and protracted cases of bodily ill usage, hardly ever dare avail themselves of the laws made for their protection: and if, in a moment of irrepressible indignation, or by the interference of neighbours, they are induced to do so, their whole effort afterwards is to disclose as little as they can, and to beg off their tyrant from his merited chastisement.

All causes, social and natural, combine to make it unlikely that women should be collectively rebellious to the power of men. They are so far in a position different from all other subject classes, that their masters require something more from them than actual service. Men do not want solely the obedience of women, they want their sentiments. All men, except the most brutish, desire to have, in the woman most nearly connected with them, not a forced slave but a willing one, not a slave merely, but a favourite. They have therefore put everything in practice to enslave their minds. The masters of all other slaves rely, for maintaining obedience, on fear; either fear of themselves, or religious fears. The masters of women wanted more than simple obedience, and they turned the whole force of education to effect their purpose. All women are brought up from the very earliest years in the belief that their ideal of character is the very opposite to that of men; not self-will, and government by self-control, but submission, and yielding to the control of others. All the moralities tell them that it is the duty of women, and all the current sentimentalities that it is their nature, to live for others; to make complete abnegation of themselves, and to have no life but in their affections. And by their affections are meant the only ones they are allowed to have—those to the men with whom they are connected, or to the children who constitute an additional and indefeasible tie between them and a man. When we put together three things—first, the natural attraction between opposite sexes; secondly, the wife's entire dependence on the husband, every privilege or pleasure she has being either his gift, or depending entirely on his will; and lastly, that the principal object of human pursuit, consideration, and all objects of social ambition, can in general be sought or obtained by her only through him, it would be a miracle if the object of being attractive to men had not become the polar star of feminine education and formation of character. And, this great means of influence over the minds of women having been acquired, an instinct of selfishness made men avail themselves of it to the utmost as a means of holding women in subjection, by representing to them meekness, submissiveness, and resignation of all individual will into the hands of a man, as an essential part of sexual attractiveness. Can it be doubted that any of the other yokes which mankind have succeeded in breaking, would have subsisted till now if the same means had existed, and had been as sedulously used, to bow down their minds to it? If it had been made the object of the life of every young plebeian to find personal favour in the eyes of some patrician, of every young serf with some seigneur; if domestication with him, and a share of his personal affections, had been held out as the prize which they all should look out for, the most gifted and aspiring being able to reckon on the most desirable prizes; and if, when this prize had been obtained, they had been shut out by a wall of brass from all interests not centering in him, all feelings and desires but those which he shared or inculcated; would not serfs and seigneurs, plebeians and patricians, have been as broadly distinguished at this day as men and women are? and would not all but a thinker here and there, have believed the distinction to be a fundamental and unalterable fact in human nature?

The preceding considerations are amply sufficient to show that custom, however universal it may be, affords in this case no presumption, and ought not to create any prejudice, in favour of the arrangements which place women in social and political subjection to men. But I may go farther, and maintain that the course of history, and the tendencies of progressive human society, afford not only no presumption in favour of this system of inequality of rights, but a strong one against it; and that, so far as the whole course of human improvement up to this time, the whole stream of modern tendencies, warrants any inference on the subject, it is, that this relic of the past is discordant with the future, and must necessarily disappear. ...

At present, in the more improved countries, the disabilities of women are the only case, save one, in which laws and institutions take persons at their birth, and ordain that they shall never in all their lives be allowed to compete for certain things. The one exception is that of royalty. Persons still are born to the throne; no one, not of the reigning family, can even occupy it, and no one even of that family can, by any means but the course of hereditary succession, attain it. All other dignitaries and social advantages are open to the whole male sex: many indeed are only attainable by wealth, but wealth may be striven for by any one, and is actually obtained by many men of the very humblest origin. The difficulties, to the majority, are indeed insuperable without the aid of fortunate accidents; but no male human being is under any legal ban: neither law nor opinion superadd artificial obstacles to the natural ones. Royalty, as I have said, is excepted: but in this case every one feels it to be an exception—an anomaly in the modern world, in marked opposition to its customs and principles, and to be justified only by extraordinary special expediencies, which, though individuals and nations differ in estimating their weight, unquestionably do in fact exist. But in this exceptional case, in which a high social function is, for important reasons, bestowed on birth instead of being put up to competition, all free nations contrive to adhere in substance to the principle from which they nominally derogate; for they circumscribe this high function by conditions avowedly intended to prevent the person to whom it ostensibly belongs from really performing it; while the person by whom it is performed, the responsible minister, does obtain the post by a competition from which no full-grown citizen of the male sex is legally excluded. The disabilities, therefore, to which women are subject from the mere fact of their birth, are the solitary examples of the kind in modern legislation. In no instance except this, which comprehends half the human race, are the higher social functions closed against any one by a fatality of birth which no exertions, and no change of circumstances, can overcome; for even religious disabilities (besides that in England and in Europe they have practically almost ceased to exist) do not close any career to the disqualified person in case of conversion.

The social subordination of women thus stands out an isolated fact in modern social institutions; a solitary breach of what has become their fundamental law; a single relic of an old world of thought and practice exploded in everything else, but retained in the one thing of most universal interest; as if a gigantic dolmen, or a vast temple of Jupiter Olympius, occupied the site of St. Paul's and received daily worship, while the surrounding Christian churches were only resorted to on fasts and festivals. This entire discrepancy between one social fact and all those which accompany it, and the radical opposition between its nature and the progressive movement which is the boast of the modern world, and which has successively swept away everything else of an analogous character, surely affords, to a conscientious observer of human tendencies, serious matter for reflection. It raises a primâ facie presumption on the unfavourable side, far outweighing any which custom and usage could in such circumstances create on the favourable; and should at least suffice to make this, like the choice between republicanism and royalty, a balanced question.

The least that can be demanded is, that the question should not be considered as prejudged by existing fact and existing opinion, but open to discussion on its merits, as a question of justice and expediency: the decision on this, as on any of the other social arrangements of mankind, depending on what an enlightened estimate of tendencies and consequences may show to be most advantageous to humanity in general, without distinction of sex. And the discussion must be a real discussion, descending to foundations, and not resting satisfied with vague and general assertions. It will not do, for instance, to assert in general terms, that the experience of mankind has pronounced in favour of the existing system. Experience cannot possibly have decided between two courses, so long as there has only been experience of one. If it be said that the doctrine of the equality of the sexes rests only on theory, it must be remembered that the contrary doctrine also has only one theory to rest upon. All that is proved in its favour by direct experience, is that mankind have been able to exist under it, and to attain the degree of improvement and prosperity which we now see; but whether that prosperity has been attained sooner, or is now greater, than it would have been under the other system, experience does not say. On the other hand, experience does say, that every step in improvement has been so invariably accompanied by a step made in raising the social position of women, that historians and philosophers have been led to adopt their elevation or debasement as on the whole the surest test and most correct measure of the civilization of a people or an age. Through all the progressive period of human history, the condition of women has been approaching nearer to equality with men. This does not of itself prove that assimilation must go on to complete equality; but it assuredly affords some presumption that such is the case.

Neither does it avail anything to say that the *nature* of the two sexes adapts them to their present functions and position, and renders these appropriate to them. Standing on the ground of common sense and the constitutions of the human mind, I deny that any one knows, or can know, the nature of the two sexes, as long as they have only been seen in their present relation to one another. If men had ever been found in society without women, or women without men, or if there had been a society of men and women in which the women were not under the control of the men, something might have been positively known about the mental and moral differences which may be inherent in the nature of each. What is now called the nature of women is an eminently artificial thing—the result of forced repression in some directions, unnatural stimulation in others. It may be asserted without scruple, that no other class of dependents have had their character so entirely distorted from its natural proportions by their relation with their masters; for, if conquered and slave races have been, in some respects, more forcibly repressed, whatever in them has not been crushed down by an iron heel has generally been let alone, and if left with any liberty of development, it has developed itself according to its own laws; but in the case of women, a hot-house and stove cultivation has always been carried on of some of the capabilities of their nature, for the benefit and pleasure of their masters. Then, because certain products of the general vital force sprout luxuriantly and reach a great development in this heated atmosphere and under this active nurture and watering, while other shoots from the same root, which are left outside in the wintry air, with ice purposely heaped all around them, have a stunted growth, and some are burnt off with fire and disappear; men, with that inability to recognise their own work which distinguishes the unanalytic mind, indolently believe that the tree grows of itself in the way they have made it grow, and that it would die if one half of it were not kept in a vapour bath and the other half in the snow.

Of all the difficulties which impede the progress of thought, and the formation of well-grounded opinions on life and social arrangements, the greatest is now the unspeakable ignorance and inattention of mankind in respect to the influences which form human character. Whatever any portion of the human species now are, or seem to be, such, it is supposed, they have a natural tendency to be: even when the most elementary knowledge of the circumstances in which they have been placed, clearly points out the causes that made them what they are. Because a cottier deeply in arrears to his landlord is not industrious, there are people who think that the Irish are naturally idle. Because constitutions can be overthrown when the authorities appointed to execute them turn their arms against them, there are people who think the French incapable of free government. Because the Greeks cheated the Turks, and the Turks only plundered the Greeks, there are persons who think that the Turks are naturally more sincere: and because women, as is often said, care nothing about politics except their personalities, it is supposed that the general good is naturally less interesting to women than to men. History, which is now so much better understood than formerly, teaches another lesson: if only by showing the extraordinary susceptibility of human nature to external influences, and the extreme variableness of those of its manifestations which are supposed to be most universal and uniform. But in history, as in travelling, men usually see only what they already had in their own minds; and few learn much from history, who do not bring much with them to its study.

Hence, in regard to that most difficult question, what are the natural differences between the two sexes—a subject on which it is impossible in the present state of society to obtain complete and correct knowledge—

while almost everybody dogmatizes upon it, almost all neglect and make light of the only means by which any partial insight can be obtained into it. This is an analytic study of the most important department of psychology, the laws of the influence of circumstances on character. For, however great and apparently ineradicable the moral and intellectual differences between men and women might be, the evidence of their being natural differences could only be negative. Those only could be inferred to be natural which could not possibly be artificial—the residuum, after deducting every characteristic of either sex which can admit of being explained from education or external circumstances. The profoundest knowledge of the laws of the formation of character is indispensible to entitle any one to affirm even that there is any difference, much more what the difference is, between the two sexes considered as moral and rational beings; and since no one, as yet, has that knowledge, (for there is hardly any subject which, in proportion to its importance, has been so little studied), no one is thus far entitled to any positive opinion on the subject. Conjectures are all that can at present be made; conjectures more or less probable, according as more or less authorized by such knowledge as we yet have of the laws of psychology, as applied to the formation of character.

CHAPTER III

To ordain that any kind of persons shall not be physicians, or shall not be advocates, or shall not be members of parliament, is to injure not them only, but all who employ physicians or advocates, or elect members of parliament, and who are deprived of the stimulating effect of greater competition on the exertions of the competitors, as well as restricted to a narrower range of individual choice.

It will perhaps be sufficient if I confine myself, in the details of my argument, to functions of a public nature: since, if I am successful as to those, it probably will be readily granted that women should be admissible to all other occupations to which it is at all material whether they are admitted or not. And here let me begin by marking out one function, broadly distinguished from all others, their right to which is entirely independent of any question which can be raised concerning their faculties. I mean the suffrage, both parliamentary and municipal. The right to share in the choice of those who are to exercise a public trust, is altogether a distinct thing from that of competing for the trust itself. If no one could vote for a member of parliament who was not fit to be a candidate, the government would be a narrow oligarchy indeed. To have a voice in choosing those by whom one is to be governed, is a means of self-protection due to every one, though he were to remain for ever excluded from the function of governing: and that women are considered fit to have such a choice, may be presumed from the fact, that the law already gives it to women in the most important of all cases to themselves: for the choice of the man who is to govern a woman to the end of life, is always supposed to be voluntarily made by herself. In the case of election to public trusts, it is the business of constitutional law to surround the right of suffrage with all needful securities and limitations; but whatever securities are sufficient in the case of the male sex, no others need be required in the case of women. Under whatever conditions, and within whatever limits, men are admitted to the suffrage, there is not a shadow of justification for not admitting women under the same. The majority of the women of any class are not likely to differ in political opinion from the majority of the men of the same class, unless the question be one in which the interests of women, as such, are in some way involved; and if they are so, women require the suffrage, as their guarantee of just and equal consideration. This ought to be obvious even to those who coincide in no other of the doctrines for which I contend. Even if every woman were a wife, and if every wife ought to be a slave, all the more would these slaves stand in need of legal protection: and we know what legal protection the slaves have, where the laws are made by their masters.

With regard to the fitness of women, not only to participate in elections, but themselves to hold offices or practise professions involving important public responsibilities; I have already observed that this consideration is not essential to the practical question in dispute: since any woman, who succeeds in an open profession, proves by that very fact that she is qualified for it. And in the case of public offices, if the political system of the country is such as to exclude unfit men, it will equally exclude unfit women: while if it is not, there is no additional evil in the fact that the unfit persons whom it admits may be either women or men. As long therefore as it is acknowledged that even a few women may be fit for these duties, the laws which shut the door on those exceptions cannot be justified by any opinion which can be held respecting the capacities of women in general. But, though this last consideration is not essential, it is far from being irrelevant. An unprejudiced view of it gives additional strength to the arguments against the disabilities of women, and reinforces them by high considerations of practical utility.

Let us at first make entire abstraction of all psychological considerations tending to show, that any of the mental differences supposed to exist between women and men are but the natural effect of the differences in their education and circumstances, and indicate no radical difference, far less radical inferiority, of nature. Let us consider women only as they already are, or as they are known to have been; and the capacities which they have already practically shown. What they have done, that at least, if nothing else, it is proved that they can do. When we consider how sedulously they are all trained away from, instead of being trained towards, any of the occupations or objects reserved for men, it is evident that I am taking a very humble ground for them, when I rest their case on what they have actually achieved. For, in this case, negative evidence is worth little, while any positive evidence is conclusive. It cannot be inferred to be impossible that a woman should be a Homer, or an Aristotle, or a Michael Angelo, or a Beethoven, because no woman has yet actually produced works comparable to theirs in any of those lines of excellence. This negative fact at most leaves the question uncertain, and open to psychological discussion. But it is quite certain that a woman can be a Queen Elizabeth, or a Deborah, or a Joan of Arc, since this is not inference, but fact. Now it is a curious consideration, that the only things which the existing law excludes women from doing, are the things which they have proved that they are able to do. There is no law to prevent a woman from having written all the plays of Shakespeare, or composed all the operas of Mozart. But Queen Elizabeth or Queen Victoria, had they not inherited the throne, could not have been intrusted with the smallest of the political duties, of which the former showed herself equal to the greatest. ...

Is it reasonable to think that those who are fit for the greater functions of politics, are incapable of qualifying themselves for the less? Is there any reason in the nature of things, that the wives and sisters of princes should, whenever called on, be found as competent as the princes themselves to *their* business, but that the wives and sisters of statesmen, and administrators, and directors of companies, and managers of public institutions, should be unable to do what is done by their brothers and husbands? The real reason is plain enough; it is that princesses, being more raised above the generality of men by their rank than placed below them by their sex, have never been taught that it was improper for them to concern themselves with politics; but have been allowed to feel the liberal interest natural to any cultivated human being, in the great transactions which took place around them, and in which they might be called on to take a part. The ladies of reigning families are the only women who are allowed the same range of interests and freedom of development as men; and it is precisely in their case that there is not found to be any inferiority. Exactly where and in proportion as women's capacities for government have been tried, in the proportion have they been found adequate.

This fact is in accordance with the best general conclusions which the world's imperfect experience seems as yet to suggest, concerning the peculiar tendencies and aptitudes characteristic of women, as women have hitherto been. I do not say, as they will continue to be; for, as I have already said more than once, I consider it presumption in any one to pretend to decide what women are or are not, can or cannot be, by natural constitution. They have always hitherto been kept, as far as regards spontaneous development, in so unnatural a state, that their nature cannot but have been greatly distorted and disguised; and no one can safely pronounce that if women's nature were left to choose its direction as freely as men's, and if no artificial bent were attempted to be given it except that required by the conditions of human society, and given to both sexes alike, there would be any material difference, or perhaps any difference at all, in the character and capacities which would unfold themselves. I shall presently show, that even the least contestable of the differences which now exist, are such as may very well have been produced merely by circumstances, without any difference of natural capacity. But, looking at women as they are known in experience, it may be said of them, with more truth than belongs to most other generalizations on the subject, that the general bent of their talents is towards the practical. This statement is conformable to all the public history of women, in the present and the past. It is not less borne out by common and daily experience. Let us consider the special nature of the mental capacities most characteristic of a woman of talent. They are all of a kind which fits them for practice, and makes them tend towards it. What is meant by a woman's capacity of intuitive perception? It means, a rapid and correct insight into present fact. It has nothing to do with general principles. Nobody every perceived a scientific law of nature by intuition, nor arrived at a general rule of duty or prudence by it. These are results of slow and careful collection and comparison of experience; and neither the men nor the women of intuition usually shine in this department, unless, indeed, the experience necessary is such as they can acquire by themselves. For what is called their intuitive sagacity makes them peculiarly apt in gathering such general truths as can be collected from their individual means of observation. When, consequently, they chance to be as well provided as men are with the results of other people's experience, by reading and education, (I use the word chance advisedly, for, in respect to the knowledge that tends to fit them for the greater concerns of life, the only educated women are the self-educated) they are better furnished than men in general with the essential requisites of skilful and successful practice. Men who have been much taught, are apt to be deficient in the sense of present fact; they do not see, in the facts which they are called upon to deal with, what is really there, but what they have been taught to expect. This is seldom the case with women of any ability. Their capacity of "intuition" preserves them from it. With equality of experience and of general faculties, a woman usually sees much more than a man of what is immediately before her. ...

HARRIET TAYLOR

arriet Taylor (1807–1858) met John Stuart Mill in 1830, while she was married to John Taylor, a wholesale druggist in London. She formed a close attachment to Mill, which lasted until the death of her husband in 1849. Taylor and Mill were married in 1851 and worked closely together until her death in 1858. Already a progressive writer when she met Mill, Taylor continued writing in support of social reforms throughout the remainder of her life. "The Enfranchisement of Women" (1851) was her most notable work.

"ENFRANCHISEMENT OF WOMEN" (SELECTIONS)

In "Enfranchisement of Women," Taylor argues against restricting women's opportunities to the domestic sphere. The only way to find out what women are capable of is to allow them to choose for themselves. She cites and argues against three sets of reasons for circumscribing women's activities: incompatibility between maternity and other roles; supposed coarsening effects of these other activities on women's characters; and undesirable social consequences of increasing competition in society, especially in the economy, which would follow from allowing women to compete. In his *Autobiography*, Mill says that "all that is most striking and profound" in *Subjection of Women* can be traced to Taylor's influence.[1] It is therefore not surprising that many arguments in "Enfranchisement" are similar to those found in *Subjection*, especially Taylor's attempt to link progress in treatment of women to overall historical development away from forcible rule in other areas of society. But Taylor goes beyond Mill in extending the realm of women's rights to the economic as well as the political: "Let every occupation be open to all, without favor or discourage- ment to any, and employments will fall into the hands of those men or women who are found by experience to be most capable of worthily exercising them."

NOTE

1. John Stuart Mill, *Autobiography* (1873; rpt. Indianapolis, 1957), p. 170.

ENFRANCHISEMENT OF WOMEN

When a prejudice, which has any hold on the feelings, finds itself reduced to the unpleasant necessity of assigning reasons, it thinks it has done enough when it has re-asserted the very point in dispute, in phrases which appeal to the pre-existing feeling. Thus, many persons think they have suf- ficiently justified the restrictions on women's field of action when they have said that the pursuits from which women are excluded are *unfeminine*, and that the *proper sphere* of women is not politics or publicity, but private and domestic life.

We deny the right of any portion of the species to decide for another portion, or any individual for another individual, what is and what is not their "proper sphere." The proper sphere for all human beings is the largest and highest which they are able to attain to. What this is, cannot be ascer- tained, without complete liberty of choice. The speakers at the Convention in America have, therefore, done wisely and right, in refusing to entertain the question of the peculiar aptitudes either of women or of men, or the limits within which this or that occupation may be supposed to be more adapted to the one or to the other. They justly maintain, that these ques- tions can only be satisfactorily answered by perfect freedom. Let every occupation be open to all, without favor or discouragement to any, and employments will fall into the hands of those men or women who are found by experience to be most capable of worthily exercising them. There need be no fear that women will take out of the hands of men any occupa- tion which men perform better than they. Each individual will prove his or her capacities, in the only way in which capacities can be proved—by trial; and the world will have the benefit of the best faculties of all its inhabitants. But to interfere beforehand by an arbitrary limit, and declare that whatever be the genius, talent, energy, or force of mind of an individual of a certain sex or class, those faculties shall not be exerted, or shall be exerted only in some few of the many modes in which others are permitted to use theirs, is not only an injustice to the individual, and a detriment to society, which loses what it can ill spare, but is also the most effectual mode of providing that, in the sex or class so fettered, the qualities which are not permitted to be exercised shall not exist.

We shall follow the very proper example of the Convention, in not entering into the question of the alleged differences in physical or mental qualities between the sexes; not because we have nothing to say, but because we have too much; to discuss this one point tolerably would need all the space we have to bestow on the entire subject. But if those who assert that the "proper sphere" for women is the domestic, mean by this that they have not shown themselves qualified for any other, the assertion evinces great ignorance of life and of history. Women have shown fitness for the highest social functions, exactly in proportion as they have been admitted to them. By a curious anomaly, though ineligible to even the lowest offices of state, they are in some countries admitted to the highest of all, the regal; and if there is any one function for which they have shown a decided vocation, it is that of reigning. Not to go back to ancient history, we look in vain for abler or firmer rulers than Elizabeth; than Isabella of Castile; than Maria Teresa; than Catherine of Russia; than Blanche, mother of Louis IX. of France; than Jeanne d'Albret, mother of Henri Quatre. There are few kings on record who contended with more difficult circumstances, or overcame them more triumphantly, than these. Even in semi-barbarous Asia, princesses who have never been seen by men, other than those of their own family, or ever spoken with them unless from behind a curtain, have as regents, during the minority of their sons, exhibited many of the most brilliant examples of just and vigorous administration. In the middle ages, when the distance between the upper and lower ranks was greater than even between women and men, and the women of the privileged class, however subject to tyranny from men of the same class, were at a less distance below them than any one else was, and often in their absence represented them in their functions and authority—numbers of heroic chatelaines, like Jeanne de Montfort, or the great Countess of Derby as late even as the time of Charles I., distinguished themselves not only by their political but their military capacity. In the centuries immediately before and after the Reformation, ladies of royal houses, as diplomatists, as governors of provinces, or as the confidential advisers of kings, equalled the first statesmen of their time; and the treaty of Cambray, which gave peace to Europe, was negociated in conferences where no other person was present, by the aunt of the Emperor Charles the Fifth, and the mother of Francis the First.

Concerning the fitness, then, of women for politics, there can be no question: but the dispute is more likely to turn upon the fitness of politics for women. When the reasons alleged for excluding women from active life in all its higher departments, are stripped of their garb of declamatory phrases, and reduced to the simple expression of a meaning, they seem to be mainly three: the incompatibility of active life with maternity, and with the cares of a household; secondly, its alleged hardening effect on the character; and thirdly, the inexpediency of making an addition to the already excessive pressure of competition in every kind of professional or lucrative employment.

The first, the maternity argument, is usually laid most stress upon: although (it needs hardly be said) this reason, if it be one, can apply only to mothers. It is neither necessary nor just to make imperative on women that they shall be either mothers or nothing; or that if they have been mothers once, they shall be nothing else during the whole remainder of their lives. Neither women nor men need any law to exclude them from an occupation, if they have undertaken another which is incompatible with it. No one proposes to exclude the male sex from Parliament because a man may be a soldier or sailor in active service, or a merchant whose business requires all his time and energies. Nine-tenths of the occupations of men exclude them *de facto* from public life, as effectually as if they were excluded by law; but that is no reason for making laws to exclude even the nine-tenths, much less the remaining tenth. The reason of the case is the same for women as for men. There is no need to make provision by law that a woman shall not carry on the active details of a household, or of the education of children, and at the same time practise a profession or be elected to Parliament. Where incompatibility is real, it will take care of itself; but there is gross injustice in making the incompatibility a pretence for the exclusion of those in whose case it does not exist. And these, if they were free to choose, would be a very large proportion—The maternity argument deserts its supporters in the case of single women, a large and increasing class of the population—a fact which, it is not irrelevant to remark, by tending to diminish the excessive competition of numbers, is calculated to assist greatly the prosperity of all. There is no inherent reason or necessity that all women should voluntarily choose to devote their lives to one animal function and its consequences. Numbers of women are wives and mothers only because there is no other career open to them, no other occupation for their feelings or their activities. Every improvement in their education and enlargement of their faculties—every thing which renders them more qualified for any other mode of life, increases the number of those to whom it is an injury and an oppression to be denied the choice. To say that women must be excluded from active life because maternity disqualifies them for it, is in fact to say, that every other career should be forbidden them in order that maternity may be their only resource.

But secondly, it is urged, that to give the same freedom of occupation to women as to men, would be an injurious addition to the crowd of competitors, by whom the avenues to almost all kinds of employment are choked up, and its remuneration depressed. This argument, it is to be observed, does not reach the political question. It gives no excuse for withholding from women the rights of citizenship. The suffrage, the jury-box, admission to the legislature and to office, it does not touch. It bears only on the industrial branch of the subject. Allowing it, then, in an economical point of view, its full force; assuming that to lay open to women the employments now monopolized by men, would tend, like the breaking down of other monopolies, to lower the rate of remuneration in those employments, let us consider what is the amount of this evil consequence, and what the compensation for it. The worst ever asserted, much worse than is at all likely to be realized, is, that if women competed with men, a man and a woman could not together earn more than is now earned by the man alone. Let us make this supposition, the most unfavorable supposition possible: the joint income of the two would be the same as before, while the woman would be raised from the position of a servant to that of a partner. Even if every woman, as matters now stand, had a claim on some man for support, how infinitely preferable is it that part of the income should be of the woman's earning, even if the aggregate sum were but little increased by it, rather than that she should be compelled to stand aside in order that men may be the sole earners, and the sole dispensers of what is earned. Even under the present laws respecting the property of women, a woman who contributes materially to the support of the family, cannot be treated in the same contemptuously tyrannical manner as one who, however she may toil as a domestic drudge, is a dependent on the man for subsistence. As for the depression of wages by increase of competition, remedies will be found for it in time. Palliatives might be applied immediately; for instance, a more rigid exclusion of children from industrial employment, during the years in which they ought to be working only to strengthen their bodies and minds for after life. Children are necessarily dependent, and under the power of others; and their labor, being not for themselves, but for the gain of their parents, is a proper subject for legislative regulation. With respect to the future, we neither believe that improvident multiplication, and the consequent excessive difficulty of gaining a subsistence, will always continue, nor that the division of mankind into capitalists and hired laborers, and the regulation of the reward of laborers mainly by demand and supply, will be for ever, or even much longer, the rule of the world. But so long as competition is the general law of human life, it is tyranny to shut out one-half of the competitors. All who have attained the age of self-government, have an equal claim to be permitted to sell whatever kind of useful labor they are capable of, for the price which it will bring.

The third objection to the admission of women to political or professional life, its alleged hardening tendency, belongs to an age now past, and is scarcely to be comprehended by people of the present time.—There are still, however, persons who say that the world and its avocations render men selfish and unfeeling; that the struggles, rivalries and collisions of business and of politics make them harsh and unamiable; that if half the species must unavoidably be given up to these things, it is the more necessary that the other half should be kept free from them; that to preserve women from the bad influences of the world, is the only chance of preventing men from being wholly given up to them.

There would have been plausibility in this argument when the world was still in the age of violence; when life was full of physical conflict, and every man had to redress his injuries, or those of others, by the sword or by the strength of his arm. Women, like priests, by being exempted from such responsibilities, and from some part of the accompanying dangers, may have been enabled to exercise a beneficial influence. But in the present condition of human life, we do not know where those hardening influences are to be found, to which men are subject, and from which women are at present exempt. Individuals now-a-days are seldom called upon to fight hand to hand, even with peaceful weapons; personal enmities and rivalries count for little in worldly transactions; the general pressure of circumstances, not the adverse will of individuals, is the obstacle men now have to make head against. That pressure, when excessive, breaks the spirit, and cramps and sours the feelings, but not less of women than of men, since they suffer certainly not less from its evils. There are still quarrels and dislikes, but the sources of them are changed. The feudal chief once found his bitterest enemy in his powerful neighbor, the minister or courtier in his rival for place; but opposition of interest in active life, as a cause of personal animosity, is out of date; the enmities of the present day arise not from great things, but small, from what people say of one another, more than from what they do; and if there are hatred, malice, and all uncharitableness, they are to found among women fully as much as among men. In the present state of civilization, the notion of guarding women from the hardening influences of the world, could only be realized by secluding them from society altogether. The common duties of common life, as at present constituted, are incompatible with any other softness in women than weakness. Surely weak minds in weak bodies must ere long cease to be even supposed to be either attractive or amiable.

But, in truth, none of these arguments and considerations touch the foundations of the subject. The real question is, whether it is right and expedient that one-half of the human race should pass through life in a state of forced subordination to the other half. If the best state of human society is that of being divided into two parts, one consisting of persons with a will and a substantive existence, the other of humble companions to these persons, attached, each of them to one, for the purpose of bringing up *his* children, and making *his* home pleasant to him; if this is the place assigned to women, it is but kindness to educate them for this; to make them believe that the greatest good fortune which can befal them, is to be chosen by some man for this purpose; and that every other career which the world deems happy or honorable, is closed to them by the law, not of social institutions, but of nature and destiny.

When, however, we ask why the existence of one-half the species should be merely ancillary to that of the other—why each woman should be a mere appendage to a man, allowed to have no interests of her own, that there may be nothing to compete in her mind with his interests and his pleasure; the only reason which can be given is, that men like it. It is agreeable to them that men should live for their own sake, women for the sake of men; and the qualities and conduct in subjects which are agreeable to rulers, they succeed for a long time in making the subjects themselves consider as their appropriate virtues. Helvetius has met with much obloquy for asserting, that persons usually mean by virtues, the qualities which are useful or convenient to themselves. How truly this is said of mankind in general, and how wonderfully the ideas of virtue, set afloat by the powerful, are caught and imbibed by those under their dominion, is exemplified by the manner in which the world were once persuaded that the supreme virtue of subjects was loyalty to kings, and are still persuaded that the paramount virtue of womanhood is loyalty to men. Under a nominal recognition of a moral code common to both, in practice self-will and self-assertion form the type of what are designated as manly virtues, while abnegation of self, patience, resignation, and submission to power, unless when resistance is commanded by other interests than their own, have been stamped by general consent as pre-eminently the duties and graces required of women. The meaning being merely, that power makes itself the centre of moral obligation, and that a man likes to have his own will, but does not like that his domestic companion should have a will different from his.

We are far from pretending that in modern and civilized times, no reciprocity of obligation is acknowledged on the part of the stronger. Such an assertion would be very wide of the truth. But even this reciprocity, which has disarmed tyranny, at least in the higher and middle classes, of its most revolting features, yet when combined with the original evil of the dependent condition of women, has introduced in its turn serious evils.

In the beginning, and among tribes which are still in a primitive condition, women were and are the slaves of men for the purposes of toil. All the hard bodily labor devolves on them. The Australian savage is idle, while women painfully dig up the roots on which he lives. An American Indian, when he has killed a deer, leaves it, and sends a woman to carry it home. In a state somewhat more advanced, as in Asia women were and are the slaves of men for the purposes of sensuality. In Europe, there early succeeded a third and milder dominion, secured not by blows, nor by locks and bars, but by sedulous inculcation on the mind; feelings also of kindness, and ideas of duty, such as a superior owes to inferiors under his protection, became more and more involved in the relation. But it did not, for many ages, become a relation of companionship, even between unequals; the lives of the two persons were apart. The wife was part of the furniture of home, of the resting-place to which the man returned from business or pleasure. His occupations were, as they still are, among men; his pleasures and excitements also were, for the most part, among men—among his equals. He was a patriarch and a despot within four walls, and irresponsible power had its effect, greater or less according to his disposition, in rendering him domineering, exacting, self-worshipping, when not capriciously or brutally tyrannical. But if the moral part of his nature suffered, it was not necessarily so, in the same degree, with the intellectual or the active portion. He might have as much vigor of mind and energy of character as his nature enabled him, and as the circumstances of his times allowed. He might write the "Paradise Lost," or win the battle of Marengo. This was the condition of the Greeks and Romans, and of the moderns until a recent date. Their relations with their domestic subordinates occupied a mere corner, though a cherished one of their lives. Their education as men, the formation of their character and faculties, depended mainly on a different class of influences.

It is otherwise now. The progress of improvement has imposed on all possessors of power, and of domestic power among the rest, an increased and increasing sense of correlative obligation. No man now thinks that his wife has no claim upon his actions but such as he may accord to her. All men, of any conscience, believe that their duty to their wives is one of the most binding of their obligations. Nor is it supposed to consist solely in protection, which, in the present state of civilization, women have almost ceased to need; it involves care for their happiness and consideration of their wishes, with a not unfrequent sacrifice of their own to them. The power of husbands has reached the stage which the power of kings had arrived at, when opinion did not yet question the rightfulness of arbitrary power, but in theory, and to a certain extent, in practice, condemned the selfish use of it. This improvement in the moral sentiments of mankind, and increased sense of the consideration due by every man to those who have no one but himself to look to, has tended to make home more and more the centre of interest, and domestic circumstances and society a larger and larger part of life, and of its pursuits and pleasures. The tendency has been strengthened by the changes of tastes and manners which have so remarkably distinguished the last two or three generations. In days not far distant, men found their excitement, and filled up their time in violent bodily exercises, noisy merriment, and intemperance. They have now, in all but the very poorest classes, lost their inclination for these things, and for the coarser pleasures generally; they have now scarcely any tastes but those which they have in common with women, and, for the first time in the world, men and women are really companions. A most beneficial change, if the companionship were between equals; but being between unequals, it produces, what good observers have noticed, though without perceiving its cause, a progressive deterioration among men in what had hitherto been considered the masculine excellences. Those who are so careful that women should not become men, do not see that men are becoming, what they have decided that women should be—are falling into the feebleness which they have so long cultivated in their companions. Those who are associated in their lives, tend to become assimilated in character. In the present closeness of association between the sexes, men cannot retain manliness unless women acquire it....

For the interest, therefore, not only of women, but of men, and of human improvement in the widest sense, the emancipation of women, which the modern world often boasts of having effected, and for which credit is sometimes given to civilization, and sometimes to Christianity, cannot stop where it is. If it were either necessary or just, that one portion of mankind should remain mentally and spiritually only half developed, the development of the other portion ought to have been made, as far as possible, independent of their influence. Instead of this, they have become the most intimate, and it may now be said, the only intimate associates of those to whom yet they are sedulously kept inferior; and have been raised just high enough to drag the others down to themselves.

Part II

Suffragists

SARAH GRIMKÉ
AND ANGELINA GRIMKÉ

S arah Grimké (1792–1873) and her younger sister Angelina (1805–1879), were born into a South Carolina slave-holding family. For many years, Sarah Grimké struggled with the moral dilemma of living in the South and thereby tacitly approving of slavery. She joined and left a number of different churches looking for guidance, eventually settling on the Congregation of Friends in Charleston. The Quakers were the only organization in the South that publicly disavowed slavery—a position the Southern establishment found abhorrent. In 1822, Grimké left the South for Philadelphia, where she and Angelina, who joined her there seven years later, were active in the society of Friends. Although the Quakers had ideas advanced far beyond those of any other Christian sect of the time—women were allowed full participation in services, slavery was condemned—the society advocated gradualism when it came to abolition, a position the Grimkés could not accept.

The Grimkés found a more morally congenial environment in the new American Anti-Slavery Society and soon became active members, speaking to groups in the North about the evils of slavery. They became controversial figures, not only because of their views on slavery, but also because cultural norms of the time did not permit women to speak publicly, especially about political issues. Much was written in the press attacking the "brazenness" of their activism. As a result of these attacks, the Grimkés came to see connections between the oppression of enslaved Africans and of women. They began to speak about God-given, natural rights that were being denied both groups. Although over the years the abolitionist movement wavered in its support of political rights for women, it provided fertile ground for broaching the issue and a constituency for political action on behalf of women's rights.

SARAH GRIMKÉ, LETTERS ON THE EQUALITY OF THE SEXES (SELECTIONS)

The selections reproduced here from Letters 1 and 12 of Sarah Grimké's *Letters on the Equality of the Sexes* (1838) show the origin of her views in her religious orientation and interest in the plight of slaves. Grimké analyzes the Biblical account of women's sphere, believing that almost everything that is said about this is incorrect. She notes the equality of Adam and Eve at their creation and in the Garden of Eden, claiming that this was not disrupted by their fall: "They both fell from innocence, and consequently from happiness, *but not from equality.*"

In Letter 12, Grimké compares the position of women and slaves. Examination of a number of laws that pertain to women shows that they "are not very unlike the slave laws of Louisiana."

LETTERS ON THE EQUALITY OF THE SEXES, AND THE CONDITION OF WOMAN.

Addressed to Mary S. Parker, President of the Boston Female Anti-Slavery Society

LETTER I

My Dear Friend,

In attempting to comply with thy request to give my views on the Province of Woman, I feel that I am venturing on nearly untrodden ground, and that I shall advance arguments in opposition to a corrupt public opinion, and to the perverted interpretation of Holy Writ, which has so universally obtained. But I am in search of truth; and no obstacle shall prevent my prosecuting that search, because I believe the welfare of the world will be materially advanced by every new discovery we make of the designs of Jehovah in the creation of woman. It is impossible that we can answer the purpose of our being, unless we understand that purpose. It is impossible that we should fufil our duties, unless we comprehend them; or live up to our privileges, unless we know what they are.

In examining this important subject, I shall depend solely on the Bible to designate the sphere of woman, because I believe almost every thing that has been written on this subject, has been the result of a misconception of the simple truths revealed in the Scriptures, in consequence of the false translation of many passages of Holy Writ. My mind is entirely delivered from the superstitious reverence which is attached to the English version of the Bible. King James's translators certainly were not inspired. I therefore claim the original as my standard, *believing that to have been inspired*, and I also claim to judge for myself what is the meaning of the inspired writers, because I believe it to be the solemn duty of every individual to search the Scriptures for themselves, with the aid of the Holy Spirit, and not be governed by the views of any man, or set of men.

We must first view woman at the period of her creation. "And God said, Let us make man in our own image, after our likeness; and let them have dominion over the fish of the sea, and over the fowl of the air, and over the cattle, and over all the earth, and over every creeping thing that creepeth upon the earth. So God created man in his own image, in the image of God created he him, male and female created he them" [Gen. 1:26–27]. In all this sublime description of the creation of man, (which is a generic term including man and woman), there is not one particle of difference intimated as existing between them. They were both made in the image of God; dominion was given to both over every other creature, but not over each other. Created in perfect equality, they were expected to exercise the vicegerence intrusted to them by their Maker, in harmony and love.

Let us pass on now to the recapitulation of the creation of man—"The Lord God formed man of the dust of the ground, and breathed into his nostrils the breath of life; and man became a living soul. And the Lord God said, it is not good that man should be alone, I will make him an help meet for him" [Gen. 2:7–18]. All creation swarmed with animated beings capable of natural affection, as we know they still are; it was not, therefore, merely to give man a creature susceptible of loving, obeying, and looking up to him, for all that the animals could do and did do. It was to give him a companion, *in all respects* his equal; one who was like himself *a free agent*, gifted with intellect and endowed with immortality; not a partaker merely of his animal gratifications, but able to enter into all his feelings as a moral and responsible being. If this had not been the case, how could she have been an help meet for him? I understand this as applying not only to the parties entering into the marriage contract, but to all men and women, because I believe God designed woman to be an help meet for man in every good and perfect work. She was a part of himself, as if Jehovah designed to make the oneness and identity of man and woman perfect and complete; and when the glorious work of their creation was finished, "the morning stars sang together, and all the sons of God shouted for joy" [Job 38:7].

This blissful condition was not long enjoyed by our first parents. Eve, it would seem from the history, was wandering along amid the bowers of Paradise, when the serpent met with her. From her reply to Satan, it is evident that the command not to eat "of the tree that is in the midst of the garden," was given to both, although the term man was used when the prohibition was issued by God. "And the woman said unto the serpent, WE may eat of the fruit of the trees of the garden, but of the fruit of the tree which is in the midst of the garden, God hath said, YE shall not eat of it, neither shall YE touch it, lest YE die" [Gen. 3:3]. Here the woman was exposed to temptation from a being with whom she was unacquainted. She had been accustomed to associate with her beloved partner, and to hold communion with God and with angels; but of satanic intelligence, she was in all probability entirely ignorant. Through the subtlety of the serpent, she was beguiled. And "when she saw that the tree was good for food, and that it was pleasant to the eyes, and a tree to be desired to make one wise, she took of the fruit thereof and did eat" [Gen. 3:6].

We next find Adam involved in the same sin, not through the instrumentality of a supernatural agent, but through that of his equal, a being whom he must have known was liable to transgress the divine command, because he must have felt that he was himself a free agent, and that he was restrained from disobedience only by the exercise of faith and love towards his Creator. Had Adam tenderly reproved his wife, and endeavored to lead her to repentance instead of sharing in her guilt, I should be much more ready to accord to man that superiority which he claims; but as the facts stand disclosed by the sacred historian, it appears to me that to say the least, there was as much weakness exhibited by Adam as by Eve. They both fell from innocence, and consequently from happiness, *but not from equality.*

LETTER XII

My Dear Sister,
There are few things which present greater obstacles to the improvement and elevation of woman to her appropriate sphere of usefulness and duty, than the laws which have been enacted to destroy her independence, and crush her individuality; laws which, although they are framed for her government, she has had no voice in establishing, and which rob her of some of her *essential rights.* Woman has no political existence. With the single exception of presenting a petition to the legislative body, she is a cipher in the nation; or, if not actually so in representative governments, she is only counted, like the slaves of the South, to swell the number of law-makers who form decrees for her government, with little reference to her benefit, except so far as her good may promote their own. I am not sufficiently acquainted with the laws respecting women on the continent of Europe, to say anything about them. But Prof. Follen, in his essay on "The Cause of Freedom in our Country," says, "Woman, though fully possessed of that rational and moral nature which is the foundation of all rights, enjoys amongst us fewer legal rights than under the civil law of continental

Europe." I shall confine myself to the laws of our country. These laws bear with peculiar rigor on married women. Blackstone, in the chapter entitled "Of husband and wife," says:—

> By marriage, the husband and wife are one person in law; that is, *the very being, or legal existence of the woman* is suspended during the marriage, or at least is incorporated and consolidated into that of the husband under whose wing, protection and cover she performs everything. For this reason, a man cannot grant anything to his wife, or enter into covenant with her; for the grant would be to suppose her separate existence, and to covenant with her would be to covenant with himself; and therefore it is also generally true, that all compacts made between husband and wife when single, are voided by the intermarriage. A woman indeed may be attorney for her husband, but that implies no separation from, but is rather a representation of, her love.

Here now, the very being of a woman, like that of a slave, is absorbed in her master. All contracts made with her, like those made with slaves by their owners, are a mere nullity. Our kind defenders have legislated away almost all our legal rights, and in the true spirit of such injustice and oppression, have kept us in ignorance of those very laws by which we are governed. They have persuaded us, that we have no right to investigate the laws, and that, if we did, we could not comprehend them; they alone are capable of understanding the mysteries of Blackstone, &c. But they are not backward to make us feel the practical operation of their power over our actions.

> The husband is bound to provide his wife with necessaries by law, as much as himself; and if she contracts debts for them, he is obliged to pay for them; but for anything besides necessaries, he is not chargeable.

Yet a man may spend the property he has acquired by marriage at the ale-house, the gambling table, or in any other way that he pleases. Many instances of this kind have come to my knowledge; and women, who have brought their husbands handsome fortunes, have been left, in consequence of the wasteful and dissolute habits of their husbands, in straitened circumstances, and compelled to toil for the support of their families.

> If the wife be indebted before marriage, the husband is bound afterwards to pay the debt; for he has adopted her and her circumstances together.

The wife's property is, I believe, equally liable for her husband's debts contracted before marriage.

If the wife be injured in her person or property, she can bring no action for redress without her husband's concurrence, and his name as well as her own: neither can she be sued, without making her husband a defendant.

This law that "a wife can bring no action," &c., is similar to the law respecting slaves. "A slave cannot bring a suit against his master, or any other person, for an injury—his master, must bring it." So if any damages are recovered for an injury committed on a wife, the husband pockets it; in the case of the slave, the master does the same.

In criminal prosecutions, the wife may be indicted and punished separately, unless there be evidence of coercion from the fact that her offence was committed in the presence, or by the command of her husband. A wife is excused from punishment for theft committed in the presence, or by the command of her husband.

It would be difficult to frame a law better calculated to destroy the responsibility of woman as a moral being, or a free agent. Her husband is supposed to possess unlimited control over her; and if she can offer the flimsy excuse that he bade her steal, she may break the eighth commandment with impunity, as far as human laws are concerned.

Our law, in general, considers man and wife as one person; yet there are some instances in which she is separately considered, as inferior to him and acting by his compulsion. Therefore, all deeds executed, and acts done by her during her coverture (i.e., marriage), are void, except it be a fine, or like matter of record, in which case she must be solely and secretly examined, to learn if her act be voluntary.

Such a law speaks volumes of the abuse of that power which men have vested in their own hands....

Women should certainly know the laws by which they are governed, and from which they frequently suffer; yet they are kept in ignorance, nearly as profound, of their legal rights, and of the legislative enactments which are to regulate their actions, as slaves....

The laws above cited are not very unlike the slave laws of Louisiana.

All that a slave possesses belongs to his master; he possesses nothing of his own, except what his master chooses he should possess.

By the marriage, the husband is absolutely master of the profits of the wife's lands during the coverture, and if he has had a living child, and survives the wife, he retains the whole of those lands, if they are estates of inheritance, during his life; but the wife is entitled only to one third if she survives, out of the husband's estates of inheritance. But this she has, whether she has had a child or not. With regard to the property of women, there is taxation without representation; for they pay taxes without having the liberty of voting for representatives.

And this taxation, without representation, be it remembered, was the cause of our Revolutionary war, a grievance so heavy, that it was thought necessary to purchase exemption from it an immense expense of blood and treasure, yet the daughters of New England, as well as of all the other States of this free Republic, are suffering a similar injustice—but for one, I had rather we should suffer any injustice or oppression, than that my sex should have any voice in the political affairs of the nation.

The laws I have quoted, are, I believe, the laws of Massachusetts, and, with few exceptions, of all the States in this Union. "In Louisiana and Missouri, and possibly, in some other southern States, a woman not only has half her husband's property by right at his death, but may always be considered as possessed of half his gains during his life; having at all times power to bequeath that amount." That the laws which have generally been adopted in the United States, for the government of women, have been framed almost entirely for the exclusive benefit of men, and with a design to oppress women, by depriving them of all control over their property, is too manifest to be denied. Some liberal and enlightened men, I know, regret the existence of these laws; and I quote with pleasure an extract from Harriet Martineau's *Society in America* [1837] as a proof of that assertion. "A liberal minded lawyer of Boston, told me that his advice to testators always is to leave the largest possible amount to the widow, subject to the condition of her leaving it to the children, but that it is with shame that he reflects that any women should owe that to his professional advice, which the law should have secured to her as a right." I have known a few instances where men have left their whole property to their wives, when they have died, leaving only minor children; but I have known more instances of "the friend and helper of many years, being portioned off like a salaried domestic," instead of having a comfortable independence secured to her, while the children were amply provided for.

As these abuses do exist, and women suffer intensely from them, our brethren are called upon in this enlightened age, by every sentiment of honor, religion and justice, to repeal these unjust and unequal laws, and restore to woman those rights which they have wrested from her. Such laws approximate too nearly to the laws enacted by slaveholders for the government of their slaves, and must tend to debase and depress the mind of that being, whom God created as a help meet for man, or "helper like unto himself," and designed to be his equal and his companion. Until such laws are annulled, woman never can occupy that exalted station for which she was intended by her Maker. And just in proportion as they are practically disregarded, which is the case to some extent, just so far is woman assuming that independence and nobility of character which she ought to exhibit.

The various laws which I have transcribed leave women very little more liberty, or power, in some respects, than the slave. "A slave," says the civil code of Louisiana, "is one who is in the power of a master, to whom he belongs. He can possess nothing, nor acquire anything, but what must belong to his master." I do not wish by any means to intimate that the condition of free women can be compared to that of slaves in suffering, or in degradation; still, I believe the laws which deprive married women of their rights and privileges, have a tendency to lessen them in their own estimation as moral and responsible beings, and that their being made by civil law inferior to their husbands, has a debasing and mischievous effect upon them, teaching them practically the fatal lesson to look unto man for protection and indulgence.

Ecclesiastical bodies, I believe, without exception, follow the example of legislative assemblies, in excluding woman from any participation in forming the discipline by which she is governed. The men frame the laws, and, with few exceptions, claim to execute them on both sexes. In ecclesiastical, as well as civil courts, woman is tried and condemned, not by a jury of her peers, but by beings, who regard themselves as her superiors in the scale of creation. Although looked upon as an inferior, when considered as an intellectual being, woman is punished with the same severity as man, when she is guilty of moral offences. Her condition resembles, in some measure, that of the slave, who, while he is denied the advantages of his more enlightened master, is treated with even great rigor of the law. Hoping that in the various reformations of the day, women may be relieved from some of their legal disabilities, I remain.

Thine in the bonds of womanhood,

Sarah M. Grimké

ANGELINA GRIMKÉ, LETTERS TO CATHERINE E. BEECHER (SELECTIONS)

In the selection reproduced here from Letter 12 of her *Letters to Catherine Beecher* (1838), Angelina Grimké notes what she has learned from looking into the rights of slaves. Her work in opposition to slavery served as "the high school in which human rights are more fully investigated and better understood than in any other." The plight of slaves calls attention to a fundamental moral principle: "Human beings have *rights*, because they are *moral* beings; the rights of *all* men grow out of their moral nature; and as all men have the same moral nature, they have essentially the same rights." What is true of men applies to women as well, and Grimké asserts their rights, including the right to a voice in how they are governed. Deprivation of this is "*a violation of human rights, a rank usurpation of power.*"

LETTERS TO CATHERINE E. BEECHER

LETTER XII.

Dear Friend: In my last, I made a sort of running commentary upon thy views of the appropriate sphere of woman, with something like a promise, that in my next, I would give thee my own.

The investigation of the rights of the slave has led me to a better understanding of my own. I have found the Anti-Slavery cause to be the high school of morals in our land—the school in which *human rights* are more fully investigated, and better understood and taught, than in any other. Here a great fundamental principle is uplifted and illuminated, and from this central light, rays innumerable stream all around. Human beings have *rights*, because they are *moral* beings: the rights of *all* men grow out of their moral nature; and as all men have the same moral nature, they have essentially the same rights. These rights may be wrested from the slave, but they cannot be alienated: his title to himself is as perfect *now*, as is that of Lyman Beecher: it is stamped on his moral being, and is, like it, imperishable. Now if rights are founded in the nature of our moral being, then the *mere circumstance of sex* does not give to man higher rights and responsibilities, than to woman. To suppose that it does, would be to deny the self-evident truth, that the 'physical constitution is the mere instrument of the moral nature.' To suppose that it does, would be to break up utterly the relations, of the two natures, and to reverse their functions, exalting the animal nature into a monarch, and humbling the moral into a slave; making the former a proprietor, and the latter its property. When human beings are regarded as *moral* beings, *sex,* instead of being enthroned upon the summit, administering upon rights and responsibilities, sinks into insignificance and nothingness. My doctrine then is, that whatever it is morally right for man to do, it is morally right for woman to do. Our duties originate, not from difference of sex, but from the diversity of our relations in life, the various gifts and talents committed to our care, and the different eras in which we live.

This regulation of duty by the mere circumstance of sex, rather than by the fundamental principle of moral being, has left to all that multifarious train of evils flowing out of the anti-christian doctrine of masculine and feminine virtues. By this doctrine, man has been converted into the warrior, and clothed with sternness, and those other kindred qualities, which in common estimation belong to his character as a *man;* whilst woman has been taught to lean upon an arm of flesh, to sit as a doll arrayed in 'gold, and pearls, and costly array,' to be admired for her personal charms, and caressed and humoured like a spoiled child, or converted into a mere drudge to suit the convenience of her lord and master. Thus have all the diversified relations of life been filled with 'confusion and every evil work.'

This principle has given to man a charter for the exercise of tyranny and selfishness, pride and arrogance, lust and brutal violence. It has robbed woman of essential rights, the right to think and speak and act on all great moral questions, just as men think and speak and act; the right to share their responsibilities, perils and toils; the right to fulfil the great end of her being, as a moral, intellectual and immortal creature, and of glorifying God in her body and her spirit which are His. Hitherto, instead of being a help meet to man, in the highest, noblest sense of the term, as a companion, a co-worker, an equal; she has been a mere appendage of his being, an instrument of his convenience and pleasure, the pretty toy with which he wiled away his leisure moments, or the pet animal whom he humored into playfulness and submission. Woman, instead of being regarded as the equal of man, has uniformly been looked down upon as his inferior, a mere gift to fill up the measure of his happiness. In 'the poetry of romantic gallantry,' it is true, she has been called, 'the last *best* gift of God to man;' but I believe I speak forth the words of truth and soberness when I affirm, that woman never was given to man. She was created, like him, in the image of God, and crowned with glory and honor; created only a little lower than the angels,—not, as is almost universally assumed, a little lower than man; on her brow, as well as on his, was placed the 'diadem of beauty,' and in her hand the sceptre of universal dominion. Gen: 1. 27, 28. 'The last *best gift* of God to man!' Where is the scripture warrant for this 'rhetorical flourish, this splendid absurdity?' Let us examine the account of her creation. 'And the rib which the Lord God had taken from man, made he a woman, and brought her unto the man.' Not as a gift—for Adam immediately recognized her *as a part of himself*—('this is now bone of my bone, and flesh of my flesh')—a companion and equal, not one hair's breadth beneath him in the majesty and glory of her moral being; not placed under his authority as a *subject,* but by his side, on the same platform of human rights, under the government of God only. This idea of woman's being 'the last best gift of God to man,' however pretty it may sound to the ears of those who love to discourse upon 'the poetry of romantic gallantry, and the generous promptings of chivalry,' has nevertheless been the means of sinking her from an *end* into a mere *means*—of turning her into an *appendage* to man, instead of recognizing her as *a part of man*—of destroying her individuality, and rights, and responsibilities, and merging her moral being in that of man. Instead of *Jehovah* being *her* king, *her* lawgiver, and *her* judge, she has been taken out of the exalted scale of existence in which He placed her, and subjected to the despotic control of man.

I have often been amused at the vain efforts made to define the rights and responsibilities of immortal beings as *men* and *women*. No one has yet found out just *where* the line of separation between them should be drawn, and for this simple reason, that no one knows just how far below man woman is, whether she be a head shorter in her moral responsibilities, or head and shoulders, or the full length of his noble stature, below him, i.e. under his feet. Confusion, uncertainty, and great inconsistencies, must exist on this point, so long as woman is regarded in the least degree inferior to man; but place her where her Maker placed her, on the same high level of human rights with man, side by side with him, and difficulties vanish, the mountains of perplexity flow down at the presence of this grand equalizing principle. Measure her rights and duties by the unerring standard of *moral being*, not by the false weights and measures of a mere circumstance of her human existence, and then the truth will be self-evident, that whatever it is *morally* right for a man to do, it is *morally* right for a woman to do. I recognize no rights but *human* rights—I know nothing of men's rights and women's rights; for in Christ Jesus, there is neither male nor female. It is my solemn conviction, that, until this principle of equality is recognised and embodied in practice, the church can do nothing effectual for the permanent reformation of the world. Woman was the first transgressor, and the first victim of power. In all heathen nations, she has been the slave of man, and Christian nations have never acknowledged her rights. Nay more, no Christian denomination or Society has ever acknowledged them on the broad basis of humanity. I know that in some denominations, she is permitted to preach the gospel; not from a conviction of her rights, nor upon the ground of her equality as a *human being*, but of her equality in spiritual gifts—for we find that woman, even in these Societies, is allowed no voice in framing the Discipline by which she is also governed. Now, I believe it is woman's right to have a voice in all the laws and regulations by which she is to be *governed*, whether in Church or State; and that the present arrangements of society, on these points, are *a violation of human rights, a rank usurpation of power*, a violent seizure and confiscation of what is sacredly and inalienably hers—thus inflicting upon woman outrageous wrongs, working mischief incalculable in the social circle, and in its influence on the world producing only evil, and that continually. *If* Ecclesiastical and Civil governments are ordained of God, *then* I contend that woman has just as much right to sit in solemn counsel in Conventions, Conferences, Associations and General Assemblies, as man—just as much right to it upon the throne of England, or in the Presidential chair of the United States.

Dost thou ask me, if I would wish to see woman engaged in the contention and strife of sectarian controversy, or in the intrigues of political partizans? I say no! never—never. I rejoice that she does not stand on the same platform which man now occupies in these respects; but I mourn, also, that he should thus prostitute his higher nature, and vilely cast away his birthright. I prize the purity of *his* character as highly as I do that of hers. As a moral being, *whatever it is morally wrong for her to do, it is morally wrong for him to do*. The fallacious doctrine of male and female virtues has well nigh ruined all that is morally great and lovely in his character: he has been quite as deep a sufferer by it as woman, though mostly in different respects and by other processes. As my time is engrossed by the pressing responsibilities of daily public duty, I have no leisure for that minute detail which would be required for the illustration and defence of these principles. Thou wilt find a wide field opened before thee, in the investigation of which, I doubt not, thou wilt be instructed. Enter this field, and explore it: thou wilt find in it a hid treasure, more precious than rubies—a fund, a mine of principles, as new as they are great and glorious.

Thou sayest, 'an ignorant, a narrow-minded, or a stupid woman, cannot feel nor understand the rationality, the propriety, or the beauty of this relation'—i.e. subordination to man. Now, verily, it does appear to me, that nothing but a narrow-minded view of the subject of human rights and responsibilities can induce any one to believe in *this subordination to a fallible being*. Sure I am, that the signs of the times clearly indicate a vast and rapid change in public sentiment, on this subject. Sure I am that she is not to be, as she has been, *'a mere second-hand agent'* in the regeneration of a fallen world, but the acknowledged equal and co-worker with man in this glorious work. Not that 'she will carry her measures by tormenting when she cannot please, or by petulant complaints or obtrusive interference, in matters which are out of her sphere, and which she cannot comprehend.' But just in proportion as her moral and intellectual capacities become enlarged, she will rise higher and higher in the scale of creation, until she reaches that elevation prepared for her by her Maker, and upon whose summit she was originally stationed, only 'a little lower than the angels.' Then will it be seen that nothing which concerns the well-being of mankind is either beyond her sphere, or above her comprehension: *Then* will it be seen 'that America will be distinguished above all other nations for well educated women, and for the influence they will exert on the general interests of society.'

But I must close with recommending to thy perusal, my sister's Letters on the Province of Woman, published in the New England Spectator, and republished by Isaac Knapp of Boston. As she has taken up this subject so fully, I have only glanced at it. That thou and all my countrywomen may better understand the true dignity of woman, is the sincere desire of

Thy Friend,

A. E. Grimké

DECLARATION OF SENTIMENTS AND RESOLUTIONS, SENECA FALLS

The Seneca Falls Declaration was the nascent woman's movement declaration of independence from traditional notions about the nature of women and their role in society. It was presented at the Wesleyan Chapel in Seneca Falls, New York, on July 19, 1848, at a meeting organized by Elizabeth Cady Stanton and Lucretia Mott as the result of conversations in the years following the 1840 World's Anti-Slavery Convention in London which they had attended as American delegates. The exclusion of women from that convention's proceedings disappointed Stanton and Mott and moved them to consider the plight of women, distinct from, but related to, the plight of African slaves. Three hundred people were in attendance when James Mott, husband of Lucretia, called the meeting to order. The Declaration of Sentiments, penned a few days before the convention by Stanton and Mott, was read to the convention.

The Declaration of Sentiments is notable not only for its claim that men and women are equal and possess the same rights, but also its attempt to root these contentions in the American tradition by drawing on the Declaration of Independence. The opening of the Declaration of Sentiments closely mirrors the earlier document, though with notable revisions: "We hold these truths to be self-evident: that all men and women are created equal...." But whereas the Declaration of Independence presents a list of abuses perpetrated by the British king against the American colonies, the Declaration of Sentiments recounts injustices men have committed against women. The first items in this series concern denying women the franchise and other political rights.

Of the 12 resolutions attached to the Declaration of Sentiments, 11 were adopted unanimously. However, the resolution calling for the enfranchisement of women was hotly debated and passed by a narrow margin only after Frederick Douglass, beloved paragon of the abolitionist movement, rose on the floor to defend it.

DECLARATION OF SENTIMENTS AND RESOLUTIONS, SENECA FALLS

When, in the course of human events, it becomes necessary for one portion of the family of man to assume among the people of the earth a position different from that which they have hitherto occupied, but one to which the laws of nature and of nature's God entitle them, a decent respect to the opinions of mankind requires that they should declare the causes that impel them to such a course.

We hold these truths to be self-evident: that all men and women are created equal; that they are endowed by their Creator with certain inalienable rights; that among these are life, liberty, and the pursuit of happiness; that to secure these rights governments are instituted, deriving their just powers from the consent of the governed. Whenever any form of government becomes destructive of these ends, it is the right of those who suffer from it to refuse allegiance to it, and to insist upon the institution of a new government, laying its foundation on such principles, and organizing its powers in such form, as to them shall seem most likely to effect their safety and happiness. Prudence, indeed, will dictate that governments long established should not be changed for light and transient causes; and accordingly all experience hath shown that mankind are more disposed to suffer, while evils are sufferable, than to right themselves by abolishing the forms to which they were accustomed. But when a long train of abuses and usurpations, pursuing invariably the same object evinces a design to reduce them under absolute despotism, it is their duty to throw off such government, and to provide new guards for their future security. Such has been the patient sufferance of the women under this government, and such is now the necessity which constrains them to demand the equal station to which they are entitled.

The history of mankind is a history of repeated injuries and usurpations on the part of man toward woman, having in direct object the establishment of an absolute tyranny over her. To prove this, let facts be submitted to a candid world.

He has never permitted her to exercise her inalienable right to the elective franchise.

He has compelled her to submit to laws, in the formation of which she had no voice.

He has withheld from her rights which are given to the most ignorant and degraded men—both natives and foreigners.

Having deprived her of this first right of a citizen, the elective franchise, thereby leaving her without representation in the halls of legislation, he has oppressed her on all sides.

He has made her, if married, in the eye of the law, civilly dead.

He has taken from her all right in property, even to the wages she earns.

He has made her, morally, an irresponsible being, as she can commit many crimes with impunity, provided they be done in the presence of her husband. In the covenant of marriage, she is compelled to promise obedience to her husband, he becoming, to all intents and purposes, her master—the law giving him power to deprive her of her liberty, and to administer chastisement.

He has so framed the laws of divorce, as to what shall be the proper causes, and in case of separation, to whom the guardianship of the children shall be given, as to be wholly regardless of the happiness of women—the law, in all cases, going upon a false supposition of the supremacy of man, and giving all power into his hands.

After depriving her of all rights as a married woman, if single, and the owner of property, he has taxed her to support a government which recognizes her only when her property can be made profitable to it.

He has monopolized nearly all the profitable employments, and from those she is permitted to follow, she receives but a scanty remuneration. He closes against her all the avenues to wealth and distinction which he considers most honorable to himself. As a teacher of theology, medicine, or law, she is not known.

He has denied her the facilities for obtaining a thorough education, all colleges being closed against her.

He allows her in Church, as well as State, but a subordinate position, claiming Apolstolic authority for her exclusion from the ministry, and, with some exceptions, from any public participation in the affairs of the Church.

He has created a false public sentiment by giving to the world a different code of morals for men and women, buy which moral delinquencies which exclude women from society, are not only tolerated, but deemed of little account in man.

He has usurped the prerogative of Jehovah himself, claiming it as his right to assign for her a sphere of action, when that belongs to her conscience and to her God.

He has endeavored, in every way that he could, to destroy her confidence in her own powers, to lessen her self-respect, and to make her willing to lead a dependent and abject life.

Now, in view of this entire disfranchisement of one-half the people of this country, their social and religious degradation—in view of the unjust laws above mentioned, and because women do feel themselves aggrieved, oppressed, and fraudulently deprived of their most sacred rights, we insist that they have immediate admission to all the rights and privileges which belong to them as citizens of the United States.

In entering upon the great work before us, we anticipate no small amount of misconception, misrepresentation, and ridicule; but we shall use every instrumentality within our power to effect our object. We shall employ agents, circulate tracts, petition the State and National legislatures, and endeavor to enlist the pulpit and the press in our behalf. We hope this Convention will be followed by a series of Conventions embracing every part of the country.

RESOLUTIONS

WHEREAS, The great precept of nature is conceded to be, that "man shall pursue his own true and substantial happiness." Blackstone in his Commentaries remarks, that this law of Nature being coeval with mankind, and dictated by God himself, is of course superior in obligation to any other. It is binding over all the globe, in all countries and at all times; no human laws are of any validity if contrary to this, and such of them as are valid, derive all their force, and all their validity, and all their authority, mediately and immediately, from this original; therefore,

Resolved, That such laws as conflict, in any way, with the true and substantial happiness of woman, are contrary to the great precept of nature and of no validity, for this is "superior in obligation to any other."

Resolved, That all laws which prevent woman from occupying such a station in society as her conscience shall dictate, or which place her in a position inferior to that of man, are contrary to the great precept of nature, and therefore of no force or authority.

Resolved, That woman is man's equal—was intended to be so by the Creator, and the highest good of the race demands that she should be recognized as such.

Resolved, That the women of this country ought to be enlightened in regard to the laws under which they live, that they may no longer publish their degradation by declaring themselves satisfied with their present position, nor their ignorance, by asserting that they have all the rights they want.

Resolved, That inasmuch as man, while claiming for himself intellectual superiority, does accord to woman moral superiority, it is pre-eminently his duty to encourage her to speak and teach, as she has an opportunity, in all religious assemblies.

Resolved, That the same amount of virtue, delicacy, and refinement of behavior that is required of woman in the social state, should also be required of man, and the same transgressions should be visited with equal severity on both man and woman.

Resolved, That the objection of indelicacy and impropriety, which is so often brought against woman when she addresses a public audience, comes with a very ill-grace from those who encourage, by their attendance, her appearance on the stage, in the concert, or in the feats of the circus.

Resolved, That woman has too long rested satisfied in the circumscribed limits which corrupt customs and a perverted application of the Scriptures have marked out for her, and that it is time she should move in the enlarged sphere which her great Creator has assigned her.

Resolved, That it is the duty of the women of this country to secure to themselves their sacred right to the elective franchise.

Resolved, That the equality of human rights results necessarily from the fact of the identity of the race in capabilities and responsibilities.

Resolved, therefore, That, being invested by the Creator with the same capabilities, and the same consciousness of responsibility for their exercise, it is demonstrably the right and duty of woman, equally with man, to promote every righteous cause by every righteous means; and especially in regard to the great subjects of morals and religion, it is self-evidently her right to participate with her brother in teaching them, both in private and in public, by writing and by speaking, by any instrumentalities proper to be used, and in any assemblies proper to be held; and this being a self-evident truth growing out of the divinely implanted principles of human nature, any custom or authority adverse to it, whether modern or wearing the hoary sanction of antiquity, is to be regarded as a self-evident falsehood, and at war with mankind.

[At last session Lucretia Mott offered and spoke to the following resolution:]

Resolved, That the speedy success of our cause depends upon the zealous and untiring efforts of both men and women, for the overthrow of the monopoly of the pulpit, and for the securing to woman an equal participation with men in the various trades, professions, and commerce.

FREDERICK DOUGLASS

F rederick Douglass (1817–1895) was born into slavery in Maryland but at the age of 21 escaped to freedom in Massachusetts. Recounting his experiences to local abolitionist groups, he became an eloquent witness against the institution of slavery and began to lecture at abolitionist meetings across the East. He fled the United States for England in 1845 when he revealed his slave master's identity in his autobiography. After his freedom was purchased by English supporters, Douglass returned to the United States and published a newspaper, the *North Star*, which became a voice for extending human rights to enslaved Africans and to American women.

EDITORIAL FROM THE NORTH STAR, JULY 28, 1848

This editorial appeared in the *North Star* on July 28, 1848. Douglass refers to the milestone of the women's rights movement—the Seneca Falls Convention—and discusses the competence women demonstrated in organizing and presiding over the meeting. He notes that some abolitionists had abandoned the antislavery cause, "lest by giving their influence in that direction they might possibly be giving countenance to the dangerous heresy that woman, in respect to rights, stands on an equal footing with man." Douglass proclaims his support for any movement "to improve and elevate the character of any members of the human family" and so supports giving women the right to vote.

EDITORIAL IN THE *NORTH STAR,* JULY 28, 1848

THE RIGHTS OF WOMEN.—One of the most interesting events of the past week, was the holding of what is technically styled a Woman's Rights Convention at Seneca Falls. The speaking, addresses, and resolutions of this extraordinary meeting were almost wholly conducted by women; and although they evidently felt themselves in a novel position, it is but simple justice to say that their whole proceedings were characterized by marked ability and dignity. No one present, we think, however much he might be disposed to differ from the views advanced by the leading speakers on that occasion, will fail to give them credit for brilliant talents and excellent dispositions. In this meeting, as in other deliberative assemblies, there were frequent differences of opinion and animated discussion; but in no case was there the slightest absence of good feeling and decorum. Several interesting documents setting forth the rights as well as grievances of women were read. Among these was a Declaration of Sentiments, to be regarded as the basis of a grand movement for attaining the civil, social, political, and religious rights of women. We should not do justice to our own convictions, or to the excellent persons connected with this infant movement, if we did not in this connection offer a few remarks on the general subject which the Convention met to consider and the objects they seek to attain. In doing so, we are not insensible that the bare mention of this truly important subject in any other than terms of contemptuous ridicule and scornful disfavor, is likely to excite against us the fury of bigotry and the folly of prejudice. A discussion of the rights of animals would be regarded with far more complacency by many of what are called the *wise* and the *good* of our land, than would be a discussion of the rights of women. It is, in their estimation, to be guilty of evil thoughts, to think that woman is entitled to equal rights with man. Many who have at last made the discovery that the negroes have some rights as well as other members of the human family, have yet to be convinced that women are entitled to any. Eight years ago a number of persons of this description actually abandoned the anti-slavery cause, lest by giving their influence in that direction they might possibly be giving countenance to the dangerous heresy that woman, in respect to rights, stands on an equal footing with man. In the judgment of such persons the American slave system, with all its concomitant horrors, is less to be deplored than this *wicked* idea. It is perhaps needless to say, that we cherish little sympathy for such sentiments or respect for such prejudices. Standing as we do upon the watch-tower of human freedom, we can not be deterred from an expression of our approbation of any movement, however humble, to improve and elevate the character of any members of the human family. While it is impossible for us to go into this subject at length, and dispose of the various objections which as often urged against such a doctrine as that of female equality, we are free to say that in respect to political rights, we hold woman to be justly entitled to all we claim for man. We go farther, and express our conviction that all political rights which it is expedient for man to exercise, it is equally so for woman. All that distinguishes man as an intelligent and accountable being, is equally true of woman; and if that government only is just which governs by the free consent of the governed, there can be no reason in the world for denying to woman the exercise of the elective franchise, or a hand in making and administering the laws of the land. Our doctrine is that "right is of no sex." We therefore bid the women engaged in this movement our humble Godspeed.

SOJOURNER TRUTH

Sojourner Truth (1795–1883), was born into slavery in New York State and gained her freedom through the New York State Emancipation Act in 1827. She discarded her slave name Isabella in 1843, the year she took to the road to speak out about rights denied to both enslaved Africans and unenfranchised women. Although the women's movement grew out of the abolition movement, African-American voices were hardly ever sought and rarely listened to when raised. Sojourner Truth was an exception. Illiterate and untutored in the art of rhetoric, she was both eloquent and a dynamic presence in the lecture hall. When she spoke, audiences rose to their feet and cheered.

AIN'T I A WOMAN

Her famous 1851 speech "Ain't I a Woman" presents an argument rarely developed by women in the suffrage movement. All the concern expressed by opponents of woman suffrage about the injury political rights might do to woman's delicate nature pointedly ignored the women who slaved in fields and survived brutal lives. If legislators saw fit for women like Sojourner Truth to "plough and to plant," to "bear the lash," and to bear 13 children and see them sold as slaves, they should not worry that the vote would do violence to women.

AIN'T I A WOMAN

REMINISCENCES BY FRANCES D. GAGE.

The leaders of the movement trembled on seeing a tall, gaunt black woman in a gray dress and white turban, surmounted with an uncouth sun-bonnet, march deliberately into the church, walk with the air of a queen up the aisle, and take her seat upon the pulpit steps. A buzz of disapprobation was heard all over the house, and there fell on the listening ear, "An abolition affair!" "Woman's rights and niggers!" "I told you so!" "Go it, darkey!" ...

There were very few women in those days who dared to "speak in meeting"; and the august teachers of the people were seemingly getting the better of us, while the boys in the galleries, and the sneerers among the pews, were hugely enjoying the discomfiture, as they supposed, of the "strong-minded." Some of the tender-skinned friends were on the point of losing dignity, and the atmosphere betokened a storm. When, slowly from her seat in the corner rose Sojourner Truth, who, till now, had scarcely lifted her head. "Don't let her speak!" gasped half a dozen in my ear. She moved slowly and solemnly to the front, laid her old bonnet at her feet, and turned her great speaking eyes to me. There was a hissing sound of disapprobation above and below. I rose and announced, "Sojourner Truth," and begged the audience to keep silence for a few moments.

The tumult subsided at once, and every eye was fixed on this almost Amazon form, which stood nearly six feet high, head erect, and eyes piercing the upper air like one in a dream. At her first word there was a profound hush. She spoke in deep tones, which, though not loud, reached every ear in the house, and away through the throng at the doors and windows.

"Wall, chilern, whar dar is so much racket dar must be somethin' out o' kilter. I tink dat 'twixt de niggers of de Souf and de womin at de Norf, all talkin' 'bout rights, de white men will be in a fix pretty soon. But what's all dis here talkin' 'bout?

"Dat man ober dar say dat womin needs to be helped into carriages, and lifted ober ditches, and to hab de best place everywhar. Nobody eber helps me into carriages, or ober mud-puddles, or gibs me any best place!" And raising herself to her full height, and her voice to a pitch like rolling thunder, she asked, "And a'n't I a woman? Look at me! Look at my arm! (and she bared her right arm to the shoulder, showing her tremendous muscular power). I have ploughed, and planted, and gathered into barns, and no man could head me! And a'n't I a woman? I could work as much and eat as much as a man—when I could get it—and bear de lash as well! And a'n't I a woman? I have borne thirteen chilern, and seen 'em mos' all sold off to slavery, and when I cried out with my mother's grief, none but Jesus heard me! And a'n't I a woman?

"Den dey talks 'bout dis ting in de head; what dis dey call it?" ("Intellect," whispered some one near.) "Dat's it, honey. What's dat got to do wid womin's rights or nigger's rights? If my cup won't hold but a pint, and yourn holds a quart, wouldn't ye be mean not to let me have my little half-measure full?" And she pointed her significant finger, and sent a keen glance at the minister who had made the argument. The cheering was long and loud.

"Den dat little man in black dar, he say women can't have as much rights as men, 'cause Christ wan't a woman! Whar did your Christ come from?" Rolling thunder couldn't have stilled that crowd, as did those deep, wonderful tones, as she stood there with outstretched arms and eyes of fire. Raising her voice still louder, she repeated, "Whar did your Christ come from? From God and a woman! Man had nothin' to do wid Him." Oh, what a rebuke that was to that little man.

Turning again to another objector, she took up the defense of Mother Eve. I can not follow her through it all. It was pointed, and witty, and solemn; eliciting at almost every sentence deafening applause; and she ended by asserting: "If de fust woman God ever made was strong enough to turn de world upside down all alone, dese women togedder (and she glanced her eye over the platform) ought to be able to turn it back, and get it right side up again! And now dey is asking to do it, de men better let 'em." Long-continued cheering greeted this. "'Bleeged to ye for hearin' on me, and now ole Sojourner han't got nothin' more to say."

Amid roars of applause, she returned to her corner, leaving more than one of us with streaming eyes, and hearts beating with gratitude. She had taken us up in her strong arms and carried us safely over the slough of difficulty turning the whole tide in our favor. I have never in my life seen anything like the magical influence that subdued the mobbish spirit of the day, and turned the sneers and jeers of an excited crowd into notes of respect and admiration. Hundreds rushed up to shake hands with her, and congratulate the glorious old mother, and bid her God-speed on her mission of "testifyin' agin concerning the wickedness of this 'ere people."

KEEP THE THING GOING WHILE THINGS ARE STIRRING

By the time of her address to the 1867 Equal Rights Association, the second selection, Sojourner Truth had become an important figure on the women's rights circuit. Because black men had gained the right to vote, Truth was concerned about the rights of black women: "And if colored men get their rights, and not colored women theirs, you see the colored men will be masters over the women and it will be just as bad as it was before."

KEEP THE THING GOING
WHILE THINGS ARE STIRRING

Mrs. Mott then introduced the venerable Sojourner Truth, who was greeted with loud cheers, after which she said:

My friends, I am rejoiced that you are glad, but I don't know how you will feel when I get through. I come from another field—the country of the slave. They have got their liberty—so much good luck to have slavery partly destroyed; not entirely. I want it root and branch destroyed. Then we will all be free indeed. I feel that if I have to answer for the deeds done in my body just as much as a man, I have a right to have just as much as a man. There is a great stir about colored men getting their rights, but not a word about the colored women; and if colored men get their rights, and not colored women theirs, you see the colored men will be masters over the women, and it will be just as bad as it was before. So I am for keeping the thing going while things are stirring; because if we wait till it is still, it will take a great while to get it going again. White women are a great deal smarter, and know more than colored women, while colored women do not know scarcely anything. They go out washing, which is about as high as a colored woman gets, and their men go about idle, strutting up and down; and when the women come home, they ask for their money and take it all, and then scold because there is no food. I want you to consider on that, chil'n. I call you chil'n; you are somebody's chil'n, and I am old enough to be mother of all that is here. I want women to have their rights. In the courts women have no right, no voice; nobody speaks for them. I wish woman to have her voice there among the pettifoggers. If it is not a fit place for women, it is unfit for men to be there.

I am above eighty years old; it is about time for me to be going. I have been forty years a slave and forty years free, and would be here forty years more to have equal rights for all. I suppose I am kept here because something remains for me to do; I suppose I am yet to help to break the chain. I have done a great deal of work; as much as a man, but did not get so much pay. I used to work in the field and bind grain, keeping up with the cradler; but men doing no more, got twice as much pay; so with the German women. They work in the field and do as much work, but do not get the pay. We do as much, we eat as much, we want as much. I suppose I am about the only colored woman that goes about to speak for the rights of the colored women. I want to keep the thing stirring, now that the ice is cracked. What we want is a little money. You men know that you get as much again as women when you write, or for what you do. When we get our rights we shall not have to come to you for money, for then we shall have money enough in our own pockets; and may be you will ask us for money. But help us now until we get it. It is a good consolation to know that when we have got this battle once fought we shall not be coming to you any more. You have been having our rights so long, that you think, like a slave-holder, that you own us. I know that it is hard for one who has held the reins for so long to give up; it cuts like a knife. It will feel all the better when it closes up again. I have been in Washington about three years, seeing about these colored people. Now colored men have the right to vote. There ought to be equal rights now more than ever, since colored people have got their freedom. I am going to talk several times while I am here; so now I will do a little singing. I have not heard any singing since I came here.

Accordingly, suiting the action to the word, Sojourner sang, "We are going home." "There, children," said she, "in heaven we shall rest from all our labors; first do all we have to do here. There I am determined to go, not to stop short of that beautiful place, and I do not mean to stop till I get there, and meet you there, too."

VICTORIA WOODHULL

Victoria Woodhull (1838–1927) was the first woman ever to address a committee of the United States Congress. Her appearance before the House Judiciary Committee to argue for the enfranchisement of women came as a surprise to many people active in the suffrage movement. Unaffiliated with the National American Woman Suffrage Association (NAWSA), Woodhull had been associated with a radical feminism that advocated sexual freedom for women. Along with her sister, Tennessee Claflin, Woodhull ran a brokerage house, financed by Cornelius Vanderbilt. Her unconventional views and unconventional domestic arrangements—she shared a household with both her first and second husbands, without ever having been divorced—caused much skepticism in the suffrage movement. However, her impressive appearance before the Judiciary Committee earned sympathy among the more strait-laced, middle-class suffrage activists.

For a while Woodhull gained admission to the inner circle of suffragists, with Susan B. Anthony and Elizabeth Cady Stanton standing behind her in the face of attacks in the press and from other suffragists. But when Woodhull began to speak out in many fora in favor of the doctrine of free love, the national suffrage movement parted ways with her.

Woodhull's flamboyance hurt the credibility of the suffrage movement for awhile, but ultimately her arguments were adopted by the movement.

ADDRESS BEFORE JUDICIARY COMMITTEE
OF U.S. HOUSE OF REPRESENTATIVES

Unlike arguments in previous selections in this volume, Woodhull's argument is essentially constitutional rather than moral. The subject of sex is not mentioned in the Constitution. Women are persons and citizens. They should be equal to men in all rights of citizenship, and so their right to vote is assured by references to "person" in the Fourteenth Amendment and "citizen" in the Fifteenth without restrictions of gender. In a self-governing country, one portion of the citizenry has no right to deprive another of the benefits of citizenship. Male citizens have no more right to restrict the privileges of women than women have the right to restrict the privileges of men.

ADDRESS OF VICTORIA C. WOODHULL
JANUARY 11, 1871.

To the Honorable the Judiciary Committee
of the House of Representatives of the Congress
of the United States:

Having most respectfully memorialized Congress for the passage of such laws as in its wisdom shall seem necessary and proper to carry into effect the rights vested by the Constitution of the United States in the citizens to vote, without regard to sex, I beg leave to submit to your honorable body the following in favor of my prayer in said memorial which has been referred to your Committee.

The public law of the world is founded upon the conceded fact that sovereignty can not be forfeited or renounced. The sovereign power of this country is perpetually in the politically organized people of the United States, and can neither be relinquished nor abandoned by any portion of them. The people in this republic who confer sovereignty are its citizens: in a monarchy the people are the subjects of sovereignty. All citizens of a republic by rightful act or implication confer sovereign power. All people of a monarchy are subjects who exist under its supreme shield and enjoy its immunities. The subject of a monarch takes municipal immunities from the sovereign as a gracious favor; but the woman citizen of this country has the inalienable "sovereign" right of self-government in her own proper person. Those who look upon woman's status by the dim light of the common law, which unfolded itself under the feudal and military institutions that establish right upon physical power, can not find any analogy in the status of the woman citizen of this country, where the broad sunshine of our Constitution has enfranchised all.

As sovereignty can not be forfeited, relinquished, or abandoned, those from whom it flows—the citizens—are equal in conferring the power, and should be equal in the enjoyment of its benefits and in the exercise of its rights and privileges. One portion of citizens have no power to deprive another portion of rights and privileges such as are possessed and exercised by themselves. The male citizen has no more right to deprive the female citizen of the free, public, political, expression of opinion than the female citizen has to deprive the male citizen thereof.

The sovereign will of the people is expressed in our written Constitution, which is the supreme law of the land. The Constitution makes no distinction of sex. The Constitution defines a woman born or naturalized in the United States, and subject to the jurisdiction thereof, to be a citizen. It recognizes the right of citizens to vote. It declares that the right of citizens of the United States to vote shall not be denied or abridged by the United States or by any State on account of "race, color, or previous condition of servitude."

Women, white and black, belong to races, although to different races. A race of people comprises all the people, male and female. The right to vote can not be denied on account of race. All people included in the term race have the right to vote, unless otherwise prohibited. Women of all races are white, black, or some intermediate color. Color comprises all people, of all races and both sexes. The right to vote can not be denied on account of color. All people included in the term color have the right to vote unless otherwise prohibited.

With the right to vote sex has nothing to do. Race and color include all people of both sexes. All people of both sexes have the right to vote, unless prohibited by special limiting terms less comprehensive than race or color. No such limiting terms exist in the Constitution. Women, white and black, have from time immemorial groaned under what is properly termed in the Constitution "previous condition of servitude." Women are the equals of men before the law, and are equal in all their rights as citizens. Women are debarred from voting in some parts of the United States, although they are allowed to exercise that right elsewhere. Women were formerly permitted to vote in places where they are now debarred therefrom. The naturalization laws of the United States expressly provide for the naturalization of women. But the right to vote has only lately been definitely declared by the Constitution to be inalienable, under three distinct conditions—in all of which woman is clearly embraced.

The citizen who is taxed should also have a voice in the subject matter of taxation. "No taxation without representation" is a right which was fundamentally established at the very birth of our country's independence; and by what ethics does any free government impose taxes on women without

giving them a voice upon the subject or a participation in the public declaration as to how and by whom these taxes shall be applied for common
public use? Women are free to own and to control property, separate and
free from males, and they are held responsible in their own proper persons,
in every particular, as well as men, in and out of court. Women have the
same inalienable right to life, liberty, and the pursuit of happiness that men
have. Why have they not this right politically, as well as men?

Women constitute a majority of the people of this country—they hold
vast portions of the nation's wealth and pay a proportionate share of the
taxes. They are intrusted with the most vital responsibilities of society; they
bear, rear, and educate men; they train and mould their characters; they
inspire the noblest impulses in men; they often hold the accumulated fortunes of a man's life for the safety of the family and as guardians of the
infants, and yet they are debarred from uttering any opinion by public vote,
as to the management by public servants of these interests; they are the
secret counselors, the best advisers, the most devoted aids in the most trying periods of men's lives, and yet men shrink from trusting them in the
common questions of ordinary politics. Men trust women in the market, in
the shop, on the highway and railroad, and in all other public places and
assemblies, but when they propose to carry a slip of paper with a name
upon it to the polls, they fear them. Nevertheless, as citizens, women have
the right to vote; they are part and parcel of that great element in which the
sovereign power of the land had birth; and it is by usurpation only that
men debar them from this right. The American nation, in its march onward
and upward, can not publicly choke the intellectual and political activity of
half its citizens by narrow statutes. The will of the entire people is the true
basis of republican government, and a free expression of that will by the
public vote of all citizens, without distinctions of race, color, occupation, or
sex, is the only means by which that will can be ascertained. As the world
has advanced into civilization and culture; as mind has risen in its dominion over matter; as the principle of justice and moral right has gained sway,
and merely physical organized power has yielded thereto; as the might of
right has supplanted the right of might, so have the rights of women
become more fully recognized, and that recognition is the result of the
development of the minds of men, which through the ages she has polished, and thereby heightened the lustre of civilization.

It was reserved for our great country to recognize by constitutional
enactment that political equality of all citizens which religion, affection, and
common sense should have long since accorded; it was reserved for
America to sweep away the mist of prejudice and ignorance, and that
chivalric condescension of a darker age, for in the language of Holy Writ,
"The night is far spent, the day is at hand, let us therefore cast off the work
of darkness and let us put on the armor of light. Let us walk honestly as in
the day." It may be argued against the proposition that there still remains

upon the statute books of some States the word "male" to an exclusion; but as the Constitution, in its paramount character, can only be read by the light of the established principle, *ita lex Scripta est,* and as the subject of sex is not mentioned, and the Constitution is not limited either in terms or by necessary implication in the general rights of citizens to vote, this right can not be limited on account of anything in the spirit of inferior or previous enactments upon a subject which is not mentioned in the supreme law. A different construction would destroy a vested right in a portion of the citizens, and this no legislature has a right to do without compensation, and nothing can compensate a citizen for the loss of his or her suffrage—its value is equal to the value of life....

Therefore, Believing firmly in the right of citizens to freely approach those in whose hands their destiny is placed under the Providence of God, your memorialist has frankly, but humbly, appealed to you, and prays that the wisdom of Congress may be moved to action in this matter for the benefit and the increased happiness of our beloved country.

ELIZABETH CADY STANTON

lizabeth Cady Stanton (1815–1902) can be described as the genius behind the woman's rights movement. Born into a wealthy, socially prominent family of lawyers and judges, she was led to her grievances about the political and domestic status of women by a variety of factors. As a child, she repeatedly saw her father advise women who came to him with legal questions that women's rights were not protected by laws. Added to this was personal disappointment. Intellectually ambitious, and encouraged by parents who allowed her to study subjects not traditionally in the female school curriculum, she achieved honors in Greek and was a top student at the co-educational academy she attended. However, when her male classmates went off to Union College, she discovered that there was not a college in the United States she could attend. Later, her marriage to Henry Stanton, a man considered too radical by her father, a man who was a vigorous supporter of human rights movements for enslaved Africans and for women, pointed nevertheless to the unhappy situation of women in society. She found herself the mother of seven children and left to her own devices, running a large household in Seneca Falls, a small New York backwater town.

The Seneca Falls Declaration (1848; see pages 99–103), the document that impelled the women's rights movement from disorganized rumblings of a few disgruntled women to a national, even worldwide, movement, was thought up by Elizabeth Cady Stanton and Lucretia Mott. Mott, a well-known speaker on the abolitionist circuit, met Stanton at the World's Anti-Slavery Convention in 1840. Although Stanton and Mott were members of the American delegation, they were excluded from participating in the convention because they were women. They found a bond in their outrage at this injustice and eight years later convened the convention that launched the women's rights movement.

Stanton was a prolific writer and speaker. She produced treatises and speeches on women's position in Western societies as well as on narrower issues of women's rights.

"THE SOLITUDE OF SELF"

In her famous 1892 speech "Solitude of Self," Stanton proclaims "the individuality of each human soul." This brings with it requirements of freedom and independence in all spheres of life. Men do not have their rights as individuals determined by the requirements of their personal relationships, as fathers, husbands, or brothers. The same should hold for women. Their rights as individuals, citizens, and women should not be subordinated to the necessities of the domestic sphere. Women require political rights in order to develop "every faculty of mind and body." They must be able to achieve their full potential, because "of the solitude and personal responsibility" of each individual life.

THE SOLITUDE OF SELF

The point I wish plainly to bring before you on this occasion is the individuality of each human soul—our Protestant idea, the right of individual conscience and judgment—our republican idea, individual citizenship. In discussing the rights of woman we are to consider, first, what belongs to her as an individual, in a world of her own, the arbiter of her own destiny, an imaginary Robinson Crusoe with her woman Friday on a solitary island. Her rights under such circumstances are to use all her facilities for her own safety and happiness.

Secondly, if we consider her as a citizen, as a member of a great nation, she must have the same rights as all the other members, according to the fundamental principles of our Government.

Thirdly, viewed as a woman, an equal factor in civilization, her rights and duties are still the same—individual happiness and development.

Fourthly, it is only the incidental relations of life, such as mother, wife, sister, daughter, which may involve some special duties and training. In the usual discussion in regard to woman's sphere, such men as Herbert Spencer, Fredrick Harrison and Grant Allen uniformly subordinate her rights and duties as an individual, as a citizen, as a woman, to the necessities of these incidental relations, some of which a large class of women never assume. In discussing the sphere of man we do not decide his rights as an individual, as a citizen, as a man, by his duties as a father, a husband, a brother or a son, some of which he may never undertake. Moreover he would be better fitted for these very relations, and whatever special work he might choose to do to earn his bread, by the complete development of all his faculties as an individual. Just so with woman. The education which will fit her to discharge the duties in the largest sphere of human usefulness, will best fit her for whatever special work she may be compelled to do.

The isolation of every human soul and the necessity of self-dependence must give each individual the right to choose his own surroundings. The strongest reason for giving woman all the opportunities for higher education, for the full development of her faculties, her forces of mind and body; for giving her the most enlarged freedom of thought and action; a complete emancipation from all forms of bondage, of custom, dependence, superstition; from all the crippling influences of fear—is the solitude and personal responsibility of her own individual life. The strongest reason why we ask for a woman a voice in the government under which she lives; in the religion she is asked to believe; equality in social life, where she is the chief factor; a place in the trades and professions, where she may earn her bread, is because of her birthright to self-sovereignty; because as an individual, she must rely on herself....

To throw obstacles in the way of a complete education is like putting out the eyes; to deny the rights of property is like cutting off the hands. To refuse political equality is to rob the ostracized of all self-respect, of credit in the market place, of recompense in the world of work, of a voice in choosing those who make and administer the law, a choice in the jury before whom they are tried, and in the judge who decides their punishment. Shakespeare's play of Titus and Andronicus contains a terrible satire on a woman's position in the nineteenth century—"Rude men seized the king's daughter, cut out her tongue, cut off her hands, and then bade her go call for water and wash her hands." What a picture of woman's position! Robbed of her natural rights, handicapped by law and custom at every turn, yet compelled to fight her own battles, and in the emergencies of life to fall back on herself for protection....

How the little courtesies of life on the surface of society, deemed so important from man towards woman, fade into utter insignificance in view of the deeper tragedies in which she must play her part alone, where no human aid is possible!

Nothing strengthens the judgment and quickens the conscience like individual responsibility. Nothing adds such dignity to character as the recognition of one's self-sovereignty, the right to an equal place, everywhere conceded—a place earned by personal merit, not an artificial attainment by inheritance, wealth, family and position. Conceding then that the responsibilities of life rest equally on man and woman from the fierce storms of life is the sheerest mockery, for they beat on her from every point of the compass, just as they do on man, and with more fatal results, for he has been trained to protect himself, to resist, to conquer....

In music women speak again the language of Mendelssohn, Beethoven, Chopin, Schumann, and are worthy interpreters of their great thoughts. The poetry and novels of the century are theirs, and they have touched the key note of reform in religion, politics and social life. They fill the editor's and professor's chair, plead at the bar of justice, walk the wards of the hospital, speak from the pulpit and the platform. Such is the type of womanhood that an enlightened public sentiment welcomes to-day, and such the triumph of the facts of life over the false theories of the past.

Is it, then, consistent to hold the developed women of this day within the same narrow political limits as the dame with the spinning wheel and knitting needle occupied in the past? No, no! Machinery has taken the labors of woman as well as man on its tireless shoulders; the loom and the spinning wheel are but dreams of the past; the pen, the brush, the easel, the chisel, have taken their places, while the hopes and ambitions of women are essentially changed.

We see reason sufficient in the outer conditions of human beings for individual liberty and development, but when we consider the self-dependence of every human soul, we see the need of courage, judgment and the exercise of every faculty of mind and body, strengthened and developed by use, in a woman as well as a man....

"ARGUMENTS IN FAVOR OF A SIXTEENTH AMENDMENT"

According to the Fifteenth Amendment to the Constitution: "The right of citizens of the United States to vote shall not be denied or abridged by the United States, or by any State, on account of race, color, or previous condition of servitude." In this 1869 speech to the National Woman's Suffrage Convention, Stanton argues for a Sixteenth Amendment that would grant women the vote. She argues that all artificial distinctions, whether of family, color, or sex, are destructive to national life. One of her striking arguments concerns adverse consequences of excluding women from political life. This has allowed the destructiveness and cruelty of the "male element" free reign, untempered by qualities in woman's nature. "Whatever is done to lift woman to her true position will help to usher in a new day of peace and perfection for the race."

ARGUMENTS IN FAVOR
OF A SIXTEENTH AMENDMENT

The Republican party to-day congratulates itself on having carried the Fifteenth Amendment of the Constitution, thus securing "manhood suffrage" and establishing an aristocracy of sex on this continent. As several bills to secure Woman's Suffrage in the District and the Territories have been already presented in both houses of Congress, and as by Mr. Julian's bill, the question of so amending the Constitution as to extend suffrage to all the women of the country has been presented to the nation for consideration, it is not only the right but the duty of every thoughtful woman to express her opinion on a Sixteenth Amendment. While I hail the late discussions of Congress and the various bills presented as so many signs of progress, I am especially gratified with those of Messrs. Julian and Pomeroy, which forbid any State to deny the right of suffrage to any of its citizens on account of sex or color.

This fundamental principle of our government—the equality of all the citizens of the republic—should be incorporated in the Federal Constitution, there to remain forever. To leave this question to the States and partial acts of Congress, is to defer indefinitely its settlement, for what is done by this Congress may be repealed by the next; and politics in the several States differ so widely, that no harmonious action on any question can ever be secured, except as a strict party measure. Hence, we appeal to the party now in power, everywhere, to end this protracted debate on suffrage, and declare it the inalienable right of every citizen who is amenable to the laws of the land, who pays taxes and the penalty of crime....

I urge a speedy adoption of a Sixteenth Amendment for the following reasons:

1. A government, based on the principle of caste and class, can not stand. The aristocratic idea, in any form, is opposed to the genius of our free institutions, to our own declaration of rights, and to the civilization of the age. All artificial distinctions, whether of family, blood, wealth, color, or sex, are equally oppressive to the subject classes, and equally destructive to national life and prosperity. Governments based on every form of aristocracy, on every degree and variety of inequality, have been tried in despotisms, monarchies, and republics, and all alike have perished. In the panorama of the past behold the mighty nations that have risen, one by one, but to fall. Behold their temples, thrones, and pyramids, their gorgeous palaces and stately monuments now crumbled all to dust. Behold every monarch in Europe at this very hour trembling on his throne. Behold the republics on this Western continent convulsed, distracted, divided, the hosts scattered, the leaders fallen, the scouts lost in the wilderness, the once

inspired prophets blind and dumb, while on all sides the cry is echoed, "Republicanism is a failure," though that great principle of a government "by the people, of the people, for the people" has never been tried. Thus far, all nations have been built on caste and failed. Why, in this hour of reconstruction, with the experience of generations before us, make another experiment in the same direction? If serfdom, peasantry, and slavery have shattered kingdoms, deluged continents with blood, scattered republics like dust before the wind, and rent our own Union asunder, what kind of a government, think you, American statesmen, you can build, with the mothers of the race crouching at your feet, while iron-heeled peasants, serfs, and slaves, exalted by your hands, tread our inalienable rights into the dust? While all men, everywhere, are rejoicing in new-found liberties, shall woman alone be denied the rights, privileges, and immunities of citizenship?...

Of all kinds of aristocracy, that of sex is the most odious and unnatural; invading, as it does, our homes, desecrating our family altars, dividing those whom God has joined together, exalting the son above the mother who bore him, and subjugating, everywhere, moral power to brute force. Such a government would not be worth the blood and treasure so freely poured out in its long struggles for freedom....

2. I urge a Sixteenth Amendment, because "manhood suffrage" or a man's government, is civil, religious, and social disorganization. The male element is a destructive force, stern, selfish, aggrandizing, loving war, violence, conquest, acquisition, breeding in the material and moral world alike discord, disorder, disease, and death. See what a record of blood and cruelty the pages of history reveal! Through what slavery, slaughter, and sacrifice, through what inquisitions and imprisonments, pains and persecutions, black codes and gloomy creeds, the soul of humanity has struggled for the centuries, while mercy has veiled her face and all hearts have been dead alike to love and hope! The male element has held high carnival thus far, it has fairly run riot from the beginning, overpowering the feminine element everywhere, crushing out all the diviner qualities in human nature, until we know but little of true manhood and womanhood, of the latter comparatively nothing, for it has scarce been recognized as a power until within the last century. Society is but the reflection of man himself, untempered by woman's thought, the hard iron rule we feel alike in the church, the state, and the home. No one need wonder at the disorganization, at the fragmentary condition of everything, when we remember that man, who represents but half a complete being, with but half an idea on every subject, has undertaken the absolute control of all sublunary matters.

People object to the demands of those whom they choose to call the strong-minded, because they say, "the right of suffrage will make the women masculine." That is just the difficulty in which we are involved today. Though disfranchised we have few women in the best sense, we have simply so many reflections, varieties, and dilutions of the masculine gender....

We ask women's enfranchisement, as the first step toward the recognition of that essential element in government that can only secure the health, strength, and prosperity of the nation. Whatever is done to lift woman to her true position will help to usher in a new day of peace and perfection for the race. In speaking of the masculine element, I do not wish to be understood to say that all men are hard, selfish, and brutal, for many of the most beautiful spirits the world has known have been clothed with manhood; but I refer to those characteristics, though often marked in woman, that distinguish what is called the stronger sex. For example, the love of acquisition and conquest, the very pioneers of civilization, when expended on the earth, the sea, the elements, the riches and forces of Nature, are powers of destruction when used to subjugate one man to another or to sacrifice nations to ambition. Here that great conservator of woman's love, if permitted to assert itself, as it naturally would in freedom against oppression, violence, and war, would hold all these destructive forces in check, for woman knows the cost of life better than man does, and not with her consent would one drop of blood ever be shed, one life sacrificed in vain....

If the civilization of the age calls for an extension of the suffrage, surely a government of the most virtuous, educated men and women would better represent the whole, and protect the interests of all than could the representation of either sex alone. But government gains no new element of strength in admitting all men to the ballot-box, for we have too much of the man-power there already....

Will the foreign element, the dregs of China, Germany, England, Ireland, and Africa supply this needed force, or the nobler types of American womanhood who have taught our presidents, senators, and congressmen the rudiments of all they know?

3. I urge a Sixteenth Amendment because, when "manhood suffrage" is established from Maine to California, woman has reached the lowest depths of political degradation....

If American women find it hard to bear the oppressions of their own Saxon fathers, the best orders of manhood, what may they not be called to endure when all the lower orders of foreigners now crowding our shores legislate for them and their daughters. Think of Patrick and Sambo and Hans and Yung Tung, who do not know the difference between a monarchy and a republic, who can not read the Declaration of Independence or Webster's spelling-book, making laws for Lucretia Mott, Ernestine L. Rose, and Anna E. Dickinson. Think of jurors and jailors drawn from these ranks to watch and try young girls for the crime of infanticide, to decide the moral code by which the mothers of this Republic shall be governed? This manhood suffrage is an appalling question, and it would be well for thinking women, who seem to consider it so magnanimous to hold their own claims in abeyance until all men are crowned with citizenship, to remember that the most ignorant men are ever the most hostile to the equality of women, as they have known them only in slavery and degradation.

Go to our courts of justice, our jails and prisons; go into the world of work; into the trades and professions; into the temples of science and learning, and see what is meted out everywhere to women—to those who have no advocates in our courts, no representatives in the councils of the nation. Shall we prolong and perpetuate such injustice, and by increasing this power risk worse oppressions for ourselves and daughters? It is an open, deliberate insult to American womanhood to be cast down under the iron-heeled peasantry of the Old World and the slaves of the New, as we shall be in the practical working of the Fifteenth Amendment, and the only atonement the Republican party can make is now to complete its work, by enfranchising the women of the nation....

As political sagacity moved our rulers thus to guard the interests of the negro for party purposes, common justice might have compelled them to show like respect for their own mothers, by counting woman too out of the basis of representation, that she might no longer swell the numbers to legislate adversely to her interests. And this desecration of the last will and testament of the fathers, this retrogressive legislation for woman, was in the face of the earnest protests of thousands of the best education, most refined and cultivated women of the North....

It is a startling assertion, but nevertheless true, that in none of the nations of modern Europe are the higher classes of women politically so degraded as are the women of this Republic to-day. In the Old World, where the government is the aristocracy, where it is considered a mark of nobility to share its offices and powers, women of rank have certain hereditary rights which raise them above a majority of the men, certain honors and privileges not granted to serfs and peasants. There women are queens, hold subordinate offices, and vote on many questions. In our Southern States even, before the war, women were not degraded below the working population. They were not humiliated in seeing their coachmen, gardeners, and waiters go to the polls to legislate for them; but here, in this boasted Northern civilization, women of wealth and education, who pay taxes and obey the laws, who in morals and intellect are the peers of their proudest rulers, are thrust outside the pale of political consideration with minors, paupers, lunatics, traitors, idiots, with those guilty of bribery, larceny, and infamous crimes.

Would those gentlemen who are on all sides telling the women of the nation not to press their claims until the negro is safe beyond peradventure, be willing themselves to stand aside and trust all their interests to hands like these? The educated women of this nation feel as much interest in republican institutions, the preservation of the country, the good of the race, their own elevation and success, as any man possibly can, and we have the same distrust in man's power to legislate for us, that he has in woman's power to legislate wisely for herself.

4. I would press a Sixteenth Amendment, because the history of American statesmanship does not inspire me with confidence in man's capacity to govern the nation alone, with justice and mercy. I have come to this conclusion, not only from my own observation, but from what our rulers say of themselves. Honorable Senators have risen in their places again and again, and told the people of the wastefulness and corruption of the present administration. Others have set forth, with equal clearness, the ignorance of our rulers on the question of finance....

THE WOMAN'S BIBLE, INTRODUCTION

The final selection from Stanton is her Introduction to *The Woman's Bible*, which was published in 1895 (and 1897). *The Woman's Bible* was the work of a "Revising Committee" organized by Stanton, and she wrote the Introduction. The depths of Stanton's radicalism are seen in her attack on traditional interpretations of the Bible, which had been used to justify women's subordination for centuries. According to traditional views, from the Creation, women were inferior and subordinate to men. Through the temptation of Eve, women had brought sin and death into the world. Stanton writes: "When in the early part of the Nineteenth Century, women began to protest against their civil and political degradation, they were referred to the Bible for an answer. When they protested against their unequal position in the church, they were referred to the Bible for an answer."

As was the case with some of Stanton's other arguments, the religious views expressed in *The Woman's Bible* were too radical for their time. At its annual convention in 1896, the National American Woman Suffrage Association passed a resolution dissociating itself from *The Woman's Bible*.

THE WOMAN'S BIBLE

INTRODUCTION

From the inauguration for the movement for woman's emancipation the Bible has been used to hold her in the "divinely ordained sphere," prescribed in the Old and New Testaments.

The canon and civil law; church and state; priests and legislators; all political parties and religious denominations have alike taught that woman was made after man, of man, and for man, an inferior being, subject to man.

Creeds codes, Scriptures and statutes, are all based on this idea. The fashions, forms, ceremonies and customs of society, church ordinances and disciplines all grow out of this idea.

Of the old English common law, responsible for woman's civil and political status, Lord Brougham said, "it is a disgrace to the civilization and Christianity of the Nineteenth Century." Of the canon law, which is responsible for woman's status in the church, Charles Kingsley said, "this will never be a good world for woman until the last remnant of the canon law is swept from the face of the earth."

The Bible teaches that woman brought sin and death into the world, that she precipitated the fall of the race, that she was arraigned before the judgment seat of Heaven, tried, condemned and sentenced. Marriage for her was to be a condition of bondage, maternity a period of suffering and anguish, and in silence and subjection, she was to play the role of a dependent on man's bounty for all her material wants, and for all the information she might desire on the vital questions of the hour, she was commanded to ask her husband at home. Here is the Bible position of woman briefly summed up.

Those who have the divine insight to translate, transpose and transfigure this mournful object of pity into an exalted, dignified personage, worthy our worship as the mother of the race, are to be congratulated as having a share of the occult mystic power of the eastern Mahatmas.

The plain English to the ordinary mind admits of no such liberal interpretation. The unvarnished texts speak for themselves. The canon law, church ordinances and Scriptures, are homogeneous, and all reflect the same spirits and sentiments.

These familiar texts are quoted by clergymen in their pulpits, by statesmen in the halls of legislation, by lawyers in the courts, and are echoed by the press of all civilized nations, and accepted by woman herself as "The Word of God." So perverted is the religious element in her nature, that with faith and works she is the chief support of the church and clergy; the very powers that make her emancipation impossible. When, in the early part of the Nineteenth Century, women began to protest against their civil and political degradation, they were referred to the Bible for an answer.

This led to a general and critical study of the Scriptures. Some, having made a fetish of these books and believing them to be the veritable "Word of God," with liberal translations, interpretations, allegories and symbols, glossed over the most objectionable features of the various books and clung to them as divinely inspired. Others, seeing the family resemblance between the Mosaic code, the canon law, and the old English common law, came to the conclusion that all alike emanated from the same source; wholly human in their origin and inspired by the natural love of domination in the historians. Others bewildered with their doubts and fears, came to no conclusion. While their clergymen told them on the one hand, that they owed all the blessings and freedom they enjoyed to the Bible, on the other, they said it clearly marked out their circumscribed sphere of action: that the demands for political and civil rights were irreligious, dangerous to the stability of the home, the state and the church. Clerical appeals were circulated from time to time conjuring members of their churches to take no part in the anti-slavery or woman suffrage movements, as they were infidel in their tendencies, undermining the very foundations of society. No wonder the majority of women stood still, and with bowed heads, accepted the situation.

Listening to the varied opinions of women, I have long thought it would be interesting and profitable to get them clearly stated in book form. To this end six years ago I proposed to a committee of women to issue a Woman's Bible, that we might have women's commentaries on women's position in the Old and New Testaments. It was agreed on by several leading women in England and America and the work was begun, but from various causes it has been delayed, until now the idea is received with renewed enthusiasm, and a large committee has been formed, and we hope to complete the work within a year.

Those who have undertaken that labor are desirous to have some Hebrew and Greek scholars, versed in Biblical criticism, to gild our pages with their learning. Several distinguished women have been urged to do so, but they are afraid that their high reputation and scholarly attainments might be compromised by taking part in an enterprise that for a time may be very unpopular. Hence we may not be able to get help from that class.

Others fear that they might compromise their evangelical faith by affiliation with those of more liberal views, who do not regard the Bible as "Word of God," but like any other book, to be judged by its merits. If the Bible teaches the equality of Woman, why does the church refuse to ordain women to preach the gospel, to fill the offices of deacons and elders, and to administer the Sacraments, or to admit them as delegates to the Synods, General Assemblies and Conferences of the different denominations? They have never yet invited a woman to join one of their Revising Committees, nor tried to mitigate the sentence pronounced on her by changing one count in the indictment served on her in paradise.

The large number of letters received, highly appreciative of the undertaking, is very encouraging to those who have inaugurated the movement, and indicate a growing self-respect and self-assertion in the women of this generation. But we have the usual array of objectors to meet and answer. One correspondent conjures us to suspend the work, as it is "ridiculous" for "women to attempt the revision of the Scriptures." I wonder if any man wrote to the late revising committee of Divines to stop their work on the ground that it was ridiculous for men to revise the Bible. Why is it more ridiculous for women to protest against her present status in the Old and New Testament, in the ordinances and discipline of the church, than in the statutes and constitution of the state? Why is it more ridiculous to arraign ecclesiastics for their false teaching and acts of injustice to women, than members of Congress and the House of Commons? Why is it more audacious to review Moses than Blackstone, the Jewish code of laws, than the English system of jurisprudence? Women have compelled their legislators in every state in this Union to so modify their statutes for women that the old common law is now almost a dead letter, Why not compel Bishops and Revising Committees to modify their creeds and dogmas? Forty years ago it seemed as ridiculous to timid, time-serving and retrograde folk for women to demand an expurgated edition of the laws, as it now does to demand an expurgated edition of the Liturgies and Scriptures. Come, come, my conservative friend, wipe the dew off your spectacles, and see that the world is moving. Whatever your views may be as to the importance of the proposed work, your political and social degradation are but an outgrowth of your status in the Bible. When you express your aversion, based on a blind feeling of reverence in which reason has no control, to the revision of the Scriptures, you do but echo Cowper, who, when asked to read Paine's "Rights of Man," exclaimed, "No man shall convince me that I am improperly governed while I *feel* the contrary."

Others say it is not *politic* to rouse religious opposition. This much-lauded policy is but another word for *cowardice*. How can woman's position be changed from that of a subordinate to an equal, without opposition, without the broadest discussion of all the questions involved in her present degradation? For so far-reaching and momentous a reform as her complete independence, an entire revolution in all existing institutions is inevitable.

Let us remember that all forms are interdependent, and that whatever is done to establish one principle on a solid basis, strengthens all. Reformers who are always compromising, have not yet grasped the idea that truth is the only safe ground to stand upon. The object of an individual life is not to carry one fragmentary measure in human progress, but to utter the highest truth clearly seen in all directions, and thus to round out and perfect a well balanced character. Was not the sum of influence exerted by John Stuart Mill on political, religious and social questions for greater than that of any statesmen or reformer who has sedulously limited his sympathies and activities to carrying one specific measure? We have many women abundantly endowed with capabilities to understand and refuse what men have thus far written. But they are all suffering from inherited ideas of their inferiority; they do not perceive it, yet such is the true explanation of their solicitous, lest they should seem to be too self-asserting.

Again there are some who write us that our work is a useless expenditure of force over a book that has lost its hold on the human mind. Most intelligent women, they say, regard it simply as the history of a rude people in a barbarous age, and have no more reverence for the Scriptures than any other work. So long as tens of thousands of Bibles are printed every year, and circulated over the whole habitable globe, and the masses in all English-speaking nations revere it as the word of God, it is vain to belittle its influence. The sentimental feelings we all have for those things we were educated to believe sacred, do not readily yield to pure reason. I distinctly remember the shudder that passed over me on seeing a mother take our family Bible to make a higher seat for her child at a table. It seemed such a desecration, I was tempted to protest against its use for such a purpose, and this, too, long after my reason had repudiated its divine authority.

To women still believing in the plenary inspiration of the Scriptures, we say give us by all means your exegesis in the light of the higher criticism learned men are now making, and illumine the Woman's Bible, with your inspiration.

Bible historians claim special inspiration for the Old and New Testaments containing most contradictory records of the same events, of miracles opposed to all known laws, of customs that degrade the female sex of all human and animal life, stated in most questionable language that could not be read in a promiscuous assembly, and call this "The Word of God."

The only points in which I differ from all ecclesiastical teaching is that I do not believe that any man ever saw or talked with God, I do not believe that God inspired the Mosaic Code, or told the historians what they said he did about woman, for all the religions on the face of the earth degrade her, and so long as woman accepts the position that they assign her, her emancipation is impossible. Whatever the Bible may be made to do in Hebrew or Greek, in plain English it does not exalt and dignify woman. My standpoint for criticism is the revised edition of 1888. I will so far honor the revising committee of nine men who have given us the best exegesis they can according to their ability, although Disraeli said the last one before he died, contained 150,000 blunders in the Hebrew, and 7,000 in the Greek.

But the verbal criticism in regard to woman's position amounts to little. The spirit is the same in all periods and languages, hostile to her as an equal.

There are some general principles in the holy books of all religions that teach love, charity, liberty, justice and equality for all the human family, there are many grand and beautiful passages, the golden rule has been echoed and re-echoed around the world. There are lofty examples of good and true men and women, all worthy our acceptance and example whose lustre cannot be dimmed by the false sentiments and vicious characters bound up in the same volume. The Bible cannot be accepted or rejected as a whole, its teachings are varied and its lessons differ widely from each other. In criticising the peccadilloes of Sarah, Rebecca and Rachel, we would not shadow the virtues of Deborah, Huldah and Vashti. In criticising the Mosaic code we would not question the wisdom of the Golden rule and the fifth Commandment. Again the church claims special consecration for its cathedrals and priesthood, parts of these aristocratic churches are too holy for women to enter, boys were early introduced into the choirs for this reason, woman singing in an obscure corner veiled. A few of the more democratic denominations accord women some privileges, but invidious discriminations of sex are found in all religious organizations, and the most bitter outspoken enemies of woman are found among clergymen and bishops of the Protestant religion.

The canon law, the Scriptures, the creeds and codes and church discipline of the leading religions bear the impress of fallible man, and not of our ideal great first cause, "the Spirit of all Good," that set the universe of matter and mind in motion, and by immutable law holds the land, the sea, the planets, revolving round the great centre of light and heat, each in its own elliptic, with millions of stars in harmony all singing together, the glory of creation forever and ever.

SUSAN B. ANTHONY

S usan B. Anthony (1820–1906), born in a small town outside Albany, New York, was the second of eight children of free-thinking and reformist Quakers, active in both the temperance and abolitionist movements. Because of her Quaker upbringing, in which women were permitted more participation in religious life than in other sects, and as a result of her father's belief in the equality of the sexes, Anthony reached adulthood feeling less aggrieved than her compatriots in the woman suffrage movement. Although she had served as a schoolteacher in upstate New York since the age of 15 earning one-quarter of what her male counterparts earned, Anthony was not engaged in issues of women's rights, although she was active in the temperance and abolitionist movements.

In 1851, visiting Seneca Falls to attend an abolitionist meeting, Anthony first met Elizabeth Cady Stanton. Together they would constitute a formidable engine of civil rights reform. Stanton was the more verbally expressive of the two, but Anthony, with her organizational skills, her untiring zeal for political action, and her unwavering certainty in the cause, was instrumental in the woman suffrage movement's ultimate success.

TRIAL OF SUSAN B. ANTHONY

A reluctant speaker and infrequent writer, Anthony left fewer documents to posterity than did Stanton. Our first selection centers on arguments she made in 1872 when she was tried for illegally voting. Anthony had led 50 women to

131

a Rochester polling place where they registered to vote. On election day, she and a number of these women voted and were arrested and charged with voting illegally. During the trial, Anthony was not allowed to testify. After her attorney Judge Selden presented her defense, the judge read instructions to the (of course) all male jury, directing them to convict her. Her attorney protested the procedure as unconstitutional and asked that the jury be individually polled. The judge dismissed the jurors. The selection presents the scene in court the next day, when Anthony was sentenced.

In her statement, Anthony presents a combination of moral and legal arguments. She protests against a judicial system, purportedly based on trial by a jury of one's peers that excludes women, a woman defendant's true peers. This degrades women "from the status of a citizen to that of a subject." The judicial system consists of laws "made by men, interpreted by men, administered by men, in favor of men, and against women." Anthony also argues, as Victoria Woodhull had before the House of Representatives, that a "broad and liberal" interpretation of the United States Constitution and recent amendments guarantees all citizens, including women, equal rights.

TRIAL OF SUSAN B. ANTHONY

It was conceded that Miss Anthony was a woman and the she voted on November 5, 1872. Judge Selden, for the second time in all his practice, offered himself as a witness, and testified that he advised her to vote, believing that the laws and Constitution of the United States gave her full authority. He then proposed to call Miss Anthony to testify as to the intention or belief under which she voted, but the Court held she was not competent as a witness in her own behalf. After making this decision, the Court then admitted all the testimony, as reported, which she gave on the preliminary examination before the commissioner, in spite of her counsel's protest against accepting the version which that officer took of her evidence. The prosecution simply alleged the fact of her having voted. Mr. Selden then addressed the judge and jury in a masterly argument of over three hours' duration....

Judge Hunt, without leaving the bench, delivered a written opinion[1] to the effect that the Fourteenth Amendment, under which Miss Anthony claimed the authority to vote, "was a protection, not to all our rights, but to our rights as citizens of the United States only; that is, the rights existing or belonging to that condition or capacity." At its conclusion *he directed the jury to bring in a verdict of guilty.*

[1]Can a judge with propriety prepare a *written* opinion before he has heard all the arguments in a case?

Miss Anthony's counsel insisted that the Court had no power to make such a direction in a criminal case and demanded that the jury be permitted to bring in its own verdict. The judge made no reply except to order the clerk to take the verdict. Mr. Selden demanded that the jury be polled. Judge Hunt refused, and at once discharged the jury without allowing them any consultation or asking if they agreed upon a verdict. Not one of them had spoken a word. After being discharged, the jurymen talked freely and several declared they should have brought in a verdict of "not guilty."

The next day Selden argued the motion for a new trial on seven exceptions, but this was denied by Judge Hunt. The following scene then took place in the courtroom:

Judge Hunt.—(Ordering the defendant to stand up). Has the prisoner anything to say why sentence shall not be pronounced?

Miss Anthony.—Yes, your honor, I have many things to say; for in your ordered verdict of guilty you have trampled under foot every vital principle of our government. My natural rights, my civil rights, my political rights, my judicial rights, are all alike ignored. Robbed of the fundamental privilege of citizenship, I am degraded from the status of citizen to that of a subject; and not only myself individually but all of my sex are, by your honor's verdict, doomed to political subjection under this so-called republican form of government.

Judge Hunt.—The Court can not listen to a rehearsal of argument which the prisoner's counsel has already consumed three hours in presenting.

Miss Anthony.—May it please your honor, I am not arguing the question, but simply stating the reasons why sentence can not, in justice, be pronounced against me. Your denial of my citizen's right to vote, is the denial of my right of consent as one of the governed, the denial of my right of representation as one of the taxed, the denial of my right to a trial by a jury of my peers as an offender against law; therefore, the denial of my sacred right to life, liberty, property and—

Judge Hunt.—The Court can not allow the prisoner to go on.

Miss Anthony.—But your honor will not deny me this one and only poor privilege of protest against this high-handed outrage upon my citizen's rights. May it please the Court to remember that, since the day of my arrest last November, this is the first time that either myself or any person of my disenfranchised class has been allowed a word of defense before judge or jury—

Judge Hunt.—The prisoner must sit down—the Court can not allow it.

Miss Anthony.—Of all my prosecutors, from the corner grocery politician who entered the complaint, to the United States marshal, commissioner, district-attorney, district-judge, your honor on the bench—not one is my peer, but each and all are my political sovereigns; and had your honor submitted my case to the jury, as was clearly your duty, even then I should have had just cause of protest, for not one of those men was my peer; but, native or foreign born, white or black, rich or poor, educated or ignorant, sober or drunk, each and every man of them was my political superior; hence, in no sense, my peer. Under such circumstances a commoner of England, tried before a jury of lords, would have far less cause to complain than have I, a woman, tried before a jury of men. Even my counsel, Hon. Henry R. Selden, who has argued my cause so ably, so earnestly, so unanswerably before your honor, is my political sovereign. Precisely as no disfranchised person is entitled to sit upon a jury, and no woman is entitled to the franchise, so none but a regularly admitted lawyer is allowed to practice in the courts, and no woman can gain admission to the bar—hence, jury, judge, counsel, all must be of the superior class.

Judge Hunt.—The Court must insist—the prisoner has been tried according to the established forms of law.

Miss Anthony.—Yes, your honor, but by forms of law all made by men, interpreted by men, administered by men, in favor of men and against women; and hence your honor's ordered verdict of guilty, against a United States citizen for the exercise of the "citizen's right to vote," simply because that citizen was a woman and not a man. But yesterday, the same man-made forms of law declared it a crime punishable with $1,000 fine and six months' imprisonment to give a cup of cold water, a crust of bread or a night's shelter to a panting fugitive tracking his way to Canada; and every man or woman in whose veins coursed a drop of human sympathy violated that wicked law, reckless of consequences, and was justified in so doing. As then the slaves who got their freedom had to take it over or under or through the unjust forms of law, precisely so now must women take it to get their right to a voice in this government; and I have taken mine, and mean to take it at every opportunity.

Judge Hunt.—The Court orders the prisoner to sit down. It will not allow another word.

Miss Anthony.—When I was brought before your honor for trial, I hoped for a broad and liberal interpretation of the Constitution and its recent amendments, which should declare all United States citizens under its protecting aegis—which should declare equality of rights the national guarantee to all persons born or naturalized in the United States. But failing to get this justice—failing, even, to get a trial by a jury *not* my peers—I ask not leniency at your hands but rather the full rigor of the law.

Judge Hunt.—The Court must insist—[Here the prisoner sat down.] The prisoner will stand up. [Here Miss Anthony rose again.] The sentence of the Court is that you pay a fine of $100 and the costs of the prosecution.

Miss Anthony.—May it please your honor, I will never pay a dollar of your unjust penalty. All the stock in trade I possess is a debt of $10,000, incurred by publishing my paper—The Revolution—the sole object of which was to educate all women to do precisely as I have done, rebel against your man-made, unjust, unconstitutional forms of law, which tax, fine, imprison and hang women, while denying them the right of representation in the government; and I will work on with might and main to pay every dollar of that honest debt, but not a penny shall go to this unjust claim. And I shall earnestly and persistently continue to urge all women to the practical recognition of the old Revolutionary maxim, "Resistance to tyranny is obedience to God."

Judge Hunt.—Madam, the Court will not order you to stand committed until the fine is paid.

[Anthony never paid the fine.]

WOMAN WANTS BREAD, NOT THE BALLOT! (SELECTIONS)

From 1868 to 1870, with Elizabeth Cady Stanton and the abolitionist Parker Pillsbury, Anthony published a weekly newspaper, the *Revolution*. In it, they argued for enlargement of women's domestic and political rights. When in 1870, the newspaper became financially insolvent, leaving Anthony with a $10,000 personal debt, Anthony embarked on a cross-country speaking tour to earn some money. "Woman Wants Bread Not the Ballot!" was one of her more successful and popular speeches. In it she outlines her belief in the political necessity of suffrage to remedy the economic and personal exploitation of women.

The title of the speech is ironic. Though women may think their primary interests are economic rather than political, Anthony argues that political rights are necessary for economic advancement. This is shown by the experience of England. After working men were enfranchised, the government not only began to address issues important to them but also to provide public education to make them qualified to wield the ballot. Decrying "the utter helplessness of disenfranchisement," Anthony argues that only the ballot can ensure women full access to bread.

WOMAN WANTS BREAD, NOT THE BALLOT!

Delivered in most of the large cities of the United States, between
1870 and 1880. The speech never was written, and this abstract
was prepared from scattered notes and newspaper reports.

My purpose tonight is to demonstrate the great historical fact that disfranchisement is not only political degradation, but also moral, social, educational and industrial degradation; and that it does not matter whether the disfranchised class live under a monarchial or a republican form of government, or whether it be white workingmen of England, negroes on our southern plantations, serfs of Russia, Chinamen on our Pacific coast, or native born, tax-paying women of this republic. Wherever, on the face of the globe or on the page of history, you show me a disfranchised class, I will show you a degraded class of labor. Disfranchisement means inability to make, shape or control one's own circumstances. The disfranchised must always do the work, accept the wages, occupy the position the enfranchised assign to them. The disfranchised are in the position of the pauper. You remember the old adage, "Beggars must not be choosers;" they must take what they can get or nothing! That is exactly the position of women in the world of work today; they can not choose. If they could, do you for a moment believe they would take the subordinate places and the inferior pay? Nor is it a "new thing under the sun" for the disfranchised, the inferior classes weighed down with wrongs, to declare they "do not want to vote." The rank and file are not philosophers, they are not educated to think for themselves, but simply to accept, unquestioned, whatever comes.

Years ago in England when the workingmen, starving in the mines and factories, gathered in mobs and took bread wherever they could get it, their friends tried to educate them into a knowledge of the causes of their poverty and degradation. At one of these "monster bread meetings," held in Manchester, John Bright said to them, "Workingmen, what you need to bring to you cheap bread and plenty of it, is the franchise;" but those ignorant men shouted back to Mr. Bright, precisely as the women of America do to us today, "It is not the vote we want, it is bread;" and they broke up the meeting, refusing to allow him, their best friend, to explain to them the powers of the franchise. The condition of those workingmen was very little above that of slavery. Some of you may remember when George Thompson came over to this country and rebuked us for our crime and our curse of slavery, how the slaveholders and their abettors shouted back to Mr. Thompson, "Look at home, look into your mines and your factories, you have slavery in England."...

Sad as is the condition of the workingmen of England today, it is infinitely better than it was twenty years ago. At first the votes of the workingmen were given to the Liberal party, because it was the leaders of that party who secured their enfranchisement; but soon the leaders of the Conservative party, seeing the power the workingmen had, began to vie with the Liberals by going into their meetings and pledging that if they would vote the Tory ticket and bring that party into control, it would give them more and better laws even than the Liberals....

And yet, notwithstanding the declaration of our Revolutionary fathers, "all men created equal," "governments derive their just powers from the consent of the governed," "taxation and representation insepara-ble"—notwithstanding all these grand enunciations, our government was founded upon the blood and bones of half a million human beings, bought and sold as chattels in the market. Nearly all the original thirteen States had property qualifications which disfranchised poor white men as well as women and negroes. Thomas Jefferson, at the head of the old Democratic party, took the lead in advocating the removal of all property qualifications, as so many violations of the fundamental principle of our government— "the right of consent." In New York the qualification was $250. Martin Van Buren, the chief of the Democracy, was a member of the Constitutional Convention held in Buffalo in 1821, which wiped out that qualification so far as white men were concerned. He declared, "The poor man has as good a right to possess it as a means of protection to himself and his family." It was because the Democrats enfranchised poor white men, both native and foreign, that that strong old party held absolute sway in this country for almost forty years, with only now and then a one-term Whig administra-tion....

The vast numbers of wage-earning men coming from Europe to this country, where manhood suffrage prevails with no limitations, find them-selves invested at once with immense political power. They organize their trades unions, but not being able to use the franchise intelligently, they con-tinue to strike and to fight their battles with the capitalists just as they did in the old countries. Neither press nor politicians dare to condemn these strikes or to demand their suppression because the workingmen hold the balance of power and can use it for the success or defeat of either party.

> [Miss Anthony here related various timely instances of strikes where force was used to prevent non-union men from taking the places of the strikers, and neither the newspapers nor political leaders ventured to sustain the officials in the necessary steps to preserve law and order, or if they did they were defeated at the next election.]

It is said women do not need the ballot for their protection because they are supported by men. Statistics show that there are 3,000,000 women in this nation supporting themselves. In the crowded cities of the East they are compelled to work in shops, stores and factories for the merest pittance. In New York alone, there are over 50,000 of these women receiving less than fifty cents a day. Women wage-earners in different occupations have organized themselves into trades unions, from time to time, and made their strikes to get justice at the hands of their employers just as men have done, but I have yet to learn of a successful strike of any body of women. The best organized one I ever knew was that of the collar laundry women of the city of Troy, N. Y., the great emporium for the manufacture of shirts, collars and cuffs. They formed a trades union of several hundred members and demanded an increase of wages. It was refused. So one May morning in 1867, each woman threw down her scissors and her needle, her starch-pan and flat-iron, and for three long months not one returned to the factories. At the end of that time they were literally starved out, and the majority of them were compelled to go back, but not at their old wages, for their employers cut them down to even a lower figure....

My friends, the condition of those collar laundry women but represents the utter helplessness of disfranchisement. The question with you, as men, is not whether you want your wives and daughters to vote, nor with you, as women, whether you yourselves want to vote; but whether you will help to put this power of the ballot into the hands of the 3,000,000 wage-earning women, so that they may be able to compel politicians to legislate in their favor and employers to grant them justice.

The law of capital is to extort the greatest amount of work for the least amount of money; the rule of labor is to do the smallest amount of work for the largest amount of money. Hence there is, and in the nature of things must continue to be, antagonism between the two classes; therefore, neither should be left wholly at the mercy of the other.

It was cruel, under the old regime, to give rich men the right to rule poor men. It was wicked to allow white men absolute power over black men. It is vastly more cruel, more wicked to give to all men—rich and poor, white and black, native and foreign, educated and ignorant, virtuous and vicious—this absolute control over women. Men talk of the injustice of monopolies. There never was, there never can be, a monopoly so fraught with injustice, tyranny and degradation as this monopoly of sex, of all men over all women. Therefore I not only agree with Abraham Lincoln that, "No man is good enough to govern another man without his consent;" but I say also that no man is good enough to govern a woman without her consent, and still further, that all men combined in government are not good enough to govern all women without their consent. There might have been some plausible excuse for the rich governing the poor, the educated governing the ignorant, the Saxon governing the African; but there can be none for making the husband the ruler of the wife, the brother of the sister, the man of the women, his peer in birth, in education, in social position, in all that stands for the best and highest in humanity.

I believe that by nature men are no more unjust than women. If from the beginning women had maintained the right to rule not only themselves but men also, the latter today doubtless would be occupying the subordinate places with inferior pay in the world of work; women would be holding the higher positions with the big salaries; widowers would be doomed to a "life interest on one-third of the family estate;" husbands would "owe service" to their wives, so that every one of you men would be begging your good wives, "Please be so kind as to 'give me' ten cents for a cigar." The principle of self-government can not be violated with impunity. The individual's right to it is sacred—regardless of class, caste, race, color, sex or any other accident or incident of birth. What we ask is that you shall cease to imagine that women are outside this law, and that you shall come into the knowledge that disfranchisement means the same degradation to your daughters as to your sons.

Governments can not afford to ignore the rights of those holding the ballot, who make and unmake every law and law-maker. It is not because the members of Congress are tyrants that women receive only half pay and are admitted only to inferior positions in the departments. It is simply in obedience to a law of political economy which makes it impossible for a government to do as much for the disfranchised as for the enfranchised. Women are no exception to the general rule. As disfranchisement always has degraded men, socially, morally and industrially, so today it is disfranchisement that degrades women in the same spheres....

We recognize that the ballot is a two-edged, nay, a many-edged sword, which may be made to cut in every direction. If wily politicians and sordid capitalists may wield it for mere party and personal greed; if oppressed wage-earners may invoke it to wring justice from legislators and extort material advantages from employers; if the lowest and most degraded classes of men may use it to open wide the sluice-ways of vice and crime; if it may be the instrumentality by which the narrow, selfish, corrupt and corrupting men and measures rule—it is quite as true that noble-minded statesmen, philanthropists and reformers may make it the weapon with which to reverse the above order of things, as soon as they can have added to their now small numbers the immensely larger ratio of what men so love to call "the better half of the people." When women vote, they will make a new balance of power that must be weighed and measured and calculated in its effect upon every social and moral question which goes to the arbitrament of the ballot-box. Who can doubt that when the representative women of thought and culture, who are today the moral backbone of our nation, sit in counsel with the best men of the country, higher conditions will be the result?

Insurrectionary and revolutionary methods of righting wrongs, imaginary or real, are pardonable only in the enslaved and disfranchised. The moment any class of men possess the ballot, it is their weapon and their shield. Men with a vote have no valid excuse for resorting to the use of illegal means to fight their battles. When the masses of wage-earning men are educated into a knowledge of their own rights and of their duties to others, so that they are able to vote intelligently, they can carry their measures through the ballot-box and will have no need to resort to force. But so long as they remain in ignorance and are manipulated by the political bosses will they continue to vote against their own interests and turn again to violence to right their wrongs.

If men possessing the power of the ballot are driven to desperate means to gain their ends, what shall be done by disfranchised women? There are grave questions of moral, as well as material interest in which women are most deeply concerned. Denied the ballot, the legitimate means with which to exert their influence, and, as a rule, being lovers of peace, they have recourse to prayers and tears, those potent weapons of women and children, and, when they fail, must tamely submit to wrong or rise in rebellion against the powers that be. Women's crusades against saloons, brothels and gambling-dens, emptying kegs and bottles into the streets, breaking doors and windows and burning houses, all go to prove that disfranchisement, the denial of lawful means to gain desired ends, may drive even women to violations of law and order. Hence to secure both national and "domestic tranquillity," to "establish justice," to carry out the spirit of our Constitution, put into the hands of all women, as you have into those of all men, the ballot, that symbol of perfect equality, that right protective of all other rights.

CARRIE CHAPMAN CATT

C arrie Chapman Catt's (1859–1947) main contributions to the woman's
suffrage movement were on a practical, rather than a theoretical, level.
She succeeded Susan B. Anthony as president of the National
American Woman Suffrage Association (NAWSA), serving from 1900–1904
and 1915–20. Catt devised the so-called "Winning Plan," the political tactics
through which the Nineteenth Amendment was eventually ratified. She was
also instrumental in founding the League of Women Voters into which
NAWSA evolved after the attainment of suffrage. According to *The History of
Woman Suffrage:*[1] "The League of Women Voters was first mentioned at the
convention of the National American Woman Suffrage Association in
Washington, D.C., Dec. 12–15, 1917, when its president, Mrs. Carrie Chapman
Catt, outlined a plan to unite the women of the five suffrage States."

NEED FOR ORGANIZATION RATHER THAN EDUCATION

The first selection reflects the movement of women's rights from the theoretical to the practical plane. Whereas the demand for woman suffrage had at one
time been a protest against injustice, as achievement of this end became not
only a possibility but also realized in several states, questions of immediate
political tactics became more important than theoretical presentations. This
development was also seen in the rise of Catt, an organizer and eminently
practical person, to a high position in the women's movement.

In her speech at the 1895 NAWSA Convention, Catt articulates her view on the movement's paramount need for organization. She claims that the slow pace of the movement's gains has been due to misplaced emphasis on "education and agitation." According to *HWS*, to the great amusement of those present, Susan B. Anthony responded to Catt's remarks, as follows: "There never yet was a young woman who did not feel that if she had the management of the work from the beginning the cause would have been carried long ago. I felt just so when I was young."[2] But five years later, Catt was Anthony's handpicked successor as president of NAWSA.

NOTES

1. Elizabeth Cady Stanton et al., eds., *History of Woman Suffrage (HWS)*, 6 Vols. (New York and Rochester, 1881–1922). Vol. V, p. 684.
2. Ibid., Vol. IV, p. 249.

NEED FOR ORGANIZATION
RATHER THAN EDUCATION

The great need of the hour is organization. There can be no doubt that the advocates of woman suffrage in the United States are to be numbered by millions, but it is a lamentable fact that our organization can count its numbers only by thousands. There are illustrious men and women in every State, and there are men and women innumerable, who are not known to the public, who are openly and avowedly woman suffragists, yet we do not possess the benefit of their names on our membership lists or the financial help of their dues. In other words, the size of our membership is not at all commensurate with the sentiment for woman suffrage. The reason for this condition is plain; the chief work of suffragists for the past forty years has been education and agitation, and not organization. The time has come when the educational work has borne its fruit, and there are States in which there is sentiment enough to carry a woman suffrage amendment, but it is individual and not organized sentiment, and is, therefore, ineffective.

SPEECH TO IOWA CONVENTION, 1894

In this speech, delivered at the 1894 Iowa Woman Suffrage Association, Catt presents an argument from expediency. Granting women the vote will help avert the "great danger" that "lies in the votes possessed by the males in the slums of the cities." Granting the vote to people "of sound mind," women as well as men, will help to counteract "the ignorant foreign vote."

SPEECH TO IOWA CONVENTION, 1894

This Government is menaced with great danger, and that danger cannot be averted by the triumph of the party of protection, nor by that of free trade, nor by the triumph of single tax or of free silver. That danger lies in the votes possessed by the males in the slums of the cities, and the ignorant foreign vote which was sought to be brought up by each party, to make political success. It made no difference whether that vote was usually found with one party or not (except that one has more respect for an open bid than for a disguised one), the corrupting influence was just the same. In the mining districts the danger has already reached this point—miners are supplied with arms, watching with greedy eyes for the moment when they can get in their deadly work of despoiling the wealth of the country. The hoodlums of Chicago gave us a forecast of their intent to reproduce the horrors of the Old World when their numbers are sufficiently increased, and every ship load of foreigners brings them nearer to their object. These men hold the government of the large cities in the hollow of their hands. There is but one way to avert the danger—cut off the vote of the slums and give to woman, who is bound to suffer all, and more than man can, of the evils his legislation has brought upon the nation, the power of protecting herself that man has secured for himself—the ballot. Put the ballot in the hands of every person of sound mind in the nation. If that would make the vote too cumbersome, cut it off at the bottom, the vote of the slums. For several years past the proportion of men to women immigrating to this country has been increasing and has reached that of seven to one. In the five years preceding and including 1890, 1,020,032 men of voting age came to this country. And as in fourteen States an immigrant may vote, according to the laws of some States, in one year, or, in some, six months (as in Kansas), or in four months (as in Wisconsin), or in three months (as in Michigan), we can get some idea of their influence with the Government. Not only is the native-born American jeopardized in life and property, but the citizens of foreign birth who desire good government. It will be readily seen that granting the vote to woman and cutting off the vote of the slums, if it could not be otherwise controlled, would result at once in good to the nation. And these good men who fear that evil would result to woman by depositing her opinion where it will be counted, who yet, like Dr. Parkhurst, call upon woman to face the dangers of walking day after day upon the streets frequented by the men who have built up Tammany, to use their influence upon voters to tear it down, when a little piece of paper deposited in a ballot-box, which would take but a small part of one day, surrounded by no greater danger, would do the work far more effectually. This shows how tenacious of power men are when once possessing it, even when they mean to use that power for good as they see it.

A LEAGUE OF WOMEN VOTERS

In this brief selection from a speech delivered in 1919, Catt calls for a nonpartisan League of Women Voters to "finish the fight" for women's rights and the improvement of American democracy. As noted earlier, Catt is given credit for first calling for such an organization. The League of Women Voters was founded in 1920 as an outgrowth of the National American Woman Suffrage Association to aid women in the intelligent use of the vote.

A LEAGUE OF WOMEN VOTERS

Every suffragist will hope for a memorial dedicated to the memory of our brave departed leaders, to the sacrifices they made for our cause, to the scores of victories won.... I venture to propose one whose benefits will bless our entire nation and bring happiness to the humblest of our citizens—the most natural, the most appropriate and the most patriotic memorial that could be suggested—a League of Women Voters to "finish the fight" and to aid in the reconstruction of the nation. What could be more natural than that women having attained their political independence should desire to give service in token of their gratitude? What could be more appropriate than that such women should do for the coming generation what those of a preceding did for them? What could be more patriotic than that these women should use their new freedom to make the country safer for their children and their children's children?

Let us then raise up a League of Women Voters, the name and form of organization to be determined by the members themselves; a league that shall be non-partisan and non-sectarian and consecrated to three chief aims: 1. To use its influence to obtain the full enfranchisement of the women of every State in our own republic and to reach out across the seas in aid of the woman's struggle for her own in every land. 2. To remove the remaining legal discriminations against women in the codes and constitutions of the several States in order that the feet of coming women may find these stumbling blocks removed. 3. To make our democracy so safe for the nation and so safe for the world that every citizen may feel secure and great men will acknowledge the worthiness of the American republic to lead.

CHARLOTTE PERKINS GILMAN

R ather than attempting to demonstrate the moral superiority of women, in her seminal book *Women and Economics* Charlotte Perkins Gilman (1860–1935) argued that women were morally, spiritually, and intellectually impoverished by their second-class citizenship. Like John Stuart Mill, Gilman claimed that extending political rights and legal protection to women would cure the narrowness of their concerns, the pettiness of their minds. She extended this argument to propose specific socialistic plans that would permit women to become productive members of society. She concluded that society would benefit from casting off a drag on its economy and doubling its productive workforce with a substantial resulting increase in overall wealth.

THE BALLOT AS AN IMPROVER OF MOTHERHOOD

The selection included here, "The Ballot as an Improver of Motherhood," is from Gilman's address to the 1896 NAWSA convention. Gilman takes on a cultural icon—motherhood. She argues that with stunted human beings in the maternal role, children cannot develop properly. Full citizenship rights will make mothers more capable of educating their children properly. Endowed with political rights, women will see themselves as part of a larger community. With this expansion of their own sense of self, mothers will be able to impart to their children an expansive, communitarian view of their roles in society.

THE BALLOT AS AN IMPROVER OF MOTHERHOOD

We have heard much of the superior moral sense of woman. It is superior in spots but not as a whole.... Here is an imaginary case which will show how undeveloped in some respects woman's moral sense still is: Suppose a train was coming with a children's picnic on board—three hundred merry, laughing children. Suppose you saw this train was about to go through an open switch and over an embankment, and your own child was playing on the track in front of it. You could turn the switch and save the train, or save your own child by pulling it off the track, but there was not time to do both. Which would you do? I have put that question to hundreds of women. I never have found one but said she would save her own child, and not one in a hundred claimed this would be absolutely right. The maternal instinct is stronger in the hearts of most women than any moral sense....

What is the suffrage going to do for motherhood? Women enter upon this greatest function of life without any preparation, and their mothers permit them to do it because they do not recognize motherhood as a business. We do not let a man practice as a doctor or a druggist, or do anything else which involves issues of life and death, without training and certificates; but the life and death of the whole human race are placed in the hands of utterly untrained young girls. The suffrage draws the woman out of her purely personal relations and puts her in relations with her kind, and it broadens her intelligence. I am not disparaging the noble devotion of our present mothers—I know how they struggle and toil—but when that tremendous force of mother love is made intelligent, fifty per cent of our children will not die before they are five years old, and those that grow up will be better men and women. A woman will no longer be attached solely to one little group, but will be also a member of the community. She will not neglect her own on that account, but will be better to them and of more worth as a mother.

JANE ADDAMS

Jane Addams (1860–1935) was a social reformer and founder of Hull House in Chicago. Addams was active in the settlement house movement, which attempted to provide recreation and educational opportunities for poor and working-class neighborhoods. Her lifetime of public service was recognized with the 1931 Nobel Peace Prize, which she shared with Nicholas Murray Butler.

WHY WOMEN SHOULD VOTE

Addams was active in a range of social causes, including pacifism and woman suffrage. Asked by the *Ladies' Home Journal* in 1910 to present a brief account of why women should be given the vote, Addams sought to overturn the traditional distinction between the domestic or private sphere and the public sphere. According to traditional views, women were relegated to the former, while the latter was the exclusive preserve of men. But Addams argued that success in the private sphere required certain policies in the public in regard to education, public health, and other areas. Women could not carry out their traditional responsibilities of caring for their families without a healthy, supportive environment. In order to make sure proper steps were taken, as an extension of their traditional domestic roles, women required the vote.

WHY WOMEN SHOULD VOTE

For many generations it has been believed that woman's place is within the walls of her own home, and it is indeed impossible to imagine the time when her duty there shall be ended or to forecast any social change which shall release her from that paramount obligation.

This paper is an attempt to show that many women today are failing to discharge their duties to their own households properly simply because they do not perceive that as society grows more complicated it is necessary that woman shall extend her sense of responsibility to many things outside of her own home if she would continue to preserve the home in its entirety. One could illustrate in many ways. A woman's simplest duty, one would say, is to keep her house clean and wholesome and to feed her children properly. Yet if she lives in a tenement house, as so many of my neighbors do, she cannot fulfill these simple obligations by her own efforts because she is utterly dependent upon the city administration for the conditions which render decent living possible. Her basement will not be dry, her stairways will not be fireproof, her house will not be provided with sufficient windows to give light and air, nor will it be equipped with sanitary plumbing, unless the Public Works Department sends inspectors who constantly insist that these elementary decencies be provided. Women who live in the country sweep their own dooryards and may either feed the refuse of the table to a flock of chickens or allow it innocently to decay in the open air and sunshine. In a crowded city quarter, however, if the street is not cleaned by the city authorities no amount of private sweeping will keep the tenement free from grime; if the garbage is not properly collected and destroyed a tenement-house mother may see her children sicken and die of diseases from which she alone is powerless to shield them, although her tenderness and devotion are unbounded. She cannot even secure untainted meat for her household, she cannot provide fresh fruit, unless the meat has been inspected by city officials, and the decayed fruit, which is so often placed upon sale in the tenement districts, has been destroyed in the interests of public health. In short, if woman would keep on with her old business of caring for her house and rearing her children she will have to have some conscience in regard to public affairs lying quite outside of her immediate household. The individual conscience and devotion are no longer effective.

Chicago One Spring Had a Spreading Contagion of scarlet fever just at the time that the school nurses had been discontinued because business men had pronounced them too expensive. If the women who sent their children to the schools had been sufficiently public-spirited and had been provided with an implement through which to express that public spirit they would have insisted that the schools be supplied with nurses in order that their own children might be protected from contagion. In other words, if women would effectively continue their old avocations they must take part in the slow upbuilding of that code of legislation which is alone sufficient to protect the home from the dangers incident to modern life. One might instance the many deaths of children from contagious diseases the germs of which had been carried in tailored clothing. Country doctors testify as to the outbreak of scarlet fever in remote neighborhoods each autumn, after the children have begun to wear the winter overcoats and cloaks which have been sent from infected city sweatshops. That their mothers mend their stockings and guard them from "taking cold" is not a sufficient protection when the tailoring of the family is done in a distant city under conditions which the mother cannot possibly control. The sanitary regulation of sweatshops by city officials is all that can be depended upon to prevent such needless destruction. Who shall say that women are not concerned in the enactment and enforcement of such legislation if they would preserve their homes?

Even women who take no part in public affairs in order that they may give themselves entirely to their own families, sometimes going so far as to despise those other women who are endeavoring to secure protective legislation, may illustrate this point. The Hull-House neighborhood was at one time suffering from a typhoid epidemic. A careful investigation was made by which we were able to establish a very close connection between the typhoid and a mode of plumbing which made it most probable that the infection had been carried by flies. Among the people who had been exposed to the infection was a widow who had lived in the ward for a number of years, in a comfortable little house which she owned. Although the Italian immigrants were closing in all around her she was not willing to sell her property and to move away until she had finished the education of her children. In the mean time she held herself quite aloof from her Italian neighbors and could never be drawn into any of the public efforts to protect them by securing a better code of tenement-house sanitation. Her two daughters were sent to an Eastern college; one June, when one of them had graduated and the other still had two years before she took her degree, they came to the spotless little house and to their self-sacrificing mother for the summer's holiday. They both fell ill, not because their own home was not clean, not because their mother was not devoted, but because next door to them and also in the rear were wretched tenements, and because the mother's utmost efforts could not keep the infection out of her own house. One daughter died and one recovered but was an invalid for two years following. This is, perhaps, a fair illustration of the futility of the individual conscience when woman insists upon isolating her family from the rest of the community and its interests. The result is sure to be a pitiful failure.

One of the Interesting Experiences in the Chicago campaign for inducing the members of the Charter Convention to recommend municipal franchise for women in the provisions of the new charter was the unexpected enthusiasm and help which came from large groups of foreign-born women. The Scandinavian women represented in many Lutheran Church societies said quite simply that in the old country they had had the municipal franchise upon the same basis as men since the seventeenth century; all the women formerly living under the British Government, in England, Australia or Canada, point out that Chicago women were asking now for what the British women had long had. But the most unexpected response came from the foreign colonies in which women had never heard such problems discussed and took the prospect of the municipal ballot as a simple device—which it is—to aid them in their daily struggle with adverse city conditions. The Italian women said that the men engaged in railroad construction were away all summer and did not know anything about their household difficulties. Some of them came to Hull-House one day to talk over the possibility of a public wash-house. They do not like to wash in their own tenements; they have never seen a washing-tub until they came to America, and find it very difficult to use it in the restricted space of their little kitchens and to hang the clothes within the house to dry. They say that in the Italian villages the women all go to the streams together; in the town they go to the public wash-house; and washing, instead of being lonely and disagreeable, is made pleasant by cheerful conversation. It is asking a great deal of these women to change suddenly all their habits of living, and their contention that the tenement-house kitchen is too small for laundry-work is well taken. If women in Chicago knew the needs of the Italian colony they would realize that any change bringing cleanliness and fresh clothing into the Italian household would be a very sensible and hygienic measure. It is, perhaps, asking a great deal that the members of the City Council should understand this, but surely a comprehension of the needs of these women and efforts toward ameliorating their lot might be regarded as matters of municipal obligation on the part of voting women.

The same thing is true of the Jewish women in their desire for covered markets which have always been a municipal provision in Russia and Poland. The vegetables piled high upon the wagons standing in the open markets of Chicago become covered with dust and soot. It seems to these women a violation of the most rudimentary decencies and they sometimes say quite simply: "If women have anything to say about it they would change all that."

If Women Follow Only the Lines of their traditional activities here are certain primary duties which belong to even the most conservative women, and which no one woman or group of women can adequately discharge unless they join the more general movements looking toward social amelioration through legal enactment.

The first of these, of which this article has already treated, is woman's responsibility for the members of her own household that they may be properly fed and clothed and surrounded by hygienic conditions. The second is a responsibility for the education of children: (*a*) that they may be provided with good schools; (*b*) that they may be kept free from vicious influences on the street; (*c*) that when working they may be protected by adequate child-labor legislation.

(*a*) The duty of a women toward the schools which her children attend is so obvious that it is not necessary to dwell upon it. But even this simple obligation cannot be effectively carried out without some form of social organization as the mothers' school clubs and mothers' congresses testify, and to which the most conservative women belong because they feel the need of wider reading and discussion concerning the many problems of childhood. It is, therefore, perhaps natural that the public should have been more willing to accord a vote to women in school matters than in any other, and yet women have never been members of a Board of Education in sufficient numbers to influence largely actual school curriculi. If they had been kindergartens, domestic science courses and school playgrounds would be far more numerous than they are. More than one woman has been convinced of the need of the ballot by the futility of her efforts in persuading a business man that young children need nurture in something besides the three r's. Perhaps, too, only women realize the influence which the school might exert upon the home if a proper adaptation to actual needs were considered. An Italian girl who has had lessons in cooking at the public school will help her mother to connect the entire family with American food and household habits. That the mother has never baked bread in Italy—only mixed it in her own house and then taken it out to the village oven—makes it all the more necessary that her daughter should understand the complications of a cooking-stove. The same thing is true of the girl who learns to sew in the public school, and more than anything else, perhaps, of the girl who receives the first simple instruction in the care of little children, that skillful care which every tenement-house baby requires if he is to be pulled through his second summer. The only time, to my knowledge, that lessons in the care of children were given in the public schools of Chicago was one summer when the vacation schools were being managed by a volunteer body of women. The instruction was eagerly received by the Italian girls, who had been "little mothers" to younger children ever since they could remember.

As a result of this teaching I recall a young girl who carefully explained to her Italian mother that the reason the babies in Italy were so healthy and the babies in Chicago were so sickly was not, as her mother had always firmly insisted, because her babies in Italy had goat's milk and her babies in America had cow's milk, but because the milk in Italy was clean and the milk in Chicago was dirty. She said that when you milked your own goat before the door you knew that the milk was clean, but when you bought milk from the grocery store after it had been carried for many miles in the country "you couldn't tell whether or not it was fit for the baby to drink until the men from the City Hall, who had watched it all the way, said that it was all right." She also informed her mother that the "City Hall wanted to fix up the milk so that it couldn't make the baby sick, but that they hadn't quite enough votes for it yet." The Italian mother believed what her child had been taught in the big school; it seemed to her quite as natural that the city should be concerned in providing pure milk for her younger children as that it should provide big schools and teachers for her older children. She reached this naïve conclusion because she had never heard those arguments which make it seem reasonable that a woman should be given the school franchise, but no other.

(*b*) **But Women are Also Beginning to Realize** that children need attention outside of school hours; that much of the petty vice in cities is merely the love of pleasure gone wrong, the overrestrained boy or girl seeking improper recreation and excitement. It is obvious that a little study of the needs of children, a sympathetic understanding of the conditions under which they go astray, might save hundreds of them. Women traditionally have had an opportunity to observe the plays of children and the needs of youth, and yet in Chicago, at least, they had done singularly little in this vexed problem of juvenile delinquency until they helped to inaugurate the Juvenile Court movement a dozen years ago. The Juvenile Court Committee, made up largely of women, paid the salaries of the probation officers connected with the court for the first six years of its existence, and after the salaries were cared for by the county the same organization turned itself into a Juvenile Protective League, and through a score of paid officers are doing valiant service in minimizing some of the dangers of city life which boys and girls encounter.

This Protective League, however, was not formed until the women had had a civic training through their semi-official connection with the Juvenile Court. This is, perhaps, an illustration of our inability to see the duty "next to hand" until we have become alert through our knowledge of conditions in connection with the larger duties. We would all agree that social amelioration must come about through the efforts of many people who are moved thereto by the compunction and stirring of the individual conscience, but we are only beginning to understand that the individual conscience will respond to the special challenge largely in proportion as the individual is able to see the social conditions because he has felt responsible for their improvement. Because this body of women assumed a public responsibility that have seen to it that every series suggesting obscenity and criminality have been practically eliminated. The police department has performed this and many other duties to which it was oblivious before simply because these women have made it realize that it is necessary to protect and purify those places of amusement which are crowded with young people every night. This is but the negative side of the policy pursued by the public authorities in the fifteen small parks of Chicago, each of which is provided with halls in which young people may meet nightly for social gatherings and dances. The more extensively the modern city endeavors on the one hand to control and on the other hand to provide recreational facilities for its young people the more necessary it is that women should assist in their direction and extension. After all, a care for wholesome and innocent amusement is what women have for many years assumed. When the reaction comes on the part of taxpayers women's votes may be necessary to keep the city to its beneficent obligations toward its own young people.

(*c*) **As the Education of Her Children** has been more and more transferred to the school, so that even children four years old go to the kindergarten, the woman has been left in a household of constantly-narrowing interests, not only because the children are away, but also because one industry after another is slipping from the household into the factory. Ever since steam power has been applied to the processes of weaving and spinning woman's traditional work has been carried on largely outside of the home. The clothing and household linen are not only spun and woven, but also usually sewed, by machinery; the preparation of many foods has also passed into the factory and necessarily a certain number of women have been obliged to follow their work there, although it is doubtful, in spite of the large number of factory girls, whether women now are doing as large a proportion of the world's work as they used to do. Because many thousands of those working in factories and shops are girls between the ages of fourteen and twenty-two there is a necessity that older women should be interested in the conditions of industry. The very fact that these girls are not going to remain in industry permanently makes it more important that some one should see to it that they shall not be incapacitated for their future family life because they work for exhausting hours and under insanitary conditions.

If woman's sense of obligation had enlarged as the industrial conditions changed she might naturally and almost imperceptibly have inaugurated the movements for social amelioration in the line of factory legislation and shop sanitation. That she has not done so is doubtless due to the fact that her conscience is slow to recognize any obligation outside of her own family circle, and because she was so absorbed in her own household that she failed to see what the conditions outside actually were. It would be interesting to know how far the consciousness that she had no vote and could not change matters operated in this direction. After all, we see only those things to which our attention has been drawn, we feel responsibility for those things which are brought to us as matters of responsibility. If conscientious women were convinced that it was a civic duty to be informed in regard to these grave industrial affairs, and then to express the conclusions which they had reached by depositing a piece of paper in a ballot-box, one cannot imagine that they would shirk simply because the action ran counter to old traditions.

To Those of My Readers Who Would Admit that although woman has no right to shirk her old obligations, that all of these measures could be secured more easily through her influence upon the men of her family than through the direct use of the ballot, I should like to tell a little story. I have a friend in Chicago who is the mother of four sons and the grandmother of twelve grandsons who are voters. She is a woman of wealth, of secured social position, of sterling character and clear intelligence, and may, therefore, quite fairly be cited as a "woman of influence." Upon one of her recent birthdays, when she was asked how she had kept so young, she promptly replied: "Because I have always advocated at least one unpopular cause." It may have been in pursuance of this policy that for many years she has been an ardent advocate of free silver, although her manufacturing family are all Republicans! I happened to call at her house on the day that Mr. McKinley was elected President against Mr. Bryan for the first time. I found my friend much disturbed. She said somewhat bitterly that she had at last discovered what the much-vaunted influence of woman was worth; that she had implored each one of her sons and grandsons, had entered into endless arguments and moral appeals to induce one of them to represent her convictions by voting for Bryan! That, although sincerely devoted to her, each one had assured her that his convictions forced him to vote the Republican ticket. She said that all she had been able to secure was the promise from one of the grandsons, for whom she had an especial tenderness because he bore her husband's name, that he would not vote at all. He could not vote for Bryan, but out of respect for her feeling he would refrain from voting for McKinley. My friend said that for many years she had suspected that women could influence men only in regard to those things in which men were not deeply concerned, but when it came to persuading a man to a woman's view in affairs of politics or business it was absolutely useless. I contended that a woman had no right to persuade a man to vote against his own convictions; that I respected the men of her family for following their own judgment regardless of the appeal which the honored head of the house had made to their chivalric devotion. To this she replyed that she would agree with that point of view when a woman had the same opportunity as a man to register her convictions by vote. I believed then as I do now, that nothing is gained when independence of judgment is assailed by "influence," sentimental or otherwise, and that we test advancing civilization somewhat by our power to respect differences and by our tolerance of another's honest conviction.

This is, perhaps, the attitude of many busy women who would be glad to use the ballot to further public measures in which they are interested and for which they have been working for years. It offends the taste of such a woman to be obliged to use indirect "influence" when she is accustomed to well-bred, open action in other affairs, and she very much resents the time spent in persuading a voter to take her point of view, and possibly to give up his own, quite as honest and valuable as hers, although different because resulting from a totally different experience. Public-spirited women who wish to use the ballot, as I know them, do not wish to do the work of men nor to take over men's affairs. They simply want an opportunity to do their own work and to take care of those affairs which naturally and historically belong to women, but which are constantly being overlooked and slighted in our political institutions.

In a Complex Community Like the Modern City all points of view need to be represented; the resultants of diverse experiences need to be pooled if the community would make for sane and balanced progress. If it would meet fairly each problem as it arises, whether it be connected with a freight tunnel having to do largely with business men, or with the increasing death rate among children under five years of age, a problem in which women are vitally concerned, or with the question of more adequate street-car transfers, in which both men and women might be said to be equally interested, it must not ignore the judgments of its entire adult population.

To turn the administration of our civic affairs wholly over to men may mean that the American city will continue to push forward in its commercial and industrial development, and continue to lag behind in those things which make a city healthful and beautiful. After all, woman's traditional function has been to make her dwelling-place both clean and fair. Is that dreariness in city life, that lack of domesticity which the humblest farm dwelling presents, due to a withdrawal of one of the naturally coöperating forces? If women have in any sense been responsible for the gentler side of life which softens and blurs some of its harsher conditions, may they not have a duty to perform in our American cities?

In closing, may I recapitulate that if woman would fulfill her traditional responsibility to her own children; if she would educate and protect from danger factory children who must find their recreation on the street; if she would bring the cultural forces to bear upon our materialistic civilization; and if she would do it all with the dignity and directness fitting one who carries on her immemorial duties, then she must bring herself to the use of the ballot—that latest implement for self-government. May we not fairly say that American women need this implement in order to preserve the home?

HENRY BLACKWELL

H enry Blackwell (1825–1909) moved to the United States from England
at the age of seven. For virtually his entire life he was active in liberal
causes, including woman suffrage. He married the suffragist Lucy
Stone in 1855—on the day of their marriage publishing a joint declaration
protesting inequities in marriage law. Blackwell was also a longtime editor of
the *Woman's Journal*.

A SOLUTION OF THE SOUTHERN QUESTION

Blackwell's most notable intellectual contribution to the movement was an
argument for granting the vote to educated white women in order to counteract the influence of uneducated voters "in the North, people of foreign
birth; in the South, people of African race, and a considerable portion of the
native white population." Blackwell does not support enfranchising all
women. Although the vote cannot be withdrawn from illiterate men, he proposes literacy requirements for women. Census data demonstrate that, with
this reform enacted, "educated, responsible voters" would be everywhere
predominant.

A SOLUTION OF THE SOUTHERN QUESTION

The practical nullification in the Southern States of the Fourteenth and Fifteenth Amendments of the United States Constitution, under the pressure of a real or imaginary necessity, constitutes the most difficult fact in American politics. The portentous spectacle of a "Solid South" tends to create and perpetuate a solid North. This fact arrays the great political parties upon sectional lines, keeps alive a deplorable race issue, and retards the moral and material interests of the country. The conflict fans the dying embers of civil strife, arouses prejudice, and generates hatred. In a case like this, where the sentiments and susceptibilities of committees numbering millions of men and women are aroused on opposite sides, crimination and recrimination are out of place. Some solution must be attained tolerably acceptable to both sections and both races—a solution which will measurably satisfy intelligent public sentiment North and South. Until this is affected, harmony will be impossible, and union and reconstruction will be incomplete.

No such solution has yet been suggested. Negro colonization and a repeal of the amendments are alike impracticable. The negro is and will be a citizen and a legal voter. Coercion, intimidation, and bribery are temporary evasions, which, if continued, will demoralize society. How can the negro vote be freely cast and fairly counted without endangering social order and political stability?

In only one way can this be done. Without disfranchising a single legal voter, white or black, educated or illiterate, legislation must bring into the body politic an additional force of intelligent voters so numerous as to give the educated, responsible citizens everywhere an assured predominance. The illiterate, irresponsible voters, who now too often constitute a legal majority, must be controlled by the honest ballots of the civilized, responsible members of the community. These ballots can only be had in sufficient numbers by adding to the suffrages of men the votes of educated women.

The evils of an illiterate suffrage are felt and deplored alike North and South. They are to-day the most potent obstacle to good government; they are also the most potent obstacle to the enfranchisement of women. The percentage of illiteracy in States where foreigners and negroes form a considerable part of the population, is somewhat greater among women than among men; and this fact, added to the inexperience of women in public affairs, is regarded by many as an insuperable objection to the extension of suffrage to women.

But this objection proceeds on the assumption that all women, if any, must be enfranchised. That does not follow. In Massachusetts no man can vote unless he can read and write, and pays a tax. Suffragists, therefore, in that State, demand the ballot only for women who can read and write. Why, then, should they ask for it in other States upon a different condition? Why ask suffrage for illiterate women in New York or South Carolina, and not in Massachusetts? True, in these other States, illiterate male suffrage is not satisfactory, then the voting of illiterate men is no reason why illiterate women should be enfranchised. On the contrary, it is the best of all reasons why such women should be excluded. Nor does the exclusion of such women furnish any reason why educated women should be disfranchised On the contrary, the admitted evils of male illiteracy, otherwise irremediable, can only be overcome by adding to the existing voters the educated women of the nation.

The time has come when this question should be considered. An educational qualification for suffrage may or may not be wise, but certainly it is not necessarily unjust. If each voter governed only himself, his intelligence would concern himself alone, but his vote helps to govern everybody else. Society, in conceding his right, has itself a right to require from him a suitable preparation. Ability to read and write is absolutely necessary as a means of obtaining accurate political information. Without it, the voter is almost sure to become the tool of political demagogues. With free schools provided by the State, every citizen can qualify himself without money and without price. Under such circumstances, there is no infringement of right in requiring an educational qualification as a pre-requisite of voting. Indeed, without this, suffrage is often little more than a name. "Suffrage is the authoritative exercise of rational choice in regard to principles, measures and men." The compassion of an unintelligent voter to a "trained monkey" who goes through the motions of dropping a paper ballot into a box, has in it an element of truth. Society, therefore, has a right to prescribe, in the admission of any new class of voters, such a qualification as everyone can attain and as will enable the voter to cast an intelligent and responsible vote.

In the development of our complex political society, we have to-day two great bodies of illiterate citizens; in the North, people of foreign birth; in the South, people of African race, and a considerable portion of the native white population. Against foreigners and negroes, as such, we would not discriminate. So far as male citizens are concerned, we cannot recall an existing political equality. But, in every State save one, there are more educated women than all the illiterate voters, white and black, native and foreign. It is simply amazing that mole-eyed politicians should resort to intimidation and bribery to secure a political preponderance for intelligence, which can be fairly and honestly had by the enfranchisement of women who can read and write.

By the United States census of 1880, there were, on the present basis of universal male suffrage, in the Southern States and the District of Columbia, 2,947,424 white voters, of whom 411,900 were illiterate; and

1,252,484 colored voters, of whom 951,444 were illiterate; making in all 4,199,908 voters, of whom 1,363,844 were illiterate. In these States there were also 2,293,698 white women over twenty-one who could write, and 236,865 colored women over twenty-one who could write; making in all 2,530,563 women over twenty-one who could write. If these educated women were made voters, their votes would offset the entire illiterate voters, white and black, who number 1,363,844; and would leave a surplus, added to the educated male voters, numbering 2,836,064, would give an educated voting majority of 4,002,783 (over four million)....

EDUCATED WOMEN SUFFRAGE AND RACE.

In Alabama, by the United States census of 1880, there were 117,756 white women over twenty-one who can write, and 118,423 negro male voters, of whom 96,408 were illiterates. In Arkansas there were 89,425 white women who can write, and 46,827 negro voters, of whom 34,300 were illiterates. In Delaware there were 27,623 white women who can write, and 6,396 negroes, of whom 3,787 were illiterates. In the District of Columbia there were 31,507 white women who can write, and 13,918 negro voters, of whom 7,520 were illiterates. In Florida there were 25,324 white women who can write, and 27,489 negro voters , of whom 19,110 were illiterate. In Georgia there were 149,895 white women who can write, and 143,471 negro voters, of whom 116,516 were illiterates. In Kentucky there were 236,092 white women who can write, and 58,642 negro voters, of whom 43,177 were illiterates. In Louisiana there were 85,926 white women who can write, and 107,977 negro voters, of whom 86,555 were illiterates. In Maryland there were 169,173 white women who can write, and 48,584 negro voters, of whom 30,873 were illiterates. In Mississippi there were 90,552 white women who can write, and 130,278 negro voters, of whom 99,068 were illiterates. In Missouri there were 383,234 white women who can write, and 33,042 negro voters, of whom 19,028 were illiterates. In North Carolina there were 143,333 white women who can write, and 105,018 negro voters, of whom 80,282 were illiterates. In South Carolina there were 75,207 white women who can write, and 118,889 negro voters, of whom 93,010 were illiterates. In Texas there were 201,014 white women who can write, and 78,639 negro voters, of whom 59,669 were illiterates. In Tennessee there were 185,572 white women who can write, and 80,250 negro voters, of whom 58,601 were illiterates. In Virginia there were 179,446 white women who can write, and 128,257 negro voters, of whom 100,210 were illiterates In West Virginia there were 102,619 white women who can write, and 6,384 negro voters, of whom 3,830 were illiterates

Thus, in every State, the white women who can write exceed in number all the negro male voters, except in Alabama, Florida, Louisiana,

Mississippi, and South Carolina, and even in these five States, the white women who can write almost equal in number the negro male voters, while the negro women who can write compare with the white woman who can write only as one in eleven.

EDUCATED WOMAN SUFFRAGE VS. ILLITERACY.

By the United States census of 1880, in Alabama there were 134,938 women who can write, and 120,858 illiterate male voters. In Arkansas there were 97,144 women who can write, and 55,649 illiterate voters. In Delaware there were 29,737 women who can write, and 6,742 illiterate male voters. In the District of Columbia there were 38,439 women who can write, and 8,870 illiterate male voters. In Florida there were 31,089 women who can write, and 23,816 illiterate male voters. In Georgia there were 169,043 women who can write, and 145,087 illiterate male voters. In Kentucky there were 250,238 women who can write, and 98,133 illiterate male voters. In Louisiana there were 103,882 women who can write, and 102,932 illiterate male voters. In Maryland there were 185,212 women who can write, and 46,025 illiterate male voters. In Mississippi there were 113,964 women who can write, and 111,541 illiterate male voters. In Missouri there were 395,184 women who can write, and 59,683 illiterate male voters. In North Carolina there were 160,094 women who can write, and 124,702 illiterate male voters. In South Carolina there were 93,394 women who can write, and 106,934 illiterate male voters. In Tennessee there were 203,823 women who can write, and 105,549 illiterate male voters. In Texas there were 215,286 women who can write, and 92,754 illiterate male voters. In Virginia there were 204,671 women who can write, and 131,684 illiterate male voters. In West Virginia there were 104,425 women who can write, and 22,885 illiterate male voters.

Thus, in every State except South Carolina, the women who can write exceed in number all the illiterates, white and black; and even in South Carolina the women who can write almost equal in number all the illiterates of both races.

The attention of Senator Morgan, of Alabama, the author of a recent article in the *Forum* entitled, "Shall Negro Majorities Rule?" is invited to the fact that if educated Southern women were enfranchised, there would no longer be a negro majority of voters in any State, nor could there be ever such a majority, until universal education shall have so civilized and enlightened both races as to deprive the senator's question of any serious significance. For what is called the "race" question in the South is really to a great extent a question of illiteracy. Is it worth while to invoke nullification and set aside constitutional guarantees to accomplish a result which can be safely attained by a consistent application of the Republican principle?

Consider, too, the gigantic stimulus to education which this political step would give. It would make the ability to read and write a badge of nobility among women. Educated mothers will ensure a higher standard of culture for both sexes. With universal education, American ideas and principles will prevail, politics will be ennobled, and a government of the people, by the people and for the people will be a government of enlightened men and women for the common interest of the home and of the State....

BELLE KEARNEY

B elle Kearney (1863–1939) became involved in woman suffrage through
extensive work in the Woman's Christian Temperance Union in which
she was a national figure. She was born in Mississippi during the Civil
War and raised in the South during Reconstruction. Her best-known publication *A Slaveholder's Daughter* (1899) deals with racial problems in the South as
well as her personal experiences.

THE SOUTH AND WOMAN SUFFRAGE

In "The South and Woman Suffrage," delivered in 1903 at the National
Suffrage Convention, Kearney declares that, with the rightfulness of
woman suffrage well established already, she will argue for its expediency.
Kearney's almost religious attachment to the South, "the holy of holies of
the Anglo-Saxon race," is on display here as she presents a detailed account
of how the South came to be burdened by 4,500,000 former slaves. Building
on and at one point quoting Henry Blackwell's "Solution to the Southern
Question," Kearney too defends woman suffrage as necessary to counteract
the threat of ignorant, enfranchised former slaves and immigrants,
although she proposes education and property qualifications for voting for
both sexes. Granting women the vote "would insure immediate and
durable white supremacy, honestly attained," and so "settle the race question in politics."

THE SOUTH AND WOMAN SUFFRAGE

[Address given by Miss Belle Kearney of Mississippi
at the National Suffrage Convention.]

The Old South had its birth in the settlement of Jamestown, Southern
Virginia, in 1607, a few months after the vessels of the British Crown
touched upon the shore of this vast continent. There the foundations were
laid of the first permanent English colony of America. It was not until thirteen years later that the Pilgrims landed at Cape Cod.

North Carolina took the initiative in securing national independence,
by instructing her delegates in Congress to concur with those from the
other colonies in declaring themselves free from the governmental power of
Great Britain, and it was Richard Henry Lee, of Virginia, who made the
motion in Congress asserting the right of the colonies to be free and independent States.

The first battle fought upon American soil in opposition to the dominion of Great Britain was that of Alamance, in North Carolina, four years
before the British fired their volley at Lexington, Mass.

The Continental army had a Virginian as commander-in-chief, George
Washington; and Thomas Jefferson, who wrote the Declaration of
Independence, was a Virginian. Through all the desperate struggles of that
period, the colonies of the South gave their splendid quota of heroes, beginning with George Rogers Clark, who conducted those two masterly cam-
paigns against the British, conquering as he went, down the glorious list to
the dauntless leaders, Marion, Sumter, and Pickens. Under Nathaniel
Greene were the illustrious Virginians, Daniel Morgan, William
Washington, and Henry Lee, the last of whom afterward became the father
of the beloved general of the Southern Confederacy, Robert E. Lee.

John Fiske, the historian, says:

The five great men who stand before all others in making the government under which we now live, and who have shaped the whole
future of American history, are George Washington, for his services in
securing the independence of the United States, and the wisdom with
which he set the new government in operation; James Madison, for
the principal part in framing the Constitution; Alexander Hamilton,
for persuading the people to adopt the Constitution, and for his bold
measures which gave strength and shape to the Federalist party;
Thomas Jefferson, for illustrating the true principles of Democracy,
and for the sagacity with which he conducted the first great change of
party supremacy in 1801; John Marshall, for his work as Chief Justice
of the United States, from 1800 to 1835, in interpreting the

Constitution, and increasing its elasticity and strength, by his profound judicial decisions.

All of the men were Virginians except Alexander Hamilton, and he was born in the West Indies. The South was, preeminently, the nation-builder.

From 1789 to 1860 there were ten presidents of the United States of Southern birth, whose administrations extended over a period of forty years. Virginia gave seven of these presidents. Strong old Andrew Jackson and James K. Polk were natives of North Carolina, and Abraham Lincoln was of Virginian ancestry and born in Kentucky.

During the seventy-one years reaching from Washington's administration to that of Lincoln, the United States may be said to have been, practically, under the dominion of Southern thought and Southern leadership.

To-day America rejoices in the wise action of one of the Virginian presidents, James Monroe, in declaring that this continent should be kept free from the intrusion of foreign nations.

The services rendered by Southern men to our great country since the Revolutionary days have been signal.

Henry Clay, the profound statesman from Kentucky, was chosen Speaker of the House of Representatives in our National Congress in 1811, and by his memorable Missouri Compromise prevented difficulties for nearly thirty years on the slavery question between the North and South.

In the war of 1812, while Captain Perry and other naval commanders won their imperishable laurels, turning the scales of battle upon the waters, the Indian power was broken in the Southwest by some Tennessee troops and a few U. S. Regulars under Andrew Jackson; and at the battle of New Orleans he gained a tremendous victory for the United States.

Under Gen. Sam Houston, a Virginian, the independence of Texas was achieved. With his name, those of the martyrs of Goliad and the heroes of the Alamo will live forever.

In the Mexican war, which gave Texas to the United States, nearly all the commanders in the American army were Southern men, from Winfield Scott and Zachary Taylor to Jefferson Davis, the last of whom held the rank of colonel.

Before the Revolution, all the colonies had negro slaves, and all started with slavery. The trade was carried on as energetically in the Northern colonies as in the Southern. New England vessels manned with sailors from that section, would bring the negroes from Africa and sell them at enormous profit in the seaports at the South. Slavery was found unprofitable in the North, because the farms were so small that the men of each family could supply all the necessary labor, and the climate was too cold for the African race.

Besides, as commerce and manufactures developed, skilled labor and experience were required, and in these the negro was inadequate. The men of the North, instead of liberating their slaves, shipped them to the South, where they were sold.

This business was so profitable that we are told, "The New England delegates to the Constitutional Convention of 1787 made certain demands of protection for these slave-traders before they would join hands with the Southern colonies for a stable form of government."

The plantations of the South were so large that they required vast numbers of laborers for their cultivation. The soil was so very rich that even unskilled workmen, if intelligently directed, would answer every purpose. Slavery was peculiarly adapted to the planting system, and, as it was recognized by the Constitution, it was continued in the South. The slave trade with foreign countries came to an end in 1808, by constitutional enactment; consequently this form of commerce became unprofitable for New England vessels. When conditions change, especially those affecting the money market, opinions usually change with them. Slavery being no longer a question of profit to the North, it gradually died out in that part of the country, and a sentiment in opposition to it began to be developed.

As the years went by, one slave State after another was admitted into the Union, and the South became a section. The same sort of civilization which existed in the Southern Colonies, preceding and following the Revolutionary war, was handed down to those States which lay upon the Gulf of Mexico and extended as far north as Maryland.

The same blood was in the veins of the men and women who founded those new commonwealths as flowed in the veins of Washington, Jefferson and Madison; the same as that which coursed through the veins of the heroes of Lexington, Concord and Bunker Hill; the same dominant blood that has conquered the earth, and will rule through the ages.

The people of the South have remained true to their royal inheritance. To-day the Anglo-Saxon triumphs in them more completely than in the inhabitants of any portion of the United States—the Anglo-Saxon ideals, continue the precious treasure of 2,000 years of effort and aspiration.

By degrees, slavery became the bone of contention in politics. In course of time it would probably have been abolished by the Southerners themselves, if they had been left to work out their own destiny and that of the black man in bonds, but a conflict of ideas gathered to a storm-center between the Puritan of the North and the Cavalier of the South, and the institution was wiped out in blood.

To-day one third of the population of the South is of the negro race, and there are more negroes in the United States than there are inhabitants in "Mexico, the third Republic of the world." In some Southern States the negroes far outnumber the whites, and are so numerous in all of them as to constitute what is called a "problem." Until the present generation, they have always lived here as slaves.

The race question is national in its bearing. Still, as the South has the bulk of the negro population, the burden of the responsibility for the negro problem rests here.

The world is scarcely beginning to realize the enormity of the situation that faces the South in its grapple with the race question which was thrust upon it at the close of the Civil War, when 4,500,000 ex-slaves, illiterate and semi-barbarous, were enfranchised. Such a situation has no parallel in history. In forging a path out of the darkness, there were no precedents to lead the way. All that has been and is being accomplished is pioneer statecraft. The South has struggled under its death weight for nearly forty years, bravely and magnanimously.

The Southern States are making a desperate effort to maintain the political supremacy of Anglo-Saxonism by amendments to their constitutions limiting the right to vote by a property and educational qualification. If the United States government had been wise enough to enact such a law when the negro was first enfranchised, it would have saved years of bloodshed in the South, and such experiences of suffering and horror among the white people here as no other were ever subjected to in an enlightened nation.

The present suffrage laws in the different Southern States can be only temporary measures for protection. Those who are wise enough to look beneath the surface will be compelled to realize the fact that they act as a stimulus to the black man to acquire both education and property, but no incentive is given to the poor whites; for it is understood, in a general way, that any man whose skin is fair enough to let the blue veins show through, may be allowed the right of franchise.

The industrial education that the negro is receiving at Tuskagee and other schools is only fitting him for power, and when the black man becomes necessary to a community by reason of his skill and acquired wealth, and the poor white man, embittered by his poverty and humiliated by his inferiority, finds no place for himself or his children, then will come the grapple between the races.

To avoid this unspeakable culmination, the enfranchisement of women will have to be effected, and an educational and property qualification for the ballot be made to apply, without discrimination, to both sexes and to both races. It will spur the poor white to keep up with the march of progression, and enable him to hold his own. The class that is not willing to measure its strength with that of an inferior is not fit to survive.

The enfranchisement of women would insure immediate and durable white supremacy, honestly attained; for, upon unquestionable authority, it is stated that "in every Southern State but one, there are more educated women than all the illiterate voters, white and black, native and foreign, combined." As you probably know, of all the women in the South who can read and write, ten out of every eleven are white. When it comes to the proportion of property between the races, that of the white outweighs that of the black immeasurably. The South is slow to grasp the great fact that the enfranchisement of women would settle the race question in politics.

The civilization of the North is threatened by the influx of foreigners with their imported customs; by the greed of monopolistic wealth, and the unrest among the working classes; by the strength of the liquor traffic, and by encroachments upon religious belief.

Some day the North will be compelled to look to the South for redemption from these evils, on account of the purity of its Anglo-Saxon blood, the simplicity of its social and economic structure, the great advance in prohibitory law, and the maintenance of the sanctity of faith, which has been kept inviolate. Just as surely as the North will be forced to turn to the South for the nation's salvation, just so surely will the South be compelled to look to its Anglo-Saxon women as the medium through which to retain the supremacy of the white race over the African.

I have heard it said in the South, "Oh, well, suffrage may be a good thing for women in other sections of the United States, but not here. Our women are different." How are they unlike those of their own sex elsewhere? They are certainly as intelligent as any upon the face of the earth; they have the same deep love for the home, the same devotion to their country.

"Oh, yes; but, you see, if the white women were allowed to vote, the negro women would have the same privilege, and that would mean the humiliation of having to meet them at the polls on a basis of equality."

That difficulty would be settled by having separate polling places. When the ballot is given to the women of the South, you will find that these distinct voting precincts for the two races will be quickly established.

It is useless for me to attempt, at this late day, to refute the objections raised against woman suffrage, for every obstacle to its progress has been met years ago, and every argument for its existence justified. It is no longer a question of right with the people, for that old battle has been fought; it is now only one of expediency, and opposition by prejudice.

To defend woman suffrage before a Louisiana audience would be a work of extreme supererogation, for this noble State has the *éclat* of having empowered by constitutional law, all taxpaying women to vote upon all questions submitted to the taxpayers. Women are permitted to exercise the right of voting in some form in forty-three foreign countries and provinces. Complete enfranchisement is enjoyed by women in the Isle of Man, New Zealand, and Federated Australia.

The passion for individual liberty, so characteristic of the Anglo-Saxon race, has been strongly demonstrated in the women of the United States.

Over 250 years ago, a woman, for the first time in America, asked the privilege of being allowed to vote. That was Margaret Brent, of Maryland, a kinswoman of Lord Baltimore. The next was the wife of John Adams, who begged for the same power over 125 years later; also Mercy Warren, and the sister of Richard Henry Lee, of Virginia. This impulse toward citizenship has been transmitted through the generations of American women.

On July 2, 1776, two days before the Declaration of Independence was adopted, the women of New Jersey were enfranchised by the State Convention held in that commonwealth; but this right was afterwards taken from them. Kentucky was the next State to allow women to vote in any degree; that boon was granted in 1838.

In 1869 full political equality was given to the women of Wyoming. Colorado, Utah and Idaho have since followed, granting unlimited suffrage to women. Besides these four States, with their full enfranchisement, there are 25 other States in this country that have partial suffrage for women. Surprising victories are constantly being gained.

Mississippi was the first State in the Union to have a State Institute and College for Girls. Mississippi claims the honor of being the first State in the Union to bestow upon married women the right of full control of their property. It is my firm belief that, before many decades, the South will astonish the world by giving complete enfranchisement to its women. As a stepping-stone to this blessed consummation, let us now make a determined effort to secure from the next Legislatures of the Southern States the recognition of the right of women to presidential suffrage. The Constitution of the United States confers upon the Legislatures of the different States the undoubted power to enable their women citizens to vote at presidential elections.

If any State, by a simple change in its election law, permits all women who can read and write and who pay a tax on property, to vote at the presidential election of 1904, the general acceptance of the women in that State would settle the question of the wisdom of woman suffrage, for the result would be vastly to increase the majority of the dominant party. Public sentiment would undergo such a revolution as to make a subsequent amendment to the State constitution, bestowing unlimited enfranchisement upon women, easy to obtain.

The South, which has wrought so splendidly in the past, surely will measure up to its responsibility in taking the forward step of woman's enfranchisement in order to render justice to its own firesides and to fix the status of the white race for future years.

Anglo Saxonism is that standard of the ages to come. It is, above all else, the granite foundation of the South. Upon that its civilization will mount; upon that it will stand unshaken.

The white people of the North and South are children of the same heroic souls who laid the foundations of civil and religious liberty in this new world, and built thereon this great Republic. We call to you, men and women, across that invisible line that divides the sections, across the passage of deathless years, to unite with us in holding this mighty country safe for the habitation of the Anglo-Saxon.

Thank God the black man was freed! I wish for him all possible happiness and all possible progress, but not in encroachments upon the holy of holies of the Anglo-Saxon race.

The Old South, with its romantic ideals, its grace, its sorrow, has passed into history. Upon the ashes of its desolation has arisen a New South, strong and beautiful, full of majesty and of power. The ambition of the Old was for States' rights, for local supremacy; that of the New is for a limitless sweep of vision, and with the elixir in its veins of an intense patriotic enthusiasm. The destiny of the South is the destiny of the Republic. It will eventually become totally merged in the being of our imperial nation.

Even now, as dearly as I love my people, sacred as I hold their traditions, loyal as I am to their interests, I say with infinitely less pride that I am a Southern woman than that I am an American.

Our sectionalism must broaden without reservation into nationalism that means sovereignty, and that points to immortality.

Part III

Suffragettes

JOHN STUART MILL

SUFFRAGE FOR WOMEN[1]

In 1865, Mill was elected to Parliament. During debate over the Reform Bill of 1867, which extended the franchise to a larger percentage of English men, Mill proposed that the word "person" be substituted for "man," thereby granting women the same voting rights as men. In his *Autobiography*, Mill describes this as "by far the most important, perhaps the only really important, public service I performed in the capacity of a Member of Parliament."[2] Mill's motion received 73 votes. Debate over this issue was the first time women's right to vote was debated in the legislature of a modern country. In the speech, the opening of which is included here, Mill argues that it is unjust to make distinctions between citizens in regard to rights and privileges without strong reasons and goes on forcefully to rebut a series of familiar arguments that had been advanced against allowing women to vote.

NOTES

1. For biographical information on Mill, see page 173.
2. John Stuart Mill, *Autobiography* (1873; rpt. Indianapolis, 1957), p. 194.

SUFFRAGE FOR WOMEN

I rise, sir, to propose an extension of the suffrage which can excite no party or class feeling in the house—which can give no umbrage to the keenest assertor of the claims either of property or of numbers; an extension which has not the faintest tendency to disturb what we have heard so much about lately, the balance of political power; which cannot afflict the most timid alarmist by any revolutionary terrors, or offend the most jealous democrat as an infringement of popular rights or a privilege granted to one class of society at the expense of another. There is nothing to distract our minds from the simple consideration whether there is any reasonable ground for excluding an entire half of the nation, not only from actual admission, but from the very possibility of being admitted within the pale of citizenship, though they may fulfil every one of the conditions legally and constitutionally sufficient in all cases but theirs. This is, under the laws of our country, a solitary case. There is no other example of an exclusion which is absolute. If it were, the law that none should have a vote but the possessors of 5,000 pounds a year, the poorest man in the community might, and now and then would, attain to the privilege. But neither birth, nor merit, nor exertion, nor intellect, nor fortune, nor even that great disposer of human affairs—accident—can enable any woman to have her voice counted in those common concerns which touch her and hers as nearly as any other person in the nation.

Now, sirs, before going any further, permit me to say that a *prima facie* case is already made out. It is not just to make distinctions, in right and privileges, between one of Her Majesty's subjects and another, unless for a positive reason. I do not mean that the suffrage, or any other political function, is an abstract right, or that to withhold it from anyone, on sufficient grounds of expediency, is a personal wrong: it is an utter misunderstanding of the principle I maintain to confound this with it: my whole argument is one of expediency. But all expediencies are not on exactly the same level. There is a kind of expediency which is called justice; and justice, though it does not demand that we should bestow political rights on everyone, does demand that we should not capriciously and without cause give those rights to one, and withhold them from another. As was most justly said by my right honorable friend, the member for South Lancashire, in the most misunderstood and misrepresented speech that I ever remember, to lay a ground for the denial of the franchise to any one it is necessary to allege either personal unfitness or public danger. Can either of these be asserted in the present case? Can it be pretended that women who manage a property or conduct a business, who pay rates and taxes, often to a large amount, and often from their own earnings, many of whom are responsible heads of families, and some of whom, in the capacity of schoolmistresses, teach more than a great many of the male electors have ever learnt, are not capable of a function of which every male householder is capable? Or is it supposed that, if they were allowed to vote, they would revolutionize the State, subvert any of our valuable institutions, or that we should have worse laws, or be, in any single respect, worse governed by means of their suffrage? (Hear, hear.)

No one thinks anything of the kind; and it is not only the general principles of justice that are infringed, or at any rate set aside by excluding women, merely as women, from the election of representatives. That exclusion is repugnant to the particular principles of the British Constitution. It violates the oldest of our constitutional axioms—a principle dear to all reformers, and theoretically acknowledged by conservatives—that taxation and representation should be co-extensive; that the taxes should be voted by those who pay them. Do not women pay taxes? Does not every women who is *sui juris* pay exactly the same as a man who has the same electoral qualifications? If having a stake in the country means anything, the owner of freehold or leasehold property has the same stake, whether it is owned by a man or a woman.

There is evidence in our constitutional records that women have voted in counties and some boroughs at former, though certainly distant, periods of history. But the house will expect that I should not rest my case on general principles, either of justice or of the Constitution, but should produce what are called practical arguments. Now I frankly admit that one very serious practical argument is entirely wanting in the case of women: they do not hold great meetings in Hyde Park (Laughter) nor demonstrations at Islington.

How far this omission can be considered to invalidate their claims I will not pretend to say. But other practical arguments—practical even in the most restricted sense of the term—are not wanting; and I am ready to state them if I may first be allowed to ask, Where are the practical objections? In general, the difficulty which people feel on this subject is not a practical objection: there is nothing practical in it; it is a mere feeling—a feeling of strangeness. The idea is so very new; at least they think so, though that is a mistake: it is a very old idea. Well, sir, strangeness is a thing which wears off. Some things were strange enough to many of us three months ago which are not at all so now; and many which are strange now will not be strange to the same person a few years hence, not to say a few months; and, as for novelty, we live in a world of novelties.

The despotism of custom is on the wane; we are not content to know that things are; we ask whether they ought to be; and in this house, I am bound to suppose that an appeal lies from custom to a higher tribunal, in which reason is judge. Now, the reasons which custom is in the habit of giving for itself on this subject are very brief: that, indeed is one of my difficulties. It is not easy to refute an interjection. Interjections, however, are the only arguments among those we usually hear on this subject which it appears to me at all difficult to refute.

The others chiefly consist of such aphorisms as these: Politics is not women's business, and would make them neglect their proper duties. Women do not desire the suffrage, and would rather not have it. Women are sufficiently represented through their male relatives. Women have power enough already. I shall perhaps be thought to have done enough in the way of answering, when I have answered all these: it may perhaps instigate any honorable gentleman who takes the trouble of replying to me, to produce something more recondite. (Hear.)

BARBARA BODICHON

Born into a liberal English family in which all the children, brothers and sisters, were given equal education and equal inheritance, Barbara Bodichon (1827–1891) was one of the earliest activists for women's rights in Britain. She helped in the passage of the Married Women's Property Act of 1882 and was instrumental in founding women's colleges at Oxford, Cambridge, and the University of London. In 1865, Bodichon, along with other like-minded women, helped spearhead the election of John Stuart Mill to Parliament.

REASONS FOR AND AGAINST THE ENFRANCHISEMENT OF WOMEN (SELECTIONS)

In the selection included here, published in 1872, Bodichon argues for a bill that would extend the vote to propertied, unmarried women, who, as it was understood, did not share in the political representation of husbands and therefore needed to be represented in Parliament. Bodichon claims that the vote will improve the lives of women. Through involvement in public affairs, they will become less concerned with the frivolous matters that typically occupy the attention of middle-class women. Involvement of women in political affairs will add to overall public spirit: "Patriotism, a healthy, lively, intelligent interest in everything which concerns the nation to which we belong, and an unselfish devotedness to the public service—these are the qualities which make a people great and happy." Having given reasons in favor of her position, Bodichon proceeds to criticize a series of arguments commonly advanced against women's right to vote.

REASONS FOR AND AGAINST
THE ENFRANCHISEMENT OF WOMEN

There are now a very considerable number of open-minded, unprejudiced people, who see no particular reason why women should not have votes, if they want them; but, they ask, what would be the good of it? What is there that women want which male legislators are not willing to give? And here let me say at the outset, that the advocates of this measure are very far from accusing men of deliberate unfairness to women. It is not as a means of extorting justice from unwilling legislators that the franchise is claimed for women. In so far as the claim is made with any special reference to class interests at all, it is simply on the general ground that under a representative government, any class which is not represented is likely to be neglected. Proverbially, what is out of sight is out of mind; and the theory that women, as such, are bound to keep out of sight, finds its most empathetic expression in the denial of the right to vote. The direct results are probably less injurious than those which are indirect; but that a want of due consideration for the interests of women is apparent in our legislation, could very easily be shown....

Among instances of hardship traceable directly to exclusion from the franchise and to no other cause, may be mentioned the unwillingness of landlords to accept women as tenants. Two large farmers in Suffolk inform me that this is not an uncommon case. They mention one estate on which seven widows have been ejected, who, if they had had votes, would have been continued as tenants.

The case of women farmers is stronger, but not much stronger, than that of women who, as heads of a business or a household, fulfil the duties of a man in the same position. Their task is often a hard one, and everything which helps to sustain their self-respect, and to give them consideration and importance in the eyes of others, is likely to lessen their difficulties and make them happier and stronger for the battle of life. The very fact that, though householders and taxpayers, they have not equal privileges with male householders and taxpayers, in itself a *deconsideration,* which seems to me invidious and useless. It casts a kind of slur on the value of their opinions; and I may remark in passing, that what is treated as of no value is apt to grow valueless. Citizenship is an honour, and not to have the full rights of a citizen is a want of honour. Obvious it may not be, but by a subtle and sure process, those who without their own consent and without sufficient reason are debarred from full participation in the rights and duties of a citizen, lose more or less of social consideration and esteem....

And among all the reasons for giving women votes, the one which appears to me the strongest, is that of the influence it might be expected to have in increasing public spirit. Patriotism, a healthy, lively, intelligent interest in everything which concerns the nation to which we belong, and an unselfish devotedness to the public service—these are the qualities which make a people great and happy; these are the virtues which ought to be most sedulously cultivated in all classes of the community. And I know no better means, at this present time, of counteracting the tendency to prefer narrow private ends to the public good, than this of giving to all women, duly qualified, a direct and conscious participation in political affairs. Give some women votes, and it will tend to make all women think seriously of the concerns of the nation at large, and their interest having once been fairly roused, they will take pains, by reading and by consultation with persons better informed than themselves, to form sound opinions. As it is, women of the middle class occupy themselves but little with anything beyond their own family circle. They do not consider it any concern of theirs, if poor men and women are ill-nursed in the workhouse infirmaries, and poor children ill-taught in workhouse schools. If the roads are bad, the drains neglected, the water poisoned, they think it is all very wrong, but it does not occur to them that it is their duty to get it put right. These farmer-women and business-women have honest, sensible minds and much practical experience, but they do not bring their good sense to bear upon public affairs, because they think it is men's business, not theirs, to look after such things. It is the belief—so narrowing and deadening in its influence—that the exercise of the franchise would tend to dissipate. The mere fact of being called upon to enforce an opinion by a vote, would have an immediate effect in awakening a healthy sense of responsibility. As far as experience goes, the power women have had as householders to vote at the School Board Elections has been an unmixed good. It has certainly drawn public attention to the education of girls, and, in many places, has awakened an ardent interest in new subjects among women themselves, by the simple fact that they had had to discuss the different opinions of the candidates. There is no reason why these women should not take an active interest in all the social questions—education, public health, prison discipline, the poor laws, and the rest—which occupy Parliament, and they would be much more likely to do so, if they felt that they had importance in the eyes of members of Parliament, and could claim a hearing for their opinions....

Everything, I say again, should be done to encourage this most important and increasing class to take their place in the army of workers for the common good, and all the forces we can bring to bear for this end are of incalculable value. For by bringing women into hearty co-operation with men, we gain the benefit not only of their work, but of their intelligent sympathy. Public spirit is like fire: a feasible spark of it may be fanned into a flame, or it may very easily be put out. And the result of teaching women that they have nothing to do with politics, is that their influence goes towards extinguishing the unselfish interest—never too strong—which men are disposed to take in public affairs....

Now, let us calmly consider all the arguments we have heard against giving the franchise to women.

Among these, the first and commonest is—Women do not want votes. Certainly that is a capital reason why women should not have votes thrust upon them. There are many men who do not care to use their votes, and there is no law compelling them to vote. The statement, however, that women do not wish to vote, is a mere assertion, and may be met by a counter-assertion. Some women do want votes, which the petitions signed, and now in course of signature, go very largely to prove. Some women manifestly do; others, let it be admitted, do not. It is impossible to say positively which side has the majority, unless we could poll all the women in question; or, in other words, without resorting to the very measure which is under discussion. Make voting possible, and we shall see how many care to avail themselves of the privilege.

But, it is said, women have other duties. The function of women is different to that of men, and their function is not politics. It is very true that women have other duties—many and various. But so have men. No citizen lives for his citizen duties only. He is a professional man, a tradesman, a family man, a club man, a thousand things as well as a voter. Of course these occupations sometimes interfere with a man's duties as a citizen, and when he cannot vote, he cannot. So with women; when they cannot vote, they cannot....

Their duties in sick-rooms and in caring for children, leave them a sufficient margin of leisure for reading newspapers, and studying the *pros* and *cons* of political and social questions. No one can mean seriously to affirm that widows and unmarried women would find the mere act of voting once in several years arduous. One day, say once in three years, might surely be spared from domestic duties. If it is urged that it is not the time spent in voting that is in question, but the thought and the attention which are necessary for forming political opinions, I reply that women of the class we are speaking of, have, as a rule, more time for thought than men, their duties being of a less engrossing character, and they ought to bestow a considerable amount of thought and attention on the questions which occupy the Legislature. Social matters occupy every day a larger space in the deliberations of Parliament, and on many of these questions women are led to think and to judge in the fulfillment of those duties which, as a matter of course, devolve upon them in the ordinary business of English life....

The argument that 'women are ignorant of politics,' would have great force if it could be shown that the mass of the existing voters are thoroughly well informed on political subjects, or even much better informed than the persons to whom it is proposed to give votes. Granted that women are ignorant of politics, so are many male householders. Their ideas are not always clear on political questions, and would probably be even more confused if they had not votes. No mass of human beings will or can undertake the task of forming opinions on matters over which they have no control, and on which they have no practical decision to make. It would by most persons be considered waste of time. When women have votes, they will read with closer attention than heretofore the daily histories of our times, and will converse with each other and with their fathers and brothers about social and political questions. They will become interested in a wider circle of ideas, and where they now think and feel somewhat vaguely, they will form definite and decided opinions....

The fear entertained by some persons that family dissension would result from encouraging women to form political opinions, might be urged with equal force against their having any opinions on any subject at all. Differences on religious subjects are still more apt to rouse the passions and create disunion than political differences. As for opinions causing disunions, let it be remembered that what is a possible cause of disunion is also a possible cause of deeply-founded union. The more rational women become, the more real union there will be in families, for nothing separates so much as unreasonableness and frivolity. It will be said, perhaps, that contrary opinions may be held by the different members of a family without bringing on quarrels, so long as they are kept to the region of theory, and no attempt is made to carry them out publicly in action. But religious differences must be shown publicly. A woman who determines upon changing her religion—say to go over from Protestantism to Romanism—proclaims her difference from her family in a public and often a very distressing manner. But no one has yet proposed to make it illegal for a woman to change her religion. After all—is it essential that brothers and sisters and cousins shall all vote on the same side?

An assertion often made, that women would lose the good influence which they now exert indirectly on public affairs if they had votes, seems to require proof. First of all, it is necessary to prove that women have this indirect influence,—then that it is good,—then that the indirect good influence would be lost if they had direct influence,—then that the indirect influence which they would lose is better than the direct influence they would gain. From my own observation I should say, that the women who have gained by their wisdom and earnestness a good indirect influence, would not lose that influence if they had votes. And I see no necessary connection between goodness and indirectness. On the contrary, I believe that the great thing women want is to be more direct and straightforward in thought, word, and deed. I think the educational advantage of citizenship to women would be so great, that I feel inclined to run the risk of sacrificing the subtle indirect influence, to a wholesome feeling of responsibility, which would, I think, make women give their opinions less rashly and more conscientiously than at present on political subjects....

The question under consideration is, not whether women ought logically to be members of Parliament, but whether, under existing circumstances, it is for the good of the State that women, who perform most of the duties, and enjoy nearly all the rights of citizenship, should be by special enactment disabled from exercising the additional privilege of taking part in the election of the representatives of the people. It is a question of expediency, to be discussed calmly, without passion or prejudice.

In England, the extension proposed would interfere with no vested interests. It would involve no change in the principles on which our Government is based, but would rather make our Constitution more consistent with itself. Conservatives have a right to claim it as a Conservative measure. Liberals are bound to ask for it as a necessary part of radical reform. There is no reason for identifying it with any class or party in the State, and it is, in fact, impossible to predict what influence it might have on party politics. The question is simply of a special legal disability, which must, sooner or later, be removed.

EMMELINE PANKHURST

E mmeline Pankhurst (1858–1928) brought new and most unladylike tactics to the women's suffrage movement. In 1903, along with her daughter, Christabel, she formed the Women's Social and Political Union
(WSPU), an organization that became known for its unapologetic militancy.
The women of WSPU used public disturbances to express suffragettes' anger
and impatience with the resistance of the British government to the enfranchisement of British women. Shocking the British public, not accustomed to
violence in middle-class ladies, the Pankhursts and their cohorts engaged in
window smashing, destroying various kinds of property, placing a bomb in
Saint Paul's Cathedral, slashing the Rokeby Venus, and leading other demonstrations that captured the attention and opprobrium of suffrage opponents
and supporters alike. They were jailed many times, and in jail embarrassed
the government with hunger strikes, which were put down through brutal
force-feeding.

MY OWN STORY (SELECTIONS)

Emerging from prison in 1912, Pankhurst delivered the following speech at
the Royal Albert Hall. She defends the militant tactics of the WSPU and
promises more of the same if demands for woman suffrage are not met. "I
incite this meeting to rebellion," she declares. *"There is something that governments care far more for than human life, and that is the security of property, and so it
is through property that we shall strike the enemy."*

Some American suffragists adopted Pankhurst's methods but never achieved the dramatic demonstrations of political rage and resulting public attention that Mrs. Pankhurst achieved in the British struggle for woman suffrage.

MY OWN STORY

GRAVE STATEMENT BY THE LEADERS

At the first reunion of the leaders after the enforced holiday, Mrs. Pankhurst and Miss Christabel Pankhurst outlined a new militant policy which Mr. and Mrs. Pethick Lawrence found themselves altogether unable to approve.

Mrs. Pankhurst and Miss Christabel Pankhurst indicated that they were not prepared to modify their intentions, and recommended that Mr. and Mrs. Pethick Lawrence should resume control of the Paper, Votes for Women, *and should leave the Women's Social and Political Union.*

Rather than make schism in the ranks of the Union Mr. and Mrs. Pethick Lawrence consented to take this course.

This was signed by all four. That night at the meeting I further explained to the members that, hard as partings from old friends and comrades unquestionably were, we must remember that we were fighting in an army, and that unity of purpose and unity of policy are absolutely necessary, because without them the army is hopelessly weakened. "It is better," I said, "that those who cannot agree, cannot see eye to eye as to policy, should set themselves free, should part, and should be free to continue their policy as they see it in their own way, unfettered by those with whom they can no longer agree."

Continuing I said: "I give place to none in appreciation and gratitude to Mr. and Mrs. Pethick Lawrence for the incalculable services that they have rendered the militant movement for Woman Suffrage, and I firmly believe that the women's movement will be strengthened by their being free to work for woman suffrage in the future as they think best, while we of the Women's Social and Political Union shall continue the militant agitation for Women Suffrage initiated by my daughter and myself and a handful of women more than six years ago."

I then went on to survey the situation in which the W. S. P. U. now stood and to outline the new militant policy which he had decided upon. This policy, to begin with, was relentless opposition, not only to the party in power, the Liberal Party, but to all parties in the coalition. I reminded the women that the Government that had tricked and betrayed us and was now plotting to make our progress towards citizenship doubly difficult, was kept in office through the coalition of three parties. There was the Liberal Party, nominally the governing party, but they could not live another day without the coalition of the Nationalist and the Labour parties. So we should say, not only to the Liberal Party but to the Nationalist Party and the Labour Party, "So long as you keep in office an anti-suffrage Government, you are parties to their guilt, and from henceforth we offer you the same opposition which we give to the people whom you are keeping in power with your support." I said further: "We have summoned the Labour Party to do their duty by their own programme, and to go into opposition to the Government on every question until the Government do justice to women. They apparently are not willing to do that. Some of them tell us that other things are more important than the liberty of women— than the liberty of working women. We say, 'Then gentlemen, we must teach you the value of your own principles, and until you are prepared to stand for the right of women to decided their lives and the laws under which they shall live, you, with Mr. Asquith and company, are equally responsible for all that has happened and is happening to women in this struggle for emancipation.' "

Outlining further our new and stronger policy of aggression, I said: "There is a great deal of criticism, ladies and gentlemen, of this movement. It always seems to me when the anti-suffrage members of the Government criticise militancy in women that it is very like beasts of prey reproaching the gentler animals who turn in desperate resistance when at the point of death. Criticism from gentlemen who do not hesitate to order out armies to kill and slay their opponents, who do not hesitate to encourage party mobs to attack defenceless women in public meetings—criticism from them hardly rings true. Then I get letters from people who tell me that they are ardent suffragists but who say that they do not like the recent developments in the militant movement, and implore me to urge the members not to be reckless with human life. Ladies and gentlemen, the only recklessness the militant suffragists have shown about human life has been about their own lives and not about the lives of others, and I say here and now that it has never been and never will be the policy of the Women's Social and Political Union recklessly to endanger human life. We leave that to the enemy. We leave that to the men in their warfare. It is not the method of women. No, even from the point of view of public policy, militancy affecting the security of human life would be out of place. *There is something that governments care far more for than human life, and that is the security of property, and so it is through property that we shall strike the enemy.* From henceforward the women who agree with me will say, 'We disregard your laws, gentlemen, we set the liberty and the dignity and the welfare of women above all such considerations, and we shall continue this war, as we have done in the past; and what sacrifice of property, or what injury to property accrues will not be our fault. It will be the fault of that Government who admit the justice of our demands, but refuses to concede them without the evidence, so they have told us, afforded to governments of the past, that those who asked for liberty were in earnest in their demands!"

I called upon the women of the meeting to join me in this new militancy, and I reminded them anew that the women who were fighting in the Suffragette army had a great mission, the greatest mission the world has ever known—the freeing of one-half the human race, and through that freedom the saving of the other half. I said to them: "Be militant each in your own way. Those of you who can express your militancy by going to the House of Commons and refusing to leave without satisfaction, as we did in the early days—do so. Those of you who can express militancy by facing party mobs at Cabinet Ministers' meetings, when you remind them of their falseness to principle—do so. Those of you who can express your militancy by joining us in our anti-Government by-election policy—do so. Those of you who can break windows—break them. Those of you who can still further attack the secret idol of property, so as to make the Government realise that property is as greatly endangered by women's suffrage as it was by the Chartists of old—do so. And my last word is to the Government: I incite this meeting to rebellion. I say to the Government: You have not dared to take the leaders of Ulster for their incitement to rebellion. Take me if you dare, but if I dare tell you this, that so long as those who incited to armed rebellion and the destruction of human life in Ulster are at liberty, you will not keep me in prison. So long as men rebels—and voters—are at liberty, we will not remain in prison, first division or no first division."

MILLICENT FAWCETT

Dame Millicent Fawcett (1847–1929), head of the National Union of Women's Suffrage Societies (NUWSS), was a tireless campaigner for women's rights in Great Britain. In her 50 years as a leader in "the Cause," Fawcett was instrumental in the almost yearly introduction of woman suffrage bills to Parliament. She had great faith in parliamentary democracy, believing that in the end, Parliament would do right by British women. Deploring the militant methods of Emmeline and Christabel Pankhurst and the Women's Social and Political Union (WSPU), she advocated lawful means of changing suffrage laws: "Let us prove ourselves worthy of citizenship, whether our claim is recognized or not," she urged members of the NUWSS in a 1914 address.[1]

A REPLY TO THE LETTER OF MR. SAMUEL SMITH, M.P., ON WOMEN'S SUFFRAGE (SELECTIONS)

The selection included here, published in 1892, is a reply Fawcett made to arguments made by Samuel Smith, M.P., against woman suffrage. One by one, she refutes Smith's arguments. We see in this letter the special flavor of the British suffrage issue. Universal suffrage for men was a hotly debated question at the time. Voting rights were extended to only male property holders, and women sought the same right for women property holders. The democratic principle of enfranchising rich and poor alike did not have wide appeal in Britain. A rising Labor movement would soon change the political climate, but when she wrote this reply, Fawcett felt called upon to assure her readers that she was not expecting the franchise for any but middle-class women. In spite of this concession to political reality, we see Fawcett as a passionate advocate for extending legal protection to women who had clearly suffered without it.

NOTE:

1. Quoted in Ray Strachey, *The Cause* (1928; rpt. London, 1978), p. 338.

MR. SAMUEL SMITH, M.P., ON WOMEN'S SUFFRAGE.

Mr. Samuel Smith, M.P. for Flintshire, has given notice of his intention to move the rejection of Sir Albert Rollit's Women's Suffrage Bill, which is down for second reading on April 27th. It seems, therefore, not inopportune to consider some of the objections urged by Mr. Smith against women's suffrage, which were printed and widely circulated among members of parliament and the public during last session....

"Women," he says, used to be "subject to some injustices, which men seemed unwilling to remedy"; but these injustices he apprehends, have been remedied one after another, therefore he thinks there is no reason to give women the protection of representation. Mr. Smith's calm assumption that the legal injustices under which women labour have all been removed, is an instance of the fortitude with which one of the kindest men is prepared to endure the misfortunes of others. It is hardly an exaggeration to say that there is scarcely an instance in which the supposed interests of men and women come into conflict in which the state of the law is not flagrantly unjust to women. The law in regard to the relation of parents to their children appears to have been framed in practical infidelity to the Divine law which gives to every child two parents, a father and a mother. The man-made law regards this as more than enough, and it therefore endeavours, in a bungling way, to deprive each child of one of its natural protectors. Where the birth of a child is legitimate, that is where it brings nothing but happiness and credit with it, the sole parent, the soul fountain of authority in the eye of the law, is the father; but where the child is illegitimate, where the birth means disgrace and shame, the sole parent recognised by the law, except under special conditions which it is easy for the father to evade, is the mother. The inequality of the divorce of law is well known and need not be expatiated on. The law in regard to the protection of children and women from criminal immorality is studded with provisions which seem framed with the express purpose of protecting the criminal and making his detection and punishment far more difficult than they ought to be. The law for the protection of property(*e.g.*, the protection of infants from money-lenders), is tenfold more stringent and more vigilantly executed than the law for the protection of the persons of young girls and women from the pursuit of vicious men. The law at present deals most inadequately with persons who trade in vice. Parents who bring up their children to send them on the streets in order to live on the proceeds of their infamy, are well known in every town and many villages. Little or no effectual attempt is made by our lawmakers to restrain them. Husbands send their wives on the streets by actual personal violence or by threats of it, and are hardly touched by the law unless they happen to complicate their villainy by mixing it with blackmailing of their male victims. Every man is a possible victim of blackmailing, and everything that law can do to stop it has, very properly, been done. What we wish to see is equal vigilance for the repression of offences of which every woman is a possible victim....

With regard to avenues of remunerative employment, every woman of the professional classes who has to get her own living knows that every profession that can be closed to women is closed. The medical profession has been at last opened after years of conflict; but the opportunities for professional study in it are very much more restricted and hampered than they are in the case of men. The older universities admit women to their examinations, but rigidly exclude them from any kind of membership. The Vice-Chancellor's certificate that women have passed tripos or other honour examinations gives them no status whatever in the university. Of course no university prizes or positions are open to them; they are permitted to use the museums and libraries of the universities only on sufferance, and they are liable at any moment to be turned out of them.

The way in which women of the industrial class are restricted in their choice of employments by the rules and political power of trades' unions is well known. Hardly a session passes without new legislative restrictions on the labour of women. The efforts of trades' unions are constantly being directed against women's labour:—"Female labour is not at present a crying evil in our trade: it would be worse than folly to allow it to become so", is a passage from the report of one of the London Bookbinders' Unions of 1891. This union succeeded in turning women out of employment of gilding and marbling the edges of books in which they had been employed for many years. Among the working class the opinion is almost universal that it is justifiable to forbid by law or forcibly prevent the labour of women wherever their labour comes into competition with that of men. A witness before the Labour Commission was describing a strike that had taken place against employing women in one of the Army Clothing factories in Ireland. Mr. Courtney asked the question: "Have not the women the privilege of living?" to which the witness replies, "They have the privilege of living as long as they do not interfere with the men" ....

It cannot for a moment be doubted that the possession of Parliamentary representation would immensely strengthen the position of women industrially. We have only to look at what the possession of the Parliamentary franchise has already done for the agricultural labourer, to be sure that if women had votes, all parties would be eager to prove their zeal in remedying any legal, educational or industrial incapacity from which they may suffer.

Mr. Smith in one passage of his letter appeals to the religious argument and to the authority of St. Paul. In this matter we appeal from Paul to a greater than Paul, to Christ. No words ever fell from His lips which were inconsistent with that elevation of womanhood which is so marked a feature of practical Christianity. That women were among the last at the cross, that they were the first at the tomb, that when all forsook Him and fled, they remained faithful; that our Saviour honoured them by specially addressing to them several of His most important conversations; that He proclaimed, what the world has not yet accepted, that there is but one moral law for the man and the woman; all these things afford indications that work for the uplifting of the lives of women from a position of subordination is in accordance with the spirit of His teaching. With regard to St. Paul, we may remember this:—that if we take his teaching about women with its context, it is obvious that he was expressing to the best of his capacity his judgment about the circumstances of this own time; and he particularly and definitely asserts in more than one place that this is so. "I have no commandment of the Lord, yet I give my judgment." Much therefore, of St. Paul's teaching about the position of women and other social matters is not accepted by any Christian Church as a practical guide for conduct at the present time. St. Paul taught and believed that celibacy was a higher state than marriage, both for men and women; but I do not think that even in the Roman Catholic Church celibacy is recommended, except for the priesthood and for sisterhoods. St. Paul thought it unseemly for a woman to pray with her head uncovered; but I have never heard of any one regarding this as having any application at the present time, and the most devout Christian women attend and conduct family worship bareheaded, just as they braid their hair, wear gold, pearls and costly array on fitting occasions without any inward accusations of conscience in the matter. If we are now to be tied by the exact letter of St. Paul's opinions on the social questions of his own time, we may expect Mr. Smith and those members of Parliament who agree with him to move, when the education estimates come on, to reduce the vote by the amount of the salaries of the women teachers, for St. Paul said, "I suffer not a woman to teach". It is no exaggeration to say that one who did so would be considered very near the confines which separate sanity from insanity. Then why in other social matters, must we not merely accept St. Paul's words in their simple natural meaning as expressing his best judgment in the special circumstances of his own time, but twist them into something quite different, *viz.*, into an argument for voting against the second reading of Sir Albert Rollit's Bill of enabling women ratepayers to vote for members of Parliament?

Part IV

Antis

HORACE BUSHNELL

Horace Bushnell (1802–1876) was educated at Yale College and began studying law at Yale before he moved over to the Divinity School. In 1833, he was ordained pastor of the North Church in Hartford, Connecticut. A prolific writer of theological tracts, he achieved considerable eminence. At different times, Bushnell was offered the presidencies of Middlebury College and the newly founded University of California at Berkeley, both of which he declined. According to the *Dictionary of American Biography*, having experienced the presence of God in his own life, Bushnell revolted against rationalistic religion in favor of religion based on human experience. Thus he occupied a place in American religion analogous to that of Coleridge in England and Schleiermacher in Germany (*q.v.*).

WOMEN'S SUFFRAGE: THE REFORM AGAINST NATURE (SELECTIONS)

The thrust of *Women's Suffrage: The Reform against Nature* (1869) is evident in its title. In this, the first of the antisuffrage selections presented in this volume, Bushnell argues from a distinctive conception of women's nature. By nature, women are not equal to men, although, Bushnell contends that, even if they were equal, it would not follow that they should receive the vote. All historical experience refutes the claim that men have a natural right to vote, and so this cannot be extended to support a natural right for women to vote.

In Chapter 3, Bushnell argues that granting women the vote would run against their nature. Moreover, as English Common Law asserts, woman is "a complementary personality." Her vote is encompassed in that of her husband. Women do not require the vote to protect their interests: "There is no deliberate willingness in men to oppress women; and as soon as any sufficient reminder comes, and a real grievance is shown, there is sure to be some adequate reform that redresses the wrong discovered." If it is objected that this argument does not take into account the needs of single women, "What we have to say is, that all women alike are made to be married, whether they are or not." In Chapter 7, Bushnell recounts undesirable changes in women's nature that would follow upon their receipt of the vote, and how suffrage would undermine the institution of marriage.

WOMEN'S SUFFRAGE: THE REFORM AGAINST NATURE

CHAPTER II

The short argument, as it is commonly put, runs thus: women are the equals of men, and have therefore an equal right to vote. In which very brief and very simple form of deduction, there are, if we are not willing to be taken by the shallowest possible fallacies, two quite plainly untrue conclusions. First, it is not certainly true that women are equal to men. They are equally women as men are men; they are equally human as men; they are so far equally entitled to protection as men, but it does not hence appear that they are equal to men. They may be superior to men; they may be inferior to men; but what is a great deal closer probably to the truth, they may be very unlike in kind to men; so unlike that in the civil state they had best, both for their own sake and for the public good, stand back from any claim of right, in the public administration of the laws. How far this unlikeness extends is not here the question. I shall undertake, at a future stage of the discussion, to state more precisely in what the relative unlikeness consists; for the present I cannot forbear citing from the *Nation,* a very short but excellently vigorous statement of the fact itself. "The unlikeness between men and women is radical and essential. It runs through all the spheres. Distinct as they are in bodily form and features, they are quite as distinct in mental and moral characteristics. They neither think, feel, wish, purpose, will, not act alike. They take the same views of nothing. The old statements that one is passive, the other active; one emotional, the other moral; one affectionate, the other rational; one sentimental, the other intellectual, are likely to be more than verified by science. Of course, these statements, whether verified or not, do not justify the imposition of arbitrary limits on opportunity or enterprise. It still remains to determine what place each can fill, what work each can do, what standard each can reach; and these nature should be left to determine. But that both can not occupy the same place, do the same work, or reach the same standard, ought, we think, to be assumed. Nature has decreed it so." Accordingly, if the two sexes are so very unlike in *kind*, there can, so far, be no predication of equality between them. And then, just so far, the argument for a right in women to vote, in consideration of their equality, is inconclusive. We do not say that a yard is equal to a pound, because the two measures have no common quality; though it may be that a yard of some one thing is equal in value to a pound of some other. We do not say, taking an example where there is more appearance of a common quality, that silk and flax are equal; and yet they may make an equally strong, or equally fine thread; but since one will make a finer lace, and the other a more splendid robe, one a superb damask, and the other a superb velvet, we do not think of saying at all, that they are equal, because they are so far different in kind. In which also we may see, that, while women and men have a great many common properties, they have also a great many which are not common—so many, that we never can be sure what we mean by it, when we say that they are equal.

Yes, but their rights are equal, some will hasten, it may be, to answer, and that is enough to support the argument. Doubtless they have a perfect and complete right to be women, as men have to be men, but it may be, still, that the having a perfect right to be either women or men, does not include any right of voting at all—that is the very question here in issue.

The second fallacy above referred to is built on an argument equally baseless; it is that, being equal to men, women have a right to vote because men have a right to vote. Here the meaning is, if there is any, that men have a natural right to vote, or a right to vote that is grounded in nature. The words *man* and *suffrage* have, in this view, a fixed relation; a universal and permanent relation; such that suffrage never was or can be denied them, save by a public wrong; for every right is a something never to be stripped away, except by a wrong. Since, then, prior to the arrival of our own American Republic, there had never been more than two or three small peoples in the world that acknowledged any right to vote at all, and these no equal right, but only rights so unequal that a very few men of grade, as in Rome, counted more than a whole bottom tier of rabble that composed the chief population of the city, we are seen to have begun our public history, by assuming that there never before had been a legitimate government in the world! If we could say that, and not be shocked by the nonsense of our assumption, we were certainly a very remarkable people. How much better and closer to the sound realities of history, to have confessed, that all the great monarchies, and the rising and falling, and dawning and vanishing, and even the merely *de facto* states, had a certain morally incipient and legitimate authority, even though they gave no right of voting at all, and never heard or even thought of such a thing. Besides, we had not then, and never since have had, ourselves, any equal right of voting as being men, saying nothing of women, under our own constitutions and liberties. Some of us have been voting on the score of our property; some on the right we have bought by military service; some on the ground of qualifications imparted by our education; some on the count of our slaves. Doubtless we that are males are all so far equal, but we never to this day have been allowed to vote on our naked equality, except in here and there a single State. How then does it fare with the argument that women have a right, on the score of their equality with men, when men themselves can not vote on the score of their own equality with one another? Besides, if any of us think to make out a natural right of voting, whether in men or women, a sufficient hunt of our psychological nature ought to find some place in it where the right, for so many ages undiscovered, inheres. It was observed, long ages ago, by such men as Plato, Aristotle, Cicero, and others, that our very nature is configured, all through, to the civil state, and the condition of civil obligation; but no man has ever yet discovered that there is a right to vote twisted in among our functions and rational categories. When that discovery is made, it will be as soon as any such natural right can be set in account, and made a basis of argument for the voting of women....

CHAPTER III

Why, if our women could but see what they are doing now, what superior grades of beauty and power they fill, and how far above equality with men they rise, when they keep their own pure atmosphere of silence, and their field of peace, how they make a realm into which the poor bruised fighters, with their passions galled, and their minds scarred with wrong—their hates, disappointments, grudges, and hard-won ambitions—may come in, to be quieted, and civilized, and get some touch of the angelic, I think they would be very little apt to disrespect their womanly subordination. It will signify any thing but their inferiority. If they are already taken with the foolish ambition of place, or of winning a public name, they may not be satisfied. But in that case they barter for this honor a great deal more than they can rightly spare. God's highest honors never go with noise, but they wait on silent worth, on the consciousness of good, on secret charities, and ministries untainted by ambition. Could they but say to the noisy nothings of this bribery, "Get thee hence, Satan," as Christ did to the same coarse nonsense of flattery, they would keep their subject-way of life as he kept his, and would think it honor enough that they also came not to be ministered unto, but to minister. And if it be the question for them, whether it is better to be classed in privilege with Jesus the subject, or with Caesar the sovereign, it should not be difficult to decide....

And yet our women will not have their subordinate, or subject state, because it makes them inferior! They want, alas! the culture of soul that is wanted to see the superiority to which they are elected. They come in the wedding grace of their Cana, or the suffering grace of their Calvary, and insist on their right to be Sinai, and play the thunders too themselves. "Give us also power," they say; and power to them is force, or an equal right of command. A most miserable and really low misconception, if only they had grace to see it. Here is their true power, in a disinterested and subject life of good. And there is a way in this to govern men, that is greatness itself and victory. What can the woman do that wants to vote, in order to be somewhat, but fume, and chafe, and tear, under what she calls the wrongs of her husband—so to make her weakness more weak, and her defeat more miserable—when if she could only consent to the true gospel and woman together, to be gentle, and patient, and right, and fearless, how certainly would she come out superior and put him at her feet. There seems to me, in this view, I confess, to be a something sacred, or angelic, in such womanhood. The morally grandest sight we see in this world is a real and ideally true woman. Send her to the polls if you will, give her an office, set the Hon. before her name, and by that time she is nobody.

As regards this question of suffrage, or the allowing of suffrage to women, there is yet another way of constructing the argument, which, though it may not be another, may be more convincing to some, viz.:—that the male and female natures together constitute the proper man, and are, therefore, both represented in the vote of the man. And the radical idea here assumed of the composite unity of the two, is attested, in fact, all over the world, in one form or another, and in different modes and degrees, whenever a marriage puts them in connection as husband and wife. The woman passes under shelter and protection, so far as even to drop her family name, and be only known under the family name of her husband. In the English common law she is said to be *femme covert*, a woman who is included, as respects all civil rights, in her husband. Her personality is so far merged in his, that she can not bring a suit any more in her own name, for it is a name no longer known to the law. The assumption is that, being in and of her husband, he will both act and answer for her, except when arraigned for crime. The Roman or civil law received by so many of the principal nations of the world, carries similar ideas with it, asserting the civil absorption of the wife in the husband in terms but slightly qualified.

The Russian law and the Chinese correspond. In all which we may see how close to nature runs the impression that woman is a complementary personality, and is rightly taken to exist in her husband, as she passes under his name in her marriage, and is consentingly covered by his protectorship.

Hence it is put forward by some, as the true answer to the claim of women's suffrage, that they are already represented in and by the vote of their husbands. But this again is only saying that they will be duly cared for and protected, by the voice their husbands have in government, when they do not govern for themselves. And nothing can be assumed more safely than that; for if by some *lache* of marital attention, helped by a certain natural gravitation toward injustice when attention sleeps, the laws may sometimes slip or subside into ways that bear oppressively on women, the wrong will be easily rectified. There is no deliberate willingness in men to oppress women; and as soon as any sufficient reminder comes, and a real grievance is shown, there is sure to be some adequate reform that redresses the wrong discovered. Our legislators, have abundantly shown their readiness, and even zeal, to remove every sort of harshness in the laws toward women; they make haste in it, and are willing even to go beyond the real equity and do, since it is for women, more than is equal, and more than they would ask legislating for themselves. If they want, indeed, a partial legislation, softer and more favorable than strict equality, their surest way to get it is to let it be the legislation of men. They will do any thing for women that has even a semblance of right.

What matter then is it, whether women have a representation by their own ballot or not? Perhaps it may better suit their ambition to be powers, than wards of the state, but it is a very fatuitous and really most unsentimental ambition. Oh! if we could only be assured as men, that we should be governed well, and safely defended in every right, secured in every privilege, without any representation at all, any right of suffrage, what better and more halcyon day of promise could heaven let down upon us. Such government would be like that of God Himself. There is no privilege in representation, no inherent right of it in any state, save that, as rulers are themselves under evil, and prone to ways of wrong as God is not, it is convenient and imparts a feeling of security, to have the subjects themselves allowed a voice in the laws, and a part in their just enforcement. It is no first principle then, as our new state reformers assume, that women have a right of representation because they are human; in that way a right of suffrage; for nobody has any such right of representation, if only he can be well governed without such right; and women are as nearly sure of that as they can be, in the fact that they are made sure by the vote and representation of their husbands.

But they are many of them single persons, it may be urged, and have therefore no husband by whose vote their rights may be protected. On this account too some of the opposers of women's suffrage, apprehending a defect in their argument based in the representative office of husbands, have conceded the right of widows and single women to vote; only requiring them to lose that right when they pass into the *femme covert* state. But this would open a way for innumerable frauds, and confusions without end. Happily the whole cast of the argument is mistaken. Women are not changed in their nature, or in any natural right, because they are married.

What we have to say is, that all women alike are made to be married, whether they are or not. The sex-nature of men and women is not altered by marriage, and according to that sex-nature, women are to be sheltered legally by men. Government is not given them, but protectors are given them, who are tender above all terms of equality. So that if it were necessary for them to be represented, and they had a right to be, the whole female order would be most effectively represented in the whole male order, without respect to any chances, or mischances, of marriage whatever.

And so there is to be secured for women a more benignant, softer kind of protectorship, which is bruised and battered by no contests, or made hard and imperious by no mere dominations of force.

CHAPTER VII

I alluded to just now, in the close of the last chapter, to one or two facts in which we get slight indications of the pitch of excitement to which women are likely to be carried in the field of political action, and also of the kinds and qualities of that excitement; how far loosened from the womanly proprieties, how fierce possibly, and bitter it may be. We have only a very few facts developed as yet, to show how this almost unknown type of progress, so called, is going to behave itself. Many persons never see any thing by their imagination, taking it for granted, that what is fact, is going to be fact, and that under all newest, most untried conditions, fact will behave just as it always has. In this way it is taken for granted, we may see, in the most innocent way possible, that women are going to be women as they always have been; to be gentle, retired, quiet, unselfish, carrying an element of dignity, and grace, and presiding good manners into the caucuses and campaign assemblies of which they are become a part; just as they did when they came in, once in four or five years, to fill a gallery and look on. And so it is computed that when they drop into place under the new reform, to be political women, they will inaugurate a kind of millennial age of good manners and respectful conduct, by which every thing in political life and society will be raised. Such kind of prognostications are simply stupid, wholly without perception. Why the change we are proposing here is radical enough, when time enough is added, to alter even the type of womanhood itself. At first, or for a short time, the effect will not be so remarkable, but in five years, and still more impressively in twenty-five, it will be showing what kind of power is in it. And if still it should go on for some hundreds of years, as it is of course expected that it will, it will become a fact organic and constituent in the race, and the very look and temperament of women will be altered. The word *woman* of course will remain to denote the female sex of man, but the personal habit and type of the sex will be no more what it is. The look will be sharp, the voice will be wiry and shrill, the action will be angular and abrupt, wiliness, self-asserting boldness, eagerness for place and power will get into the expression more and more distinctly, and become inbred in the native habit. Hitherto we have been calling the female sex the fair sex, and that word *fair* represents in bloom and beauty just what the elect virtues of womanhood—the trust, the unselfishness, the deep kindliness, the ethereal grace and cheer, the facile and free-playing inspirations—call for as their fit expression. Accordingly, when these softer virtues go by, giving way to the ambitions of candidacy, and the subtle intrigues of party, they will carry off with them the fair colors, the flushes of clean sensibility, and the delicate, smooth lines of form and feature, and we shall have, instead, a race of forward, selfish, politician-women coming out in their resulting type, thin, hungry-looking, cream-tartar faces, bearing a sharper look of talent, yet somehow touched with blight and fallen out of luster. If it could be expected, that as they change type physiologically, they will become taller and more brawny, and get bigger hands and feet, and a heavier weight of brain, it would not be so much to their disadvantage, and perhaps there will be some little approach to compensation in this way, but there is far more reason to fear that the fight they are to be in, being a fight against nature, will make them at the same time thinner, sharp-featured, lank and dry, just as all disappointed, over-instigated natures always are.

I speak thus of the physiological changes, or changes of type, that are going to be wrought in womanhood, not because it is a matter of principal concern with me, that women should keep their beauty, but simply that, by these external, physiological tokens, I may raise a more adequate conception of the immense moral transformation that is going to be wrought in their personal temperament and character. Nevertheless, it is a truth most deeply grounded, that women are bound, in God's name, to save their beauty. For this is the honor and power of their subject state. Man rules by the precedence of quantity and self-asserting energy, and woman by the subject sovereignty of beauty, personal and moral together, which she can little afford to lose by a sally to gain the noisier, coarser kind that does not belong to her—which also she will as certainly fail of, as the governing of men she is after, is both against their nature and her own.

Be this as it may, it will be a very great oversight in us not to perceive that this introduction of women to an active part in political affairs will be followed by an immense change in the womanly habit and character, and a change about equally undesirable to both sexes....

And here is the melancholy fact, as regards this boasted reform, that it loosens every joint of the family state, and is really meant to do it, as we plainly see by many of the appeals set forth. Thus a leading woman apostle of this reform gives out for her declared sentiment, that "true marriage, like true religion, dwells in the sanctuary of the soul, beyond the cognizance or sanction of state or church;" ridicules the notion that a man's wife "is his property if once married, no matter whether her affections are his or another's;" laughs at his indignations, "if any one else has dared to call out what he never could;" and finally, as if to stir up discontent with marriage, in a way of enlisting the discontented in her cause, exclaims—"Oh, what a sham is the marriage we see about us, though sanctioned in our courts, and baptized at our altars, where cunning priests take toll for binding virtue with vice, angels of grace and goodness with devils in malice and malignity; beauty with deformity, joyous youth with gilded old age—palsied, blasted, with nothing to give its victim in white veil and orange blossoms but a state of luxury and sensualism." Whether these citations are meant to be as shocking as they certainly are, I do not know, and it is of no great importance to inquire. Enough to see what kind of *animus* struggles in the utterance, and that marriage is gone down forever in the argument and reform, that are working their way by appeals so revolting. Nobody can talk in this way of marriage, who would not head a general coming out of it, and is not ready to offer that kind of leadership.

Any one can see that a reform thus carried, carries with it discontent with marriage, and to just the same extent insures a legislation to facilitate divorce. Nobody is to blame, in this kind of casuistry, for the bad marriages, but the priests and the laws, and the woman party has a right of course to be quit, as soon as new passions rise to ask it, or the old ones die to make it a riddance. Being perfectly equal, and put upon her equality with her husband for the right to vote, she must prove her equality somehow, when she comes to the voting and how shall she do it, but by asserting her independence in a vote upon the other side? Such contrary vote need not do any fatal harm, it is true, and yet there is a loosening touch in it, so that if some feeling of hurt has been stirred by hot passages of debate before, or may be afterward, there is a considerable beginning of divorce in it. No wise scheme of polity will consentingly multiply such occasions of damage, in a relation at once so sacred and so delicate. Besides, where the two parties in marriage are known to be opposite in their party affinities, there will be private collodings sought, that will greatly expose the frailty of the woman, and as greatly tempt the jealousy of the man. Sometimes when the husband is up as a candidate, an opposing party, who are willing to see mischief, will set up his wife against him, and whether she consents or not, will run her into the major vote, on purpose to put him in derision. Sometimes a wife in bad blood will get herself nominated against her husband, for the purpose of bringing him under contempt and preparing the divorce she wants.

The general scheme of women's suffrage works against marriage, as we thus perceive, to make it less sacred and less permanent and just as much less beneficial. Frequent divorces check the rate of populations, as the Romans found to their cost. Frequent divorces are the bane of all family peace and order before they come, and the extinction of all true family life and nurture after they come. Hapless beings, too, are the children, that being heirs just now to a parentage and a home, are only heirs henceforth to a family quarrel. Now the dear feeling they had of their parentage is succeeded by the only question left, viz.: Who was to blame? which if they can settle it brings no comfort, and which, if they can not, brings scarcely less. Sad and decadent is the history of any people who have forgotten how to sanctify marriage, and whose children go to the records of divorce instead of the records of marriage, to find their fathers and mothers.

FRANCIS PARKMAN

F rancis Parkman (1823–1893) is generally regarded as one of the foremost American historians. He wrote several classic works, dealing mainly with the colonial period, most notably his seven-part *France and England in North America* (1865–1884). His other works include *The Oregon Trail* (1849) and *The Conspiracy of Pontiac* (1851).

SOME OF THE REASONS AGAINST WOMAN SUFFRAGE

Published in 1888, "Some of the Reasons against Woman Suffrage" presents a battery of reasons, though generally giving only a few paragraphs to each. For instance, Parkman argues that the man is the natural head of the household and that granting women the vote would undermine his authority. Other arguments include the claim that the rigors of politics would be too much for women's strength and that, because women are "impulsive and excitable," they would not use the privilege of voting well or wisely. Parkman's elliptical presentation of these arguments indicates how widespread they were at the time, and so the probability that readers would recognize them and find them convincing.

Probably Parkman's most interesting argument recalls the views of the great English conservative theorist, Edmund Burke. Parkman argues that to accede to the claim that women have a right to vote is to pursue an abstract doctrine to its destructive conclusion. The suffragist's demand "is that government of abstractions and generalities which found its realization in the French Revolution, and its apostle in the depraved and half-crazy man of genius, Jean Jacques Rousseau."

SOME OF THE REASONS AGAINST WOMAN SUFFRAGE

THE POWER OF SEX.

It has been said that the question of the rights and employment of women should be treated without regard to sex. It should rather be said that those who consider it regardless of sex do not consider it at all. It will not do to exclude from the problem the chief factor in it, and deal with women only as if they were smaller and weaker men. Yet these have been the tactics of the agitators for female suffrage, and to them they mainly owe what success they have had. Hence their extreme sensitiveness whenever the subject is approached on its most essential side. If it could be treated like other subjects, and discussed fully and freely, the cause of the self-styled reformers would have been hopeless from the first. It is happy for them that the relations of women to society cannot be so discussed without giving just offense. Their most important considerations can be touched but slightly; and even then offense will be taken.

Whatever liberty the best civilization may accord to women, they must always be subject to restrictions unknown to the other sex, and they can never dispense with the protecting influences which society throws about them. A man, in lonely places, has nothing to lose but life and property; and he has nerve and muscles to defend them. He is free to go whither he pleases, and run what risks he pleases. Without a radical change in human nature, of which the world has never given the faintest sign, women cannot be equally emancipated. It is not a question of custom, habit, or public opinion; but of an all-pervading force, always formidable in the vast number of men in whom it is not controlled by higher forces. A woman is subject, also, to many other restrictions, more or less stringent, necessary to the maintenance of self-respect and the respect of others, and yet placing her at a disadvantage, as compared to men, in the active work of the world. All this is mere truism, but the plainest truism may be ignored in the interest of a theory or a "cause."

Again, everybody knows that the physical and mental constitution of woman is more delicate than in the other sex; and, may we add, the relations between mind and body are more intimate and subtile. It is true that they are abundantly so in men; but their harder organism is neither so sensitive to disturbing influences nor subject to so many of them.

It is these and other inherent conditions, joined to the engrossing nature of a woman's special functions, that have determined through all time her relative position. What we have just said—and we might have said much more—is meant as a reminder that her greatest limitations are not of human origin. Men did not make them, and they cannot unmake them. Through them, God and Nature have ordained that those subject to them shall not be forced to join the harsh conflicts of the world militant. It is folly to ignore them, or try to counteract them by political and social quackery. They set at naught legislatures and peoples.

SELF-COMPLACENCY OF THE AGITATORS.

Here we may notice an idea which seems to prevail among the woman suffragists, that they have argued away the causes which have always determined the substantial relations of the sexes. This notion arises mainly from the fact that they have had the debate very much to themselves. Their case is that of the self-made philosopher who attacked the theory of gravitation, and, because nobody took the trouble to answer him, boasted that he had demolished it, and called it an error of the past.

The frequent low state of health among American women is a fact as undeniable as it is deplorable.

In this condition of things, what do certain women demand for the good of their sex? To add to the excitements that are wasting them other and greater excitements and cares too much for their strength other and greater cares. Because they cannot do their own work, to require them to add it to the work of men, and launch them into the turmoil where the most robust sometimes fail. It is much as if a man in a state of nervous exhaustion were told by his physician to enter at once for a foot-race or a boxing-match.

POWER SHOULD GO WITH RESPONSIBILITY.

To hold the man responsible and yet deprive him of power is neither just nor rational. The man is the natural head of the family, and is responsible for its maintenance and order. Hence he ought to control the social and business agencies which are essential to the successful discharge of the trust imposed upon him. If he is deprived of any part of this control, he should be freed also in the same measure from the responsibilities attached to it.

ALTERNATIVES OF WOMAN SUFFRAGE.

Woman suffrage must have one of two effects. If, as many of its advocates complain, women are subservient to men, and do nothing but what they desire, then woman suffrage will have no other result than to increase the power of the other sex; if, on the other hand, women vote as they see fit, without regarding their husbands, then unhappy marriages will be multiplied and divorces redoubled. We cannot afford to add to the elements of domestic unhappiness.

POLITICAL DANGERS OF WOMAN SUFFRAGE.

One of the chief dangers of popular government is that of inconsiderate and rash legislation. In impatience to be rid of one evil, ulterior consequences are apt to be forgotten. In the haste to redress one wrong, a door may be opened to many. This danger would be increased immeasurably if the most impulsive and excitable half of humanity had an equal voice in the making of laws, and in the administration of them. Abstract right would then be made to prevail after a fashion somewhat startling. A lady of intelligence and admirable intentions, an ardent partisan on principles of pure humanitarianism, confessed that, in the last presidential election, Florida had given a majority for the Democrats; but insisted that it was right to count it for Hayes, because other States had been counted wrongfully for Tilden. It was impossible to make her comprehend that government conducted on such principles would end in anarchy. (In politics, the virtues of women would sometimes be as dangerous as their faults.)

If the better class of women flatter themselves that they can control the others, they are doomed to disappointment. They will be outvoted in their own kitchens, without reckoning the agglomerations of poverty, ignorance, and vice, that form a startling proportion of our city populations. It is here that the male vote alone threatens our system with its darkest perils. The female vote would enormously increase the evil, for it is often more numerous, always more impulsive and less subject to reason, and almost always devoid of the sense of responsibility. Here the bad politician would find his richest resources. He could not reach the better class of female voters, but the rest would be ready to his hand. Three fourths of them, when not urged by some pressing need or contagious passion, would be moved, not by principles, but by personal predilections.

THE FEMALE POLITICIAN.

It is not woman's virtues that would be prominent or influential in the political arena. They would shun it by an invincible repulsion; and the opposite qualities would be drawn into it. The Washington lobby has given us some means of judging what we may expect from the woman "inside politics." If politics are to be purified by artfulness, effrontery, insensibility, a pushing self-assertion, and a glib tongue, then we may look for regeneration; for the typical female politician will be richly endowed with all these gifts.

Thus accoutred for the conflict, she may fairly hope to have the better of her masculine antagonist. A woman has the inalienable right of attacking without being attacked in turn. She may strike, but must not be struck, either literally or figuratively. Most women refrain from abusing their privilege of non-combatants; but there are those in whom the sense of impunity breeds the cowardly courage of the virago.

In reckoning the resources of the female politicians, there is one which can by no means be left out. None know better than women the potency of feminine charms aided by feminine arts. The woman "inside politics" will not fail to make use of an influence so subtle and strong, and of which the management is peculiarly suited to her talents. If—and the contingency is in the highest degree probable—she is not gifted with charms of her own, she will have no difficulty in finding and using others of her sex who are. If report is to be trusted, Delilah has already spread her snares for the congressional Samson, and the power before which the wise fail and the mighty will fall has been invoked against the sages and heroes of the Capitol. When "woman" is fairly "inside politics" the sensation press will reap a harvest of scandals more lucrative to itself than profitable to public morals. And, as the zeal of one class of female reformers has been, and no doubt will be, largely directed to their grievances in matters of sex, we shall have shrill-tongued discussions of subjects which had far better be left alone.

It may be said that the advocates of female suffrage do not look to political women for the purifying of politics, but to the votes of the sex at large. The two, however, cannot be separated. It should be remembered that the question is not of a limited and select female suffrage, but of a universal one. To limit would be impossible. It would seek the broadest areas and the lowest depths, and spread itself through the marshes and malarious pools of society....

IS WOMAN SUFFRAGE A RIGHT OR A WRONG?

It has been claimed as a right that a woman should vote. It is no right, but a wrong, that a small number of women should impose on all the rest political duties which there is no call for their assuming, which they do not want to assume, and which, if duly discharged, would be a cruel and intolerable burden. This pretense of the female suffragists was reduced to an absurdity when some of them gravely affirmed that, if a single woman wanted to vote, all the others ought to be required to do so.

Government by doctrines of abstract right, of which the French Revolution set the example and bore the fruits, involves enormous danger and injustice. No political right is absolute and of universal application. Each has its conditions, qualifications, and limitations. If these are disregarded, one right collides with another, or with many others. Even a man's right to liberty is subject to the condition that he does not use it to infringe the rights of his neighbors. It is in the concrete, and not in the abstract, that rights prevail in every sound and wholesome society. They are applied where they are applicable. A government of glittering generalities quickly destroys itself. The object of government is the accomplishment of a certain result, the greatest good of the governed; and the ways of reaching it vary in different countries and different social conditions. Neither liberty nor the suffrage are the end; they are nothing but means to reach it; and each should be used to the extent in which it is best adapted to its purpose. If the voting of women conduces to the greatest good of the community, then they ought to vote, and otherwise they ought not. The question of female suffrage thus becomes a practical question, and not one of declamation.

What would be the results of the general application of the so-called right to vote, a right which, if it exists at all, must be common to all mankind? Suppose that the populations of Turkey, the Soudan, or Zululand were to attempt to exercise it and govern themselves by universal popular suffrage. The consequence would be anarchy, and a quick return to despotism as a relief. The same would be the case, in less degree, among peoples more civilized, yet not trained to self-government by the habits and experience of generations. In fact, there are but a few of the most advanced nations in whom the universal exercise of the pretended "inalienable right" to vote would not produce political and social convulsions. The truth is this: If the exercise of the suffrage by any individual or body of individuals involves detriment to the whole people, then the right to exercise it does not exist.

It is the right and the duty of the people to provide itself with good government, and this great practical right and duty is imperative and paramount; whatever conflicts with it must give away. The air-blown theory of inalienable right is unworthy the good sense of the American people. The most rational even of the suffragists themselves have to rely on it. ....

PRACTICAL VERSUS SENTIMENTAL GOVERNMENT.

The real issue is this: Is the object of government the good of the governed, or is it not? A late writer on woman suffrage says that it is not. According to her, the object of government is to give his or her rights to everybody.

Others among the agitators do not venture either on this flat denial or this brave assertion, but only hover about them with longing looks. Virtually they maintain that the object of government is the realization of certain ideas or theories. They believe in principles, and so do we; they believe in rights, and so do we. But as the sublime may pass into the ridiculous, so the best principles may be transported into regions of folly or diabolism. There are minds so constituted that they can never stop till they have run every virtue into its correlative weakness or vice. Government should be guided by principles; but they should be sane and not crazy, sober and not drunk. They should walk on solid ground, and not roam the clouds hanging to a bag of gas.

Rights may be real or unreal. Principles may be true or false; but even the best and truest cannot safely be pushed too far, or in the wrong direction. The principle of truth itself may be carried into absurdity. The saying is old that truth should not be spoken at all times; and those whom a sick conscience worries into habitual violation of the maxim are imbeciles and nuisances. Religion may pass into morbid enthusiasm or wild fanaticism, and turn from a blessing to a curse. So the best of political principles must be kept within bounds of reason, or they will work mischief. That is the greatest and most difficult of sciences, the science of government, dealing with interests so delicate, complicated, and antagonistic, becomes a perilous guide when it deserts the ways of temperance.

SHALL WE STAND BY AMERICAN PRINCIPLES?

The suffragists' idea of government is not practical, but utterly unpractical. It is not American, but French. It is that government of abstractions and generalities which found its realization in the French Revolution, and its apostle in the depraved and half-crazy man of genius, Jean Jacques Rousseau. The French had an excuse for their frenzy in the crushing oppression they had just flung off and in their inexperience of freedom. We have no excuse. Since the nation began we have been free and our liberty is in danger from nothing but its own excesses. Since France learned to subject the ideas of Rousseau to the principles of stable freedom embodied in the parliamentary government of England and in our own republicanism, she has emerged from alternate tumult and despotism to enter the paths of hope and progress.

The government of abstractions has been called, sometimes the *a priori,* and sometimes the sentimental, method. We object to this last term, unless it is carefully defined. Sentiments, like principles, enter into the life of nations as well as that of individuals; and they are vital to both. But they should be healthy, and not morbid; rational, and not extravagant. It is not common sense alone that makes the greatness of states; neither is it sentiments and principles alone. It is these last joined with reason, reflection, and moderation. Through this union it is that one small island has become the mighty mother of nations; and it is because we ourselves, her greatest offspring, have chosen the paths of Hampden, Washington, and Franklin, and not those of Rousseau, that we have passed safe through every danger, and become the wonder and despair of despotism.

Out of the wholesome fruits of the earth, and the staff of life itself, the perverse chemistry of man distils delirious vapors, which, condensed and bottled, exalt his brain with glorious fantasies, and then leave him in the mud. So it is with the unhappy suffragists. From the sober words of our ancestors they extract the means of mental inebriety. Because the fathers of the republic gave certain reasons to emphasize their creed that America should not be taxed because America was not represented in the British Parliament, they cry out that we must fling open floodgates to vaster tides of ignorance and folly, strengthen the evil of our system and weaken the good, feed old abuses, hatch new ones, and expose all our large cities—we speak with deliberate conviction—to the risk of anarchy.

Neither Congress, nor the States, nor the united voice of the whole people could permanently change the essential relations of the sexes. Universal female suffrage, even if decreed, would undo itself in time; but the attempt to establish it would work deplorable mischief. The question is, whether the persistency of a few agitators shall plunge us blindfold into the most reckless of all experiments; whether we shall adopt this supreme device for developing the defects of women, and demolish their real power to build an ugly mockery instead. For the sake of womanhood, let us hope not. In spite of the effect on the popular mind of the incessant repetition of a few trite fallacies, and in spite of the squeamishness that prevents the vast majority averse to the movement from uttering a word against it, let us trust that the good sense of the American people will vindicate itself against this most unnatural and pestilent revolution. In the full and normal development of womanhood lie the best interests in the world. Let us labor earnestly for it; and, that we may not labor in vain, let us save women from the barren perturbations of American politics. Let us respect them; and, that we may do so, let us pray for deliverance from female suffrage.

GROVER CLEVELAND

Grover Cleveland (1837–1908) was the twenty-second and twenty-fourth president of the United States. After the end of his second term, he remained active in public affairs, lecturing and writing. One issue that interested him was woman suffrage, which he opposed.

WOULD WOMAN SUFFRAGE BE UNWISE?

For the May 1905 *Ladies' Home Journal,* Cleveland wrote a brief article against women's clubs. The growth of "woman's clubbism" was "not only harmful but a menace" to both women's character and the sanctity of the home.[1] He also went on to present some reasons why women should not be given the vote. In the article presented here, from the October 1905 *Ladies' Home Journal,* Cleveland elaborates on his earlier statements. The most forceful of his battery of arguments rests on adverse consequences of granting women the vote. The votes of the thoughtful and conscientious would be outweighed by those of "the disreputable, the ignorant, the thoughtless, the purchased and the coerced." A brief look at the states that had granted suffrage shows the consequences to be on balance harmful.

NOTE

1. Grover Cleveland, "Woman's Mission and Woman's Clubs," *Ladies' Home Journal,* 22 (May 1905), pp. 3–4.

WOULD WOMAN SUFFRAGE BE UNWISE?

"Even if Every Woman Should Exercise the Suffrage, the Votes of the Thoughtful and Conscientious Would Almost Certainly be Largely Outweighed by Those of the Disreputable, the Ignorant, the Thoughtless, the Purchased and the Coerced"

No standard of advanced civilization can receive intelligent sanction that fails to yield to genuine womanhood the highest place among the social agencies that refine humanity and make the world better. And of course it is equally certain that the nearer social conditions approach perfect excellence the more tender and careful will be the homage and consideration accorded by all decent men to unperverted womanhood. If, however, these sentiments are to indicate a spirit of true and sterling manliness they must rest upon something better than the shallow gallantry which, while professing admiration for womankind, indulges in a sort of pitying toleration of feminine subordination and frailty.

Thoughtful and right-minded men base their homage and consideration for woman upon an instinctive consciousness that her unmasculine qualities, whether called weaknesses, frailties, or what we will, are the sources of her characteristic and especial strength within the area of her legitimate endeavor. They know that if she is not gifted with the power of clear and logical reasoning she has a faculty of intuition which by a shorter route leads her to abstract moral truth; that if she deals mistakenly with practical problems it is because sympathy or sentiment clouds her perception of the relative value of the factors involved; that if she is unbusinesslike her trustfulness and charitableness stand in the way of cold-blooded calculation; that if she is occasionally stubborn it is because her beliefs take a strong hold upon her; and that if she is sometimes fitful and petulant it is but the prelude to bright smiles and sunny endearments. They know she is loving, long-suffering, self-sacrificing and tender, because God has made her so; and with it all they gratefully realize that whatever she has or lacks, the influence and ministrations of woman give firm rooting and sure growth to man's best efforts.

THE PLACES ASSIGNED TO MEN AND WOMEN

It is a mistake to suppose that any human reason or argument is needful or adequate to the assignment of the relative positions to be assumed by man and woman in working out the problems of civilization. This was done long ago by a higher intelligence than ours. I believe that trust in Divine wisdom, and ungrudging submission to Divine purposes, will enable dutiful men and women to know the places assigned to them, and will incite them to act well their parts in the sight of God. It should also be easy for such as these to see how wisely the work of human progress has been distributed, and how exactly the refining, elevating influence of women, especially in her allotted sphere of home and in her character of wife and mother, supplements man's strenuous struggles in social and political warfare. In actual war it is the men who go to battle, enduring hardship and privation, and suffering disease and death for the cause they follow. They are deservedly praised for bravery and patriotism. It is the mothers, wives and maids betrothed, who, neither following the camp nor fighting in battle, constitute at home an army of woman's constancy and love, whose yearning hearts make men brave and patriotic. They teach from afar lessons of patient fortitude, and transmit through mysterious agencies, to soldiers in the field, the spirit of endurance and devotion. Soldiers who have fought, and those who praise or eulogize them, never forget to accord to woman the noble service of inspiration she has thus wrought with womanly weapons wielded in her appointed place.

WOMAN'S TRUEST INFLUENCE IN POLITICS

So in political warfare, it is perfectly fitting that actual strife and battle should be apportioned to man, and that the influence of woman, radiating from the homes of our land, should inspire to lofty aims and purposes those who struggle for the right. I am thoroughly convinced that woman can in no better way than this usefully serve the cause of political betterment, and preserve her present immeasurable power of good. It is sane intelligence, and not sentimental delusion, that discovers between the relative duties and responsibilities of man and woman, as factors in the growth of civilization, a natural equilibrium, so nicely adjusted to the attributes and limitations of both that it cannot be disturbed without social confusion and peril. It is therefore not surprising that a multitude of good American men and women, who certainly are not lacking in solicitude for their country's welfare, are troubled lest this equilibrium should be jostled out of balance by the dissemination of notions which present a distorted view of the saving grace of womanhood as a constructive influence and a potent force in our homes, and in the moral activities of our nation. These good people believe that this saving grace cannot be protected and perpetuated in its ordained beauty and strength, except by protecting and perpetuating in their ordained loyalty and purity all the distinctive traits and attributes of woman's nature. They repudiate the idea that these things have been outrun by advance and progress and are no longer worth saving. On the contrary, their patriotic thoughtfulness and clear intelligence lead them to see that, now and for all time to come, the work and mission of women within the sphere to which God has adjusted them, must constitute the immutable and unchangeable foundations of all that human enlightenment can build.

FALSE DOCTRINES TAUGHT BY CERTAIN WOMEN

None of use can deny that we have unhappily fallen upon a time when doctrines are taught by women, and to women, which tend with more or less directness to the subversion of sane and wholesome ideas of the work and mission of womanhood, and lead to a fanciful insistence upon sharing in the stern, rugged and unwomanly duties and responsibilities allotted to man. As is usually the case when a radical and unnatural change is the object of effort, those most extreme and pronounced in opinion have forged to the front and assumed leadership. In outspoken discontent with the station and opportunity American women now enjoy, these clamorous leaders openly demand their equal participation with men in the right of suffrage and in every other political right and privilege. Many other women, more considerate and conservative, who refuse to indorse these demands, nevertheless by amiably tolerating them, or by advocating other less direct attempts to enlarge the character of woman's endeavor, encourage and aid, perhaps unconsciously and unintentionally, female suffrage radicalism.

In this magazine, a few months ago, I ventured to publish some views I entertain touching woman's clubs and their tendencies. I am afraid a portion of what I wrote has been a little misunderstood by some women of genuine disposition, whose good opinion I would be glad to retain. Nevertheless, I have no intention of attempting to make my meaning plainer, or of modifying the opinions I have expressed relating specifically to woman's clubs. I desire to supplement those opinions by declaring that, while they have elicited considerable approval from women, I have been hardy less gratified to discover in the expressions of many who have dissented a tone of charming womanliness and moderation, which has confirmed me in the belief that there need be no apprehension that such women are prepared deliberately and willfully to undermine woman's legitimate mission; but what I fear more and more is the result of their good-natured and indirect affiliation with those more radically disposed—who, with noisy discontent and possibly with not too much disinclination for notoriety, exploit in the newspapers their unpleasant temper, and their indifferent attempts to commend woman suffrage, accompanied occasionally by something very like unwomanly abuse and misrepresentation.

GENERAL WOMAN SUFFRAGE IS INEXPEDIENT

I desire here to make a statement which I am willing to have regarded somewhat in the light of a confession. In my former article in *The Journal* a reference was made in the following terms to the movement on foot to secure for woman the right to vote and otherwise participate in public affairs:

"Let it here be distinctly understood that no sensible man has fears of injury to the country on account of such participation. It is its dangerous undermining effect on the characters of the wives and mothers of our land that we fear." The subject under discussion was the unfavorable effect of woman's clubs on American womanhood; and it is tolerably apparent, from what immediately followed the above-quoted indulgent allusion to female participation in public affairs, that such allusion was incidental and illustrative of the main topic. So far as I am concerned, although I then saw no prospect of the accomplishment of this participation, as appears from other parts of the same article, I believed that general woman suffrage would be an inexpedient and venturesome experiment. I am willing, however, to admit that it was only after a more thorough appreciation of what female suffrage really means that I became fully convinced that its inauguration would vastly increase the unhappy imperfections and shortcomings of our present man-voting suffrage, and that it was only after a better knowledge of the spirit and disposition that stand behind it, gained from recent experience and observation, that I was entirely persuaded that its especial susceptibility to bad leadership and hurtful influences would constitute it another menacing condition to those which already vex and disturb the deliberate and intelligent expression of the popular will.

It will not do to suppose that a majority of the sensible and responsible women of the land desire suffrage and admittance to the activities of politics. On the contrary, there is now a great preponderance of these who either actively oppose all movements in this direction or are contentedly indifferent. A few years ago the question of allowing municipal suffrage in Massachusetts to women was submitted to all the voters of that State who were eligible to vote for school committees. The number of women at that time qualified to register and ballot on the question was about 575,000. Of these, more than 550,000 declined to vote. The total woman's vote cast in favor of the proposition was smaller than had sometimes been cast in school elections. There were forty-seven towns in which not one woman's ballot was cast in the affirmative, and in each of one hundred and thirty-eight other towns fifteen women or less so voted.

I think twenty States which refuse to women all other suffrage privileges permits them to vote for school officers, either without restriction or under certain conditions. It is alleged, however, that the number who avail themselves of this privilege is commonly very small. It is said with apparent authority that at the elections for school officers, which ought to interest all women who in good faith desire to be really useful by means of their suffrage, the proportion of women who vote in the State of New York is estimated at two per cent., in Connecticut at from one to two and a half per cent., and in Massachusetts ordinarily at not more that three or four per cent. The decrease of their desire to vote on this question is indicated by such statistics as these: in the city of Chicago 29,815 women registered as voters in 1894; but in 1898 the number was only 1488. In the year 1895, in the city of Cleveland, 5831 women registered; but in 1898 this number was reduced to 82.

THE WOMAN'S CLUB AS AN ALLY OF FEMALE SUFFRAGE

In the face of such an adverse majority and such indifference among their own sex it is not unreasonable to assume that the propagandists of female suffrage who continue to goad on the cause, rely considerably for final success, upon the aid of the numerous woman's clubs, which, whatever their declared objects may be, are apt to pave the way to the reception of woman-suffrage radicalism. I have lately received a letter from a thoroughly conscientious lady which illustrates the gradation from membership in a moderate woman's club to the most extreme affiliations: While protesting in a delightfully womanly way against my views in regard to woman's clubs she frankly admitted the consequences, in her own case, of acquiring the club habit. She first joined a literary club for the "mutual improvement and culture" of its members, then an art club, then a civic club, and finally, having thus been brought within the influence of certain missionaries in the cause of female municipal suffrage, she became, and continues to be, an ardent convert to that doctrine. I do not claim that many instances have fallen under my observation which so completely demonstrate how apparently innocent club membership leads to unanticipated extremity. It is not unusual, however, for women in all stages of such membership to admit that the formation of the club habit is one of its frequent accompaniments. Our knowledge of human nature does not permit us to discredit the shrewdness of the advocates of female suffrage, who frequently encourage all sorts of woman's clubs, perfectly understanding how this habit can be utilized to open the female mind to the acceptance of their creed.

Another encouragement to those who propagate the doctrine of woman suffrage grows out of their reliance upon the chivalric consideration which the men of our nation, in the halls of legislation and everywhere, have for the female sex. A woman speaking in opposition to female suffrage before a Senate Committee a few years ago said:

"It is not the tyranny but the chivalry of men that we American women have to fear. The men of America want to give us everything we really need; and the danger is that they will mistake a minority for a majority."

A distinguished writer in dealing with the question declared:

"A woman has the inalienable right of attacking without being attacked in turn. She may strike, but must not be struck either literally or figuratively."

This is precisely as it should be—especially when women are within the sacred precincts of true womanhood. But after all is said or conceded, the question remains, whether, when woman deliberately breaks away from womanly environments and enters the arena of challenge and disputation, man's duty and reason should be silenced in deference to her demands and his mental forces given over to easy-going and undutiful gallantry.

THE BALLOT IS NOT WOMAN'S INHERENT RIGHT

Nothing can be more palpable than that a safe regulation of our suffrage lies at the very foundation of American free institutions; and of course nothing more important than this can engage the attention of those who make our laws. Legislators should never neglect the dictates of chivalry in their treatment of woman; but this does not demand that a smirking appearance of acquiescence should conceal or smother a thoughtful lawmaker's intelligent disapproval of female suffrage. It is one of the chief charms of women that they are not especially amenable to argument; but that is not a reason why, when they demand the ballot as an inherent right, they should not be reminded that suffrage is a privilege which attaches neither to man nor to woman by nature. Nor could it be deemed discourteous if, when they claim the right to vote because women are taxed as owners of property, it is pointed out to them that they are not the only persons taxed as property-holders from whom the ballot is withheld, and that under present conditions there is always a complete willingness to do every possible thing, by way of legislation, to secure and protect their property rights. Our statute books are full of proof of this.

I suppose it was only a willingness to indulge in flattering pleasantry that led a distinguished jurist, when lately addressing a large audience of young women at one of our prominent female colleges, to intimate that within the present generation the suffrage might be extended to women in every State, and to excite the enthusiastic applause of his emotional hearers by the hint that before they became gray-haired there might "sit in the White House a women who, like Queen Victoria, will shed lustre upon this country as Victoria shed lustre upon England."

SOME RESULTS IN WOMAN-SUFFRAGE STATES

Those most active in pushing the demand for woman suffrage point in its vindication to what they deem wholesome legislation accomplished in the few States where such suffrage has been granted. I am afraid, however, that in dealing with this feature of the question these advocates occasionally take a mistaken view of the relationship between cause and effect. I believe it will be found that, if the wise and progressive legislation in these woman-suffrage States is weighed against such legislation in States where woman suffrage is withheld, the balance will certainly not be found against the latter. As bearing upon the credit due to woman votes for legislation where full female suffrage has been adopted, it is worth noting that the male voters exceptionally outnumber the female voters in all these localities.

It is sometimes claimed that woman suffrage would have the effect of elevating and refining politics. Neither its short trial in four States containing in the aggregate a population very slightly in excess of one-third the population of the city of New York nor our political experience or observation supports this claim. The State in which full female suffrage prevails are Colorado, Utah, Idaho and Wyoming. In the first two of these States the proportion of female voters is considerably greater than in the others; and yet the voters of Utah have lately elected through their Legislature to the United States Senate a man whose fitness is now the subject of a pending Senatorial investigation, and not long ago they elected to Congress another man whom that body rejected. These incidents may not go far toward discrediting woman suffrage, but they certainly do not indicate its invariably refining and elevating tendency.

NOT A CREDITABLE SHOWING IN COLORADO

I hope it will not be deemed ungracious if I refer to another circumstance which is at least interesting as a coincidence. Of the four States permitting full woman suffrage, Colorado should certainly be regarded as affording the best illustration of its results, as this State is most like the older States of the East in point of urban population, in the variety and extent of its business interests and in the proportion of women to men among its residents of voting age. Less than two years ago a member of the House of Representatives from that State, holding his place by virtue of an apparent majority of the direct votes of the men and woman of his district, resigned his seat for the reason, as he openly declared, that fraudulent votes had been cast for him in the election. An investigation of the case by a Congressional Committee developed the fact that some of the most glaring frauds were committed by women. A New York newspaper in February, 1904, published a summary of the evidence taken by the committee, from which it appeared that one woman, admitting her participation in these frauds, confessed among other political sins that she gave directions to the women who were to do repeating at the polls, and that two other women were associated with her in the manipulation of ballots, one of whom arranged to have a fight started at the election place, to afford opportunity to throw out the watchers and challengers of the other party. The resigning Congressman, with a show of characteristic masculine gallantry, gave it as his opinion that of the persons implicated very few were women—"not more than one in ten at the outside." It seems to me that this statement falls far short of mitigating the situation. The most gluttonous suffrage corruptor in the world ought to be a happy scoundrel if he could "implicate" in bringing about his ends ten out of every hundred voters.

ONE DELUSION OF FEMALE SUFFRAGE

I have sometimes wondered if the really good women who are inclined to approve this doctrine of female suffrage are not deluding themselves with purely sentimental views of the subject. Have they not in some way allowed the idea to gain a place in their minds that if the suffrage were accorded to women it would be the pure, the honest, the intelligent and the patriotic of the sex who would avail themselves of it? If they are drifting on the smooth surface of such a pleasing conceit as this it behooves them to take soundings and locate landmarks. They can perhaps thus bring themselves to a realization of the fact that among women, as is, unfortunately, the case now among men, it would not be the best and the most responsible that would most diligently use their voting powers, and that, even if every woman in the land should exercise the suffrage, the votes of the thoughtful and conscientious would almost certainly be largely outweighed by those of the disreputable, the ignorant, the thoughtless, the purchased and the coerced. It is not to the purpose to say that even with all this the condition among women with suffrage would be no worse than it now is among men. We need something better for the improvement of our suffrage, not an addition of the bad already existing. Do respectable and public-spirited women who favor female suffrage have a vague idea that all women endowed with the franchise can be taught to exercise the privilege intelligently and honestly? Who is to undertake this duty, and how? They may rely upon it that the condition of civic fitness in which the suffrage finds the great mass of women will grow worse instead of better. Vested with the power of suffrage equally with the best of their sex, the unintelligent and characterless would be inclined to resist the approach of those who assume with an air of superiority to give them instruction in voting duty. Nor could such approach be expected to end with mere resistance to teaching and influence. We all know how much further women go than men in their social rivalries and jealousies. Woman suffrage would give to the wives and daughters of the poor a new opportunity to gratify their envy and mistrust of the rich. Meantime these new voters would become either the purchased or cajoled victims of plausible political manipulators, or the intimidated and helpless voting vassals of imperious employers.

This phase of the suffrage question cannot better be presented than in the following words of another: "Women change politics less than politics change women."

THE EFFECT OF THE BALLOT ON WOMAN

I take the following quotation from a book I have lately read, written by a very painstaking and conscientious woman who has spent much time in personal investigation of all questions pertaining to woman's welfare and improvement. She is zealously in favor of woman's clubs, and, it seems to me, would be glad to advocate woman suffrage if she could; but not being a theorist, but a careful, practical investigator, her experience and observation do not permit her to go to that length. After spending considerable time and mingling with all sorts of people in Colorado, where the problem of woman suffrage can be better studied than anywhere else in the United States, she presents the result of her examination in language which I appropriate as my concluding words:

"However suffrage may be regarded as an abstract problem, it is not to be denied that in Colorado its use by women has, whatever else it may have done or failed to do, brought grave disaster upon those women. The possession of the ballot and the employment of that possession have hurt the women of Colorado as women can least afford to be hurt.... Her ideals have been lowered; the delicacy of her perception of right and wrong has been dulled. Whatever good she may be able to render to her State and to the Nation by her vote, can that good, however great, compensate for the injury which she has wrought to that State and to the Nation by reason of the blow she has dealt her own womanhood?"

ANNIE NATHAN MEYER

nnie Nathan Meyer (1867–1951) was an educator and author of novels
and plays. A founder and original trustee of Barnard College, she
might have been expected to have a high opinion of women and their
potential. But she opposed woman suffrage and questioned arguments in its
favor based on the purported moral superiority of the female sex.

WOMAN'S ASSUMPTION OF SEX SUPERIORITY (SELECTIONS)

In the selection included here, published in the 1904 *North American Review,*
Meyer presents an argument from expediency against woman suffrage to
counter arguments from expediency in favor of suffrage that are seen in previous selections (e.g., Henry Blackwell's "Solution of the Southern Question" on
pages 156–161, and Belle Kearney's "The South and Woman Suffrage," on
pages 162–169).

Meyer does not question women's intellectual suitability for the franchise but argues that they lack the moral development to make them responsible voters. She claims that women are capable of the same venality men
demonstrate in public affairs.

Suffragists point out signally virtuous women and claim that enfranchising women will raise the moral tenor of politics. But according to Meyer,
one must remember "that a vote to one woman will be a vote to all women,
vicious and virtuous, ignorant and educated, lowest and highest." Failing to
see in women "any evidence of the character that is needed in our public life,"
Meyer also questions whether participation in public life is an effective way
for them to develop the requisite qualities.

WOMAN'S ASSUMPTION
OF SEX SUPERIORITY

I am quite sure that, in the political arena, I should dread the advent of women as voters and office-holders a little more than that of the tiger. Of course, to the speaker, Woman typified and summed up all that was honorable, pure, noble, uplifting. To her, even the fact that the emblematic "lady" referred to was really a goddess was in no way disconcerting. It was assumed by many campaigners that the interest taken in the campaign by the women was in itself a conclusive arraignment of Tammany, was in itself a proof that the Fusion party stood for honest government. Of course, such an assumption when it is made by a man is not to be seriously challenged; but when it is made by a large proportion (still, I am persuaded, happily, by a minority) of women, then it becomes worth while to examine woman's claim to moral superiority, to examine it soberly and seriously.

The exercise by woman of the power to vote has been held up by these women again and again as a panacea for the chief evils, if not all evils, that now threaten to undermine the moral life of America. As even these women must be aware that in voting the majority prevails, this is clearly an assumption that the majority of women may be counted upon as a force that would make for political righteousness. It is strangely difficult to keep this inference before the public. The popular method of argument is: "Mrs. Thus-and-So is a splendid woman; would she not give us a more intelligent vote than the ignorant hod-carrier?" The fact that the vote of Mrs. Thus-and-So will be pitted against that of Mrs. Hod-carrier, never seems to be considered. It must be remembered that the suffrage—at least in America—is almost certain to be refused to all women, or given to all women; that a vote to one woman will be a vote to all women, vicious and virtuous, ignorant and educated, lowest and highest.

Let me say right here, as emphatically as possible, that while I challenge the assumption that women as a sex could contribute a regenerative force to the body politic, yet I do not deny the fact that there are many fine, true women who could be relied upon to cast their votes every time for the right. That I further think that most of these women do not wish the suffrage, that they have a clearer idea of their sex as a whole and a profounder appreciation of their real duties, does not concern us at present. The question, shorn of all disingenuousness, of all sentimentality, is just this: What could the sex bring to the service of the state to offset the degeneration of public life, to offset the indifference, the sloth, the moral cowardice, the greed, the dishonesty that are seriously menacing the moral life of our Republic?

When a man is chosen by his party as a candidate for office, his career is scrutinized, the question is asked, What has he done in his private career that implies a promise of success in a public career? Similarly, when women offer themselves for political duty (and in no spirit of humility, but with smug self-satisfaction and assumption of superior virtue), is it not just to scrutinize their past, to ask, What special character, what special force, what special talent have they shown in fulfilling their apportioned duties in the past? Is there anything to warrant a faith that they would discharge this new duty faithfully and ably? It is idle for women to say that it is not fair to scrutinize their past, because it was not a past of their own seeking; to claim that incompetency in domestic life bears no relation to incompetency in political life, that the shirking of disagreeable duties would not mean the shirking of (supposedly) agreeable ones. Idle, and futile, I say, because we are probing deeper than that! We do not wish to know if their heads are equal to the problems of government; it does not concern us if they are not fitted for domestic duties—if they dislike them; it is not brains, nor aptitudes, not even ability that are vital, it is character. Character is one force needed in American life to-day. And character may be more safely judged from the way in which we perform disagreeable duties than from the way in which we perform agreeable ones. The question is not so much whether certain tasks allotted to women in the past have been well or ill performed; but it is—it doubly, trebly, is: Having been confronted with these tasks, in what manner have they approached them? Have they shirked them or have they done their best? Have they done the work they found to be done, willingly, conscientiously, patiently, uncomplainingly? Have they been satisfied to do it without applause, without public reward? Have they brought to bear on this work the best they had, the best they could become? Have they never reached forth to grasp the more spectacular work of others, while turning their backs on their own? In short, have they any claim to such characteristics as, if contributed to American public life to-day, could purify and ennoble it?

I have spoken of the lack of character as the real lack in American public life to-day. Is there any question of this? To what is due the general neglect of the disagreeable part of political duty, but to a lack of character? What explains the too common custom of paying for concessions instead of fighting for one's just dues, but a lack of character? What, the yielding to blackmail, the seeking of the line of least resistance? What, the venality, the greed, and the acceptance of a double standard of honesty—political and commercial? What does all this signify, but a lack of character?

Perhaps the enlarged opportunities enjoyed by women during the past forty years have qualified them in some directions for the suffrage. Certainly, their mental qualifications will not be so sweepingly questioned as when the subject first arose for debate. But it is my firm conviction that the development of woman's character has by no means kept step with that of her intellect. I think this is a serious arraignment of the women's colleges, one to which several of the leading colleges are awakening, and to the correction of which the best friends of woman's education are addressing themselves. There is no longer question of the capacity of woman's brain to be trained to wield the suffrage. But, alas! it can never be repeated often enough that it is not brains that are needed just now. There is a cry welling up from the surcharged hearts of those who tremble for the steadfastness of American government: but it is not a cry for brains—it is a cry for character.

"Put United Womanhood," they say, (a resounding phrase much made use of—as if all women could be united on anything save puffed sleeves or pocketless skirts!), "Put United Womanhood into politics, and we shall have character. You will no longer see the Boss one instant the epitome of all that is evil, and the next, worthy to fold his legs under your mahogany." But is this true? Is there even a shadow of truth in it? Have women, then, as a sex been so brave in fighting the conventional standpoint? Show me that more than a handful of women have the courage to ostracize the "great catch" that they know has no right to associate with their daughters, and I shall take heart. Give me the slightest inkling that women will fight the tyrannous hand of the Labor-Unions, now stifling the manhood of our business as well as of our laboring world. Give me the faintest hope that women will refuse to pay for what should come to them freely, that women will resist all favoritism, all unfairness! What is there in the past that can vouch for the future? Will the woman who quails before the departing cook, stand firm before the District Leader? Will the woman who submits to the tyranny of her volatile dressmaker, resist the voluble walking delegate? Will the woman who has made a mess of the domestic question, straighten out the tangles of the industrial and financial world? And, finally, will a woman who has shirked the noblest duty on God's earth, not shirk the lesser duties to which she, strangely enough, aspires? I hope I am not unduly severe. I am not more severe than are the women themselves who decry the moral weakness of the average man. In the very charge of inferiority launched against men by women, they present the strongest possible indictment of their own sex. These men, who are so weak, so corrupt, so far below the standard of the women—had they no mothers? With so many grafters, so many "respectable" tools of a machine, is it possible that a great many women have not betrayed their trust? Do not tell me that the casting of a bit of paper in a box once a year can offset the daily influence of a mother, or that votes can be better gained from a political platform than at the home fireside.

I fail to see in women any evidence of the character that is needed in our public life. I fail to see that they are even on the right track to attain it. I think there is no school so eminently unfit for the development of character as that of the public platform, which women are seeking more and more. I think there is a grave danger to the moral force of womanhood in woman's increasing participation in organized effort, in public life. To say nothing of the wire-pulling, of the unscrupulousness in attaining an end, of the unfairness, of the love of office, of the insincerity which reveal themselves in the large organizations of women, with discouraging and startling resemblance to the methods of their weaker brethren, I hold that there is certain to come a deterioration which I like to name "Platform Virtue." One who feeds on applause learns how easily it is gained, grows impatient of any task which does not win it, is apt to scorn such work as is not in the public eye. The most subtle moral danger lies in the fact that it is so easy to be noble, to be generous, to be unselfish, on the public platform—in one's typewritten Confession of Faith. How is the strength to be given to work on, to fight on quietly, unknown, uninterviewed, unrewarded, certainly unapplauded, when the enunciation of a few well-rounded periods yields such delightful recognition! An audience is the most good-natured, indifferent censor in the world. It seldom probes below the surface; in the rare cases in which it does, its memory is conveniently short. Just as the kindergarten methods, in the opinion of some educators, have lost for our children a certain sturdiness, a certain grim power of overcoming difficulties, so the platform habit, the club habit, the President and Secretary habit have entailed upon our women serious losses. The daily uncomplaining attention to household details that make for comfort and a restful home atmosphere; the tender, unseen care given to the children; the brooding over, watching and painstaking upbuilding of character; the brave, inspiring encouragement of the wearied wage-earner—for these things has not taste been lost?

It is so perilously easy, on the one hand, to be an angel of loving-kindness to some class of workers for whom one has founded a protecting organization, and, on the other, in the privacy of one's home, to withhold from one's servants the most ordinary human consideration. It is so easy to appeal on the platform to the highest, purest motives, to implore others to do their duty, and in the home to shirk from the most elementary duties, not only of motherhood, but of wifehood. It is so easy to be suave and delightful, gracious and charming, on the platform, and at home nervous, unstrung, impatient, fretful. The hardening processes of the age may be exemplified most strongly in the evolution of the very newest new woman. She who, twenty-five years ago, refused marriage in favor of her so-called "career," at least was willing to make a sacrifice of her emotional needs. She of to-day has no idea of renouncing marriage, but remoulds its old-fashioned idea of obligation—at times with an overriding of nature that would be comic if it were not tragic.

Are we, then to throw over entirely our cherished idea, that woman is the morally superior sex? Well, I think the women have been banking a little too heavily upon certain claims. I think that, if they had lived for centuries in the same freedom and under the same temptations as men, they would have shown far less self-control and power of resistance; and this opinion might find support in some of the conditions known to exist in the social life of our own community. Perhaps some brave twentieth-century

Fielding will arise and write an up-to-date parody of "Pamela": it will be instructive.

Even of so masculine a vice as drunkenness, there is something to be said. The assertion of sex superiority is not proven because there are fewer drunkards among women than men. Dare any one affirm that, since women have entered into industrial competition, into public life with its drain on the nervous strength, there has been less drunkenness than before? On the contrary, every one knows that the use of stimulants among women is increasing rapidly.

Notwithstanding the usual tone that pervades the speeches at a Woman's Rights Meeting (and there is a degree of bitterness, of contempt, of positive enmity against men that is not dreamed of by the average person), I believe that the work now done by the men would not be improved by being done by women.

It may seem so on the surface, but I am not wholly reactionary. I do not think that all virtue or all character is buried in the graves of our ancestresses. There is much that may be gained from all the discussion, all the unrest and change of the past half century, if only the trained women who should be the leaders will take their covetous eyes from the careers of the men, and, casting them backward over the past, will say: "Let us see how much better we can do the woman's work in the future. Let us see what training and science can do to make that work more helpful and more intelligent." I have hope for the future, because I know there are many strong women working quietly for this end. They are not the women who are supposed to represent us; they are certainly not those who periodically assure the Legislature that they do. They are seldom found on a platform. They are not presidents of clubs. They are not be-badged "chairmen" of committees; they do not belong to Mothers' Congresses, but they are accomplishing their end in a sincere, an unspectacular, the only lasting way, through the weight of personal character, the effect of personal example, through the divine influence that is so dangerously slipping away from this organization-worshipping, this number-idolizing, world of ours—I mean, the impulse of the *personal touch.* I have hope, because many of the excesses of women will be righted after women have grasped a little longer the baubles they have yearned for, after they have seen how valueless are these baubles in their hands. Then, I cannot but think, they will learn to value the things they have so blithely let go.

WILLIAM EWART GLADSTONE

William Ewart Gladstone (1809–1898), one of the dominant English political leaders of the nineteenth century, was four times Prime Minister (1868–74, 1880–85, 1886, 1892–94). As leader of the Liberal Party, Gladstone was instrumental in a series of important reforms, including vote by secret ballot, establishment of a civil service based on competitive examinations, abolition of the sale of army commissions, and parliamentary reform. Gladstone was a great orator and moral figure, yet he staunchly opposed extending the vote to women.

FEMALE SUFFRAGE

Gladstone's most notable pronouncement on the question of woman suffrage was a letter to Samuel Smith, published in 1892, which is reproduced here. Intensely religious, Gladstone endorsed conventional assumptions concerning the distinctiveness of women's nature. Though he will not say whether the social roles of women or men are higher, they are irrevocably fixed by natural differences. Gladstone's main concern is fear that enfranchising women will damage them: "The fear I have is, lest we should invite her unwittingly to trespass upon the delicacy, the purity, the refinement, the elevation of her own nature, which are the present sources of its power."

FEMALE SUFFRAGE

1, CARLTON GARDENS,
April 11, 1892.

DEAR MR. SAMUEL SMITH,

In reply to your letter, I cannot but express the hope that the House of Commons will not consent to the second reading of the Bill for Extending the Parliamentary Suffrage to Women, which will come before it on the 27th instant.

The Bill is a narrow Bill, inasmuch as it excludes from its operation the entire body of married women; who are not less reflective, intelligent, and virtuous, than their unmarried sisters, and who must I think be superior in another great element of fitness, namely the lifelong habit of responsible action. If this change is to be made, I certainly have doubts, not yet dispelled, whether it ought to be made in the shape which would thus be given it by a halting and inconsistent measure.

But it is a change which obviously, and apart from disputable matter, ought not to be made without the fullest consideration and the most deliberate assent of the nation as well as of the Parliament. Not only has there been no such assent, but there has not been even an approach to such consideration. The subject has occupied a large place in the minds of many thoughtful persons, and of these a portion have become its zealous adherents. Just weight should be allowed to their sentiments, and it is desirable that the arguments on both sides should be carefully and generally scrutinised: but the subject is as yet only sectional, and has not really been taken into view by the public mind at large. Can it be right, under these circumstances, that the principle of a change so profound should be adopted? Cannot its promoters be content with that continuance and extension of discussion, which alone can adequately sift the true merits of their cause?

I offer this suggestion in the face of the coming Election. I am aware that no legitimate or effectual use can be made of it for carrying to an issue a question at once so great and so novel; but I do not doubt, considering the zeal and ability which are enlisted in its favour, that the occasion might be made available for procuring an increase of attention to the subject, which I join with them in earnestly desiring.

There are very special reasons for circumspection in this particular case. There has never within my knowledge been a case in which the franchise has been extended to a large body of persons generally indifferent about receiving it. But here, in addition to a widespread indifference, there is on the part of large numbers of women who have considered the matter for themselves, the most positive objection and strong disapprobation. Is it not clear to every unbiased mind that before forcing on them what they conceive to be a fundamental change in their whole social function, that is to say in their Providential calling, at least it should be ascertained that the womanly mind of the country, at present so largely strange to the subject, is in overwhelming proportion, and with deliberate purpose, set upon securing it?

I speak of the change as being a fundamental change in the whole social function of woman, because I am bound in considering the Bill to take into view not only what it enacts, but what it involves. The first of these, though important, is small in comparison with the last.

What the Bill enacts is simply to place the individual woman on the same footing in regard to Parliamentary elections, as the individual man. She is to vote, she is to propose or nominate, she is to be designated by the law as competent to use and to direct, with advantage not only to the community but to herself, all those public agencies which belong to our system of Parliamentary representation. She, not the individual woman, marked by special tastes, possessed of special gifts, but the woman as such, is by this change to be plenarily launched into the whirlpool of public life, such as it is in the nineteenth, and such as it is to be in the twentieth century.

So much for what the Bill enacts: now for what it involves, and involves in the way of fair and rational, and therefore of morally necessary, consequence. For a long time, we drew a distinction between competency to vote and competency to sit in Parliament. But long before our electorate had attained to the present popular proportions, this distinction was felt to involve a palpable inconsistency, and accordingly it died away. It surely cannot be revived: and if it cannot be revived, then the woman's vote carries with it, whether by the same Bill or by a consequential Bill, the woman's seat in Parliament. These assertions ought to be strictly tested. But, if they cannot be confuted, do not let them be ignored.

If the woman's vote carries with it the woman's seat, have we at this point reached our terminus, and found a standing ground which we can in reason and in justice regard as final? Capacity to sit in the House of Commons now legally and practically draws in its train capacity to fill every office in the State. Can we alter this rule and determine to have two categories of Members of Parliament, one of them, the established and the larger one, consisting of persons who can travel without check along all the lines of public duty and honour, the other, the novel and the smaller one, stamped with disability for the discharge of executive, administrative, judicial, or other public duty? Such a stamp would I apprehend be a brand. There is nothing more odious, nothing more untenable, than an inequality in legal privilege which does not stand upon some principle in its nature broad and clear. Is there here such a principle, adequate to show that when capacity to sit in Parliament has been established, the title to discharge executive and judicial duty can be withheld? Tried by the test of feeling, the distinction would be offensive. Would it stand better under the laws of logic? It would stand still worse, if worse be possible. For the proposition we should have to maintain would be this. The legislative duty is the highest of all public duties; for this we admit your fitness. Executive and judicial duties rank below it: and for these we declare you unfit.

I think it impossible to deny that there have been and are women individually fit for any public office however masculine its character; just as there are persons under the age of twenty-one better fitted than many of those beyond it for the discharge of the duties of full citizenship. In neither case does the argument derived from exceptional instances seem to justify the abolition of the general rule. But the risks involved in the two suppositions are immeasurably different. In the one, individual judgment and authority plainly would have to distinguish between childhood and manhood, and to specify a criterion of competency in each case, which is now more conveniently fixed by the uniformity of law. In the other, a permanent and vast difference of type has been impressed upon women and men respectively by the Maker of both. Their differences of social office rest mainly upon causes, not flexible and elastic like most mental qualities, but physical and in their nature unchangeable. I for one am not prepared to say which of the two sexes has the higher and which has the lower province. But I recognize the subtle and profound character of the differences between them, and I must again, and again, and again, deliberate before aiding in the issue of what seems an invitation by public authority to the one to renounce as far as possible its own office, in order to assume that of the other. I am not without the fear lest beginning with the State, we should eventually be found to have intruded into what is yet more fundamental and more sacred, the precinct of the family, and should dislocate, or injuriously modify, the relations of domestic life.

As this is not a party question, or a class question, so neither is it a sex question. I have no fear lest the woman should encroach upon the power of the man. The fear I have is, lest we should invite her unwittingly to trespass upon the delicacy, the purity, the refinement, the elevation of her own nature, which are the present sources of its power. I admit that we have often, as legislators, been most unfaithful guardians of her rights to moral and social equality. And I do not say that full justice has in all things yet been done; but such great progress has been made in most things, that in regard to what may still remain the necessity for violent remedies has not yet been shown. I admit that in the Universities, in the professions, in the secondary circles of public action, we have already gone so far as to give a shadow of plausibility to the present proposals to go farther; but it is a shadow only, for we have done nothing that plunges the woman as such into the turmoil of masculine life. My disposition is to do all for her which is free from that danger and reproach, but to take no step in advance until I am convinced of its safety. The stake is enormous. The affirmation pleas are to my mind not clear, and, even if I thought them clearer, I should deny that they were pressing.

Such being the state of the evidence, and also such the immaturity of the public mind, I earnestly hope that the House of Commons will decline to give a second reading to the Woman's Suffrage Bill.

> I remain, dear Mr. S. Smith,
> Very faithfully yours,
> *W. E. Gladstone*

REPLY TO MR. GLADSTONE'S LETTER ON WOMAN SUFFRAGE

Along with Gladstone's letter, we include a response by "a Member of the Women's Liberal Federation," also published in 1892. The author counters Gladstone's main arguments. For instance, Gladstone exaggerates the extent to which suffrage will disrupt "the whole social function of woman." If this is true, how is it that the women of Wyoming, who have enjoyed the rights of suffrage for more than 20 years, are still as womanly as Englishwomen? Gladstone emphasizes differences between men and women that are "physical and unchangeable." But history has shown that men and women are able to evolve and so change with circumstances. Women's distinctive qualities are not preserved by denying them their "just rights," but "by upholding that which makes her a human being in its full sense, free of choice, with issues as vast as those you possess yourself; a soul as divine; an immortality as profound."

A REPLY TO MR. GLADSTONE'S LETTER ON WOMAN SUFFRAGE

SIR,

I have been one of those women—perhaps altogether in the minority—who have refrained in the course of our work for a great cause, from taking sides on the question of Woman Suffrage, with the hope that some clearer light might be thrown upon it by one whom we regard as a great leader. But now that we women have received your expression of opinion upon it, I for one feel it may not be amiss to offer a reply, and on the large ground that no considerations of expediency, no temporary end, however important, should ever be allowed to lead us aside from principles which are based, not upon caprice, prejudice, or momentary conditions, but eternal justice.

Permit me, Sir, briefly to review your arguments.

"The Bill does not include married women." The conferring of the franchise has always been progressive in character; there has been some substantial opposition to conferring the vote on married women, an opposition in which I do not share, and with which I have no sympathy, which is entirely absent in the cases for which that Bill would have provided. Moreover, the "lifelong habit of responsible action" is surely exercised by those women who are alone and have been widows for years, who have had to provide for and bring up families and single women who are working for a living, and have the sole management of their property, and not infrequently the care of relatives' children.

Again, when you assert that there has been not only no assent to this reform, but no approach to it, you certainly very seriously overstate the facts. The question of Woman Suffrage has been before the nation for the last twenty-five years, and frequently before Parliament, and has been steadily supported by intelligent women and men, and by the press in an increasing degree. But for the pains taken to suppress its discussion in Parliament of late—all the more easy to arrange from the fact that *no* class of women is represented—the public education would have been far more complete even than it is. The change can hardly be termed "profound" either. Measures involving far more positive and extensive action on the part of women have been passed, and have been found to be both useful and beneficial to the community. For a striking example of a woman to whom ideas of this kind are never applied, we need only refer to our Queen.

You assert that a certain proportion of women are hostile to the franchise. Probably they are. Probably they are also excellent women in many respects, although lacking in that growing appreciation of the just and right as such, which marks the women no less than the men of a younger generation, and is one of the most hopeful signs of our day. But are they obliged to use their vote if they possess it? And should they be permitted to coerce other women by their own narrower views? If the possession of the franchise involves what you describe as a "fundamental change in the whole social function of woman", how is it that the women of Wyoming, in the United States, are quite as womanly as Englishwomen, and that the State in question has shown such a marked social and electoral improvement since women were nobly included among its electors, even at the risk—found to be groundless—of the State being excluded from representation in the Union?

Even if the act of voting plunged women into the "whirlpool of public life", just as much may be said with regard to the stage, ballet-dancing, and other occupations, which not only actually do this, but bring women into direct and frequent contact with objectionable men, and publicly expose them to the gaze of those who are generally far from exalted in mind or morals. But to tell the truth, the association of which your esteemed wife herself is the President, presents aspects in its public work and meeting far more in accordance with your description than the simple exercise of the franchise. Of this you must certainly be aware. And does any thinking person consider this an objection to the valuable work of that association?

The assertion that the woman's vote carries with it the woman's seat, is pure speculation. It is outside the domain of practical politics in our day altogether, and need not even be discussed. The time may eventually come when natural capacity and high principle may count for something more than difference of sex with regard to any office; but we are very far from such an ideal state of human life, and I might add, far below it. Using your own words in other relations it may well be said that "nothing is more odious, nothing more untenable, than an inequality in legal privilege", which is based on the mere physical differences of man and woman, and which disregards all those higher qualities of mind and soul which both possess in common.

I take it, the aim of all politics—unfortunate term!—should be the amelioration of human life, the growth of progress and reform, the breaking down of selfish and unfraternal privileges and barriers, whether of race, caste, creed, or sex—and in this woman must share with man.

You add, Sir, in the close of your letter, that a "permanent and vast difference of type has been impressed upon women and men respectively by the Maker of both," and state that their "differences of social office" are "physical and unchangeable". But they are also temporary, and not only temporary as regards the individual, but as regards the race. Evolution clearly shows us that even physical nature is plastic, and that man himself becomes at a certain stage of his evolution creative, and that he has been at all times a creative force, and a producer of environments on our planet. Sex may embrace not only one plane, but many planes, until we ascend from the physical to the spiritual, where it ceases to operate. For the spiritual is eternal; there is no sex in soul, and therefore, "In *Christ Jesus* (or the divine nature), there is neither male nor female". And men and women, as such, and now, possess infinitely more in common, than apart. No, Sir, it is not by depriving woman, or any portion of womanhood, of just rights, that you can preserve "her delicacy, purity and refinement", it is not by accentuating sex that you can promote the "elevation of her own nature"; it is by upholding that which makes her a human being in its full sense, free of choice, with issues as vast as those you possess yourself; a soul as divine; an immortality as profound. If "delicacy and refinement" are the results of the old system of regarding womanhood, what are we to say of our musichalls, our casinos, of such a spectacle as the Strand presents any night in London, and of the various diversions which are brought forward for the dubious amusements of men? In these sex is the supreme and central attraction, and unfortunately "the present sources of its power" are very far from being on the plane which would make man noble and woman free.

In carrying the idea of womanly dependence beyond the domain of sentiment, which is its sole legitimate expression, and converting it into a system of religious and legal oppression and moral inequality, a foul wrong has been perpetrated, not only on womanhood but on the entire race, whose excessive and perverted sexual instincts show the natural consequences. We have no quarrel with sentiments of nature expressed in *freedom;* we oppose that repressive system which deprives woman of her spiritual birthright, and is subversive of all that is exalted in life.

There remains no further argument in your letter deserving of pressing notice, and in furnishing what may be justly considered logically unanswerable rejoinders to the statements and opinions given in its pages, I earnestly trust you may be led at no distant date to remove a growing stain upon the Liberal cause, to reconsider the question of Woman Suffrage, and to look at it in the clear and simple light of Justice.

I remain, Sir,
Yours very respectfully,
S. E. G.

The Rt. Hon. W. E. GLADSTONE, M.P.
June, 1892.

AN APPEAL AGAINST
FEMALE SUFFRAGE

The appearance of "An Appeal against Female Suffrage" in the June 1889 issue of *The Nineteenth Century* marked the beginning of an organized antisuffrage movement in Britain. A petition, signed by 104 notable women, the "Appeal" presents in capsule form a series of arguments: that men and women have separate spheres; that suffrage would have unfortunate effects on women's character and position; that the extension of suffrage to women is beset with practical difficulties; that the proposed reform is hasty. It is interesting to note that the authors of the "Appeal" embrace "all recent efforts" that had given women greater participation in community affairs, including the right to vote for and serve as members of School boards and other public bodies. But the authors staunchly oppose further progress: "We believe that the emancipating process has now reached the limits fixed by the physical constitution of women...." In *Women's Suffrage: A Short History of a Great Movement* (1912), the suffragette leader Millicent Fawcett notes that many signers of this petition later moved to the prosuffrage side of the issue. But the arguments they expressed in the "Appeal" did not undergo similar evolution.

"AN APPEAL AGAINST FEMALE SUFFRAGE."

We, the undersigned, wish to appeal to the common sense and the educated thought of the men and women of England against the proposed extension of the Parliamentary suffrage to women.

1. While desiring the fullest possible development of the powers, energies, and education of women, we believe that their work for the State, and their responsibilities towards it, must always differ essentially from those of men, and that therefore their share in the working of the State machinery should be different from that assigned to men. Certain large departments of the national life are of necessity worked exclusively by men. To men belong the struggle of debate and legislation in Parliament; the hard and exhausting labour implied in the administration of the national resources and powers; the conduct of England's relations towards the external world; the working of the army and navy; all the heavy, laborious, fundamental industries of the State, such as those of mines, metals, and railways; the lead and supervision of English commerce, the management of our vast English finance, the service of that merchant fleet on which our food supply depends. In all these spheres women's direct participation is made impossible either by the disabilities of sex, or by strong formations of custom and habit resting ultimately upon physical difference, against which it is useless to contend. They are affected indeed, in some degree, by all these national activities; therefore they ought in some degree to have an influence on them all. This influence they already have, and will have more and more as the education of women advances. But their direct interest in these matters can never equal that of men, whose whole energy of mind and body is daily and hourly risked in them. Therefore it is not just to give women direct power of deciding questions of Parliamentary policy, of war, of foreign or colonial affairs, of commerce and finance equal to that possessed by men. We hold that they already possess an influence on political matters fully proportioned to the possible share of women in the political activities of England.

At the same time we are heartily in sympathy with all the recent efforts which have been made to give women a more important part in those affairs of the community where their interests and those of men are equally concerned; where it is possible for them not only to decide but to help in carrying out, and where, therefore, judgment is weighted by a true responsibility, and can be guided by experience and the practical information which comes from it. As voters for or members of School Boards, Boards of Guardians, and other important public bodies, women have now opportunities for public usefulness which must promote the growth of character, and at the same time strengthen among them the social sense and habit. All these changes of recent years, together with the great improvements in women's education which have accompanied them, we cordially welcome. But we believe that the emancipating process has now reached the limits fixed by the physical constitution of women, and by the fundamental difference which must always exist between their main occupations and those of men. The care of the sick and the insane; the treatment of the poor; the education of children; in all these matters, and others besides, they have made good their claim to larger and more extended powers. We rejoice in it. But when it comes to questions of foreign or colonial policy, or of grave constitutional change, then we maintain that the necessary and normal experience of women—speaking generally and in the mass—does not and can never provide them with such materials for sound judgment as are open to men.

To sum up: we would give them their full share in the State of social effort and social mechanism; we look for their increasing activity in that higher State which rests on thought, conscience, and moral influence; but we protest against their admission to direct power in that State, which *does* rest upon force—the State in its administrative, military and financial aspects—where the physical capacity, the accumulated experience and inherited training of men ought to prevail without the harassing interference of those who, though they may be partners with men in debate, can in these matters never be partners with them in action.

2. If we turn from the *right* of women to the suffrage—a right which on grounds just given we deny—to the effect which the possession of the suffrage may be expected to have on their character and position and on family life, we find ourselves no less in doubt. It is urged that the influence of women in politics would tell upon the side of morality. We believe that it does so tell already, and will do so with greater force as women by improved education fit themselves to exert it more widely and efficiently. But it may be asked, On what does this moral influence depend? We believe that it depends largely on qualities which the natural position and functions of women as they are at present tend to develop, and which might be seriously impaired by their admission to the turmoil of active political life. These qualities are, above all, sympathy and disinterestedness. Any disposition of things which threatens to lessen the national reserve of such forces as these we hold to be a misfortune. It is notoriously difficult to maintain them in the presence of party necessities and in the heat of party struggle. Were women admitted to this struggle, their natural eagerness and quickness of temper would probably make them hotter partisans than men. As their political relations stand at present, they tend to check in them the disposition to partisanship, and to strengthen in them the qualities of sympathy and disinterestedness. We believe that their admission to the suffrage would precisely reverse this condition of things, and that the whole nation would suffer in consequence. For whatever may be the duty and privilege of the parliamentary vote for men, we hold that citizenship is not

dependent upon or identical with the possession of the suffrage. Citizenship lies in the participation of each individual in effort for the good of the community. And we believe that women will be more valuable citizens, will contribute more precious elements to the national life without the vote than with it. The quickness to feel, the willingness to lay aside prudential considerations in a right cause, which are amongst the peculiar excellencies of women, are in their right place when they are used to influence the more highly trained and developed judgment of men. But if this quickness of feeling could be immediately and directly translated into public action, in matters of vast and complicated political import, the risks of politics would be enormously increased, and what is now a national blessing might easily become a national calamity. On the one hand, then, we believe that to admit women to the ordinary machinery of political life would inflame the partisanship and increase the evils, already so conspicuous, of that life, would tend to blunt the special moral qualities of women, and so to lessen the national reserves of moral force; and, on the other hand, we dread the political and practical effects which, in our belief, would follow on such a transformation as is proposed, of an influence which is now beneficent largely because it is indirect and gradual.

3. Proposals for the extension of the suffrage to women are beset with grave political difficulties. If votes be given to unmarried women on the same terms as they are given to men, large numbers of women leading immoral lives will be enfranchised on the one hand, while married women, who, as a rule, have passed through more of the practical experiences of life than the unmarried, will be excluded. To remedy part of this difficulty it is proposed by a large section of those who advocate the extension of the suffrage to women, to admit married women with the requisite property qualification. This proposal—an obviously just one if the suffrage is to be extended to women at all—introduces changes in family life, and in the English conception of the household, of enormous importance, which have never been adequately considered. We are practically invited to embark upon them because a few women of property possessing already all the influence which belongs to property, and a full share of that public protection and safety which is the fruit of taxation, feel themselves aggrieved by the denial of the parliamentary vote. The grievance put forward seems to us wholly disproportionate to the claim based upon it.

4. A survey of the manner in which this proposal has won its way into practical politics leads us to think that it is by no means ripe for legislative solution. A social change of momentous gravity has been proposed; the mass of those immediately concerned in it are notoriously indifferent; there has been no serious and general demand for it, as is always the case if a grievance is real and reform necessary; the amount of information collected is quite inadequate to the importance of the issue; and the public has gone through no sufficient discipline of discussion on the subject. Meanwhile

pledges to support female suffrage have been hastily given in the hopes of strengthening existing political parties by the female vote. No doubt there are many conscientious supporters of female suffrage amongst members of Parliament; but it is hard to deny that the present prominence of the question is due to party considerations of a temporary nature. It is, we submit, altogether unworthy of the intrinsic gravity of the question that it should be determined by reference to the passing needs of party organisation. Meanwhile we remember that great electoral changes have been carried out during recent years. Masses of new electors have been added to the constituency. These new elements have still to be assimilated; these new electors have still to be trained to take their part in the national work; and while such changes are still fresh, and their issues uncertain, we protest against any further alteration in our main political machinery, especially when it is an alteration which involves a new principle of extraordinary range and significance, closely connected with the complicated problems of sex and family life.

5. It is often urged that certain injustices of the law towards women would be easily and quickly remedied were the political power of the vote conceded to them; and that there are many wants, especially among working women, which are now neglected, but which the suffrage would enable them to press on public attention. We reply that during the past half century all the principal injustices of the law towards women have been amended by means of the existing constitutional machinery; and with regard to those that remain, we see no signs of any unwillingness on the part of Parliament to deal with them. On the contrary, we remark a growing sensitiveness to the claims of women, and the rise of a new spirit of justice and sympathy among men, answering to those advances made by women in education, and the best kind of social influence, which we have already noticed and welcomed. With regard to the business or trade interests of women—here, again, we think it safer and wiser to trust to organisation and self-help on their own part, and to the growth of a better public opinion among the men workers, than to the exercise of a political right which may easily bring women into direct and hasty conflict with men.

In conclusion: nothing can be further from our minds than to seek to depreciate the position or the importance of women. It is because we are keenly alive to the enormous value of their special contribution to the community, that we oppose what seems to us likely to endanger that contribution. We are convinced that the pursuit of a mere outward equality with men is for women not only vain but demoralising. It leads to a total misconception of woman's true dignity and special mission. It tends to personal struggle and rivalry, where the only effort of both the great divisions of the human family should be to contribute the characteristic labour and the best gifts of each to the common stock.

WOMEN'S SUFFRAGE: A REPLY

The "Appeal" received a reply in the July 1889 issue of *The Fortnightly Review*. Over two thousand women signed a petition "to express their approval of the proposed extension of the Parliamentary Franchise to Women, which they believe would be beneficial both to them and of the State." For reasons of space, only some 500 names were printed in *The Fortnightly Review*. Here we reproduce the article that accompanied the petition

The "Reply" directly addresses the arguments of the "Appeal." For instance, the latter presents claims concerning women's distinctive nature and how this makes them suited only for activities different from men's. The "Reply" argues that these differences give women interests different from men's, which can be protected only by the vote. To the "Appeal's" claim that "all the principal injustices of the law towards women" have been addressed by existing constitutional machinery, the "Reply" presents an entire litany of discriminatory laws and practices that had not been addressed. Especially notable is the "Reply's" observation concerning the social and economic background of the women who had produced the antisuffrage document: "The names of women who live by their work are very scantily represented." Raised in comfort and security, these women are insulated from the conditions of women who work for a living. "The position of women of the industrial classes is one where the protection of representation would be of special use," as they are constantly threatened by legislation hostile to their interests that favors the interests of men.

WOMEN'S SUFFRAGE: A REPLY.

One hundred and four ladies have appealed in the June number of *The Nineteenth Century* to "the common-sense and educated thought of the men and women of England against the proposed extension of the Parliamentary suffrage to women."

For more than twenty years the supporters of woman's suffrage have been appealing to "the common-sense and educated thought" of the men and women of their country, to show cause why those women who fulfil the qualifications demanded by law of male electors and have been admitted with good results and with no appreciable harm whatever, to various other franchises, should still be denied the exercise of the parliamentary vote. "Common-sense" may take fright at an entirely new experiment. It was not unnatural that persons of a cautious disposition should view with apprehension any change in the status of women which it was feared might endanger the quiet of home life, and introduce an element of discord between men and women. This apprehension was even felt at one time in regard to the admission of ladies to hear debates in the House of Commons. But experience and a more cultivated common-sense have removed these fears. Women have been admitted to many kinds of electoral privileges and to much public work involving grave responsibility, and none of the apprehended evils have followed. Nature is very strong; women have not ceased to be women because they have learnt Latin, or voted for County Councillors, or become Poor Law Guardians. The "Ewig Weibliche" has not only survived all this, it has been strengthened. The specially womanly work of the care and education of children, the nursing of the sick, the reclamation of the wreckage of society, the study of the purely domestic arts, are now undertaken by women with more system and more devotion than at any previous period.

The ladies who sign the protest avow their belief that the influence of women in politics tells on the side of morality. "Common-sense" appears to indicate that any force which tells on the side of morality in politics would be of benefit to the State if it were given a legitimate and constitutional form of expression through admission to the franchise. The protesting ladies, however, fear that the beneficial moral influence now exerted by women on politics would be "seriously impaired by their admission to the turmoil of active political life." It should not be forgotten that whether women vote or not, all parties in the State are now inviting them to take part in the turmoil of active political life. Within a few days of the appearance of the protest, Lord Salisbury was addressing the ladies of the Primrose League and Mr. Gladstone was addressing the ladies of the Liberal Federation, and each party leader was calling on women to enter into the fight to help his own side. As a matter of fact, no contested election now passes without each party availing itself of the help of women. It is not intended here to argue whether this is desirable or undesirable in itself; but it must be obvious that it is a state of things which puts the quiet, retiring woman, to whom the publicity and rowdyism of elections are distasteful, at a disadvantage. It would be easy for such a woman to walk to the polling booth and give a vote; but so long as women may make speeches and canvass electors but not vote, the quiet, typically domestic woman is precluded from the only expression of her political views which would not be repugnant or impossible to her.

It is certainly strange to hear ladies who are foremost in inviting women to organize themselves on this side or that of the greatest constitutional struggle which has taken place during the last two hundred years, gravely asserting, as they do in this protest, that it would be a misfortune to admit women to share in the ordinary machinery of political life. Women form a part of "the machinery" already; and the very same ladies, or some of them, who deprecate, in *The Nineteenth Century*, the introduction of women into political controversy, are, as presidents and vice-presidents of political associations, urging upon their fellow-countrywomen the duty of mastering difficult and complicated political problems, and describing to them how they should organize themselves, and what work they should undertake, with the view of influencing the verdict of the country at the next general election. It would be almost incredible, if it were not true, that some of the very ladies who are working most actively in this way and urging other women to work, assert in this protest that the necessary and normal experience of women "does not and can never provide them with such materials for forming a sound judgment," in questions of grave constitutional change, "as are open to men." The comparison with men cannot but remind us that, in Lord Tennyson's words, we have for good or ill taken "the suffrage of the plough." The woman householder and property-owner, whom it is proposed to enfranchise, need not fear comparison in education, in knowledge, in variety of experience, and generally speaking, in materials for forming a sound judgment in questions involving grave constitutional change, with the vast mass of the newly enfranchised electors. If personal fitness for the intelligent exercise of the franchise be the main consideration, the women who would be enfranchised cannot be held to be less fit to vote than the chimney-sweeps and labourers who vote already. Not here and there one, but in thousands of cases all over the country, women, as employers of labour, enable a number of men to possess votes, while they, whose education and means of forming a judgment on political questions may be presumed to be superior to that of the men they employ, are precluded from voting. One of the things that recommends women's suffrage to many minds is the undoubted fact that it would tend to raise the average of intelligence and education among the electorate.

The ladies' protest gives prominence to the fact that women's work for the State is different from that of men, and that many minor differences follow as a natural consequence from the fundamental difference of sex. This difference is one of the strongest claims which women have to representation. If men and women were exactly alike, and thought and felt alike on all subjects, if their work in the world were exactly the same, women would not suffer, and the State would not suffer, from the non-representation of one part of the homogeneous mass. But being different, that wherein they differ remains unrepresented. It is a loss to the State that women's knowledge of home and domestic life, their experience on such subjects as the care of children and the service of the poor, should not have its weight in influencing the representation of the country and the course of legislation. It is not urged that these things, of which women have a special knowledge, should have a preponderating influence; but if Parliament is to be the mirror of the nation, they should have their place in the representative system. More than one instance could be adduced in which blunders have been made in Parliament because, while the naval, military, banking, agricultural, and other interests were fully and zealously represented, the interests of the home and domestic life were too much forgotten. If every member of Parliament had ten or twelve per cent. of women among his constituents he would be much more apt than he is at present to think, when any new bill is placed in his hands, "How will this affect home-life? what will the women in my constituency think of this?"

Equally gratuitous with the assumption that "common-sense" supports the exclusion of a valuable moral force from representation, is the assertion that the demand for women's suffrage proceeds merely from a few women of property who feel themselves aggrieved by the denial of the parliamentary vote. It may be noted in passing that the names of the women who live by their work are very scantily represented in *The Nineteenth Century* protest; whilst those who are in ordinary parlance spoken of as working women are conspicuously absent. On the other hand, hundreds of thousands of women, chiefly of the working class, have for years been petitioning Parliament for the suffrage. The largest halls in all the largest towns of the country have been filled to overflowing by women of all classes making the same demand. In working women's clubs the subject of women's suffrage is not much discussed because, to quote one of the members, "you can't discuss when you're all agreed." Large numbers of the poorer classes of professional women, those who maintain themselves by teaching and writing, are warmly in favour of an extension of the suffrage of their own sex. It is desired to speak with all personal respect of the ladies who signed *The Nineteenth Century* protest; they have as great a right to express their opinions as those who disagree with them (that is, if all women are not out of court, because of their alleged "lack of material for forming a sound judgment on questions of grave constitutional change"). But the obvious criticism of the list of names in *The Nineteenth Century* is that they are those of ladies who "have but fed on the roses and lain in the lilies of life." They have been surrounded by every comfort, unpurchased by effort on their part. The names of very many are chiefly known through those of the distinguished men who have fought the battle of life for them. Hardly one has stood alone in the world to "journey her stage and earn her wage" with no one but herself to look to for help. May it not be hoped that these ladies will see that "the materials for forming a sound judgment on this question of grave constitutional change" are more likely to be possessed by those to whom fortune has decreed a less sheltered nook from the storms of life?

Mrs. Henry Sidgwick, whose work in connection with education has brought her into contact with large numbers of women who earn their living by teaching, was speaking a few weeks ago on the aspect of women's suffrage in regard to the needs of this class. She said her

> "educational work at Cambridge had brought her largely into connection with women of the professional classes who were working for their own support, and often for that of their families as well; and it was from their point of view that the question of women's suffrage

naturally presented itself to her. She thought it was often forgotten how numerous those women were, how large a proportion of the women of the more educated classes were unmarried and dependent on themselves. They were apt to lead somewhat isolated lives, and, being out of sight, to be out of mind. Nevertheless, they were existent, and large numbers of them were very active and useful members of society. And it seemed anomalous and indefensible that they should be left to struggle for existence—just as they would if they were men—should have the burdens of responsible and independent citizens, as men had, and yet that whatever protection to their interests Parliamentary representation would afford them should be withheld from them."

The position of women of the industrial classes is one where the protection of representation would be of special use. Their industrial position is constantly liable to be threatened by hostile legislation. Trade unions are exceedingly and naturally jealous of the competition of women's labour. They are powerfully represented in Parliament, and hardly a session passes without some attempt being made to protect by law the trade interests of men, and to hamper and restrict the industrial employment of women. The case of the pit-brow women is not yet forgotten. It may be contended that this instance is favourable to those who argue that women can protect their interests without representation. It is true that, by vigorous effort, by stumping the country, by scattering broadcast photographs of the women in their working clothes, by diligent "lobbying" in the House of Commons, and also because the interests of the women coincided with those of their employers, the pit-brow women have held their own. But who can tell how soon the attack on their industry will be renewed? The representatives of the men's and women's side of the question met not very long ago. One who spoke on behalf of the men's trades union said, "You have won now, but we shall win in the long run, because we have votes and you have not." If the women were represented as well as the men, attempts to deprive women by law of an honest and healthy way of earning a living would never be made, and, consequently, much friction and mutual anger, always so much to be deprecated between the sexes, would be avoided.

The ladies in *The Nineteenth Century* support their case by stating that "all the principal injustices of the law towards women have been amended by means of the existing constitutional machinery." They may not know that the law still recognises in a mother no legal rights over her children during the lifetime of her husband. A husband may remove his children entirely from their mother, not allowing her even to see them or correspond with them, and this for no moral fault on her part, but just because he chooses to have it so. The inequality of the divorce law is another well-known instance of the cases in which the existing constitutional machinery has remained placidly content with a state of things unjust to women. The inequalities of the law of intestacy, as regards men and women, are so flagrant as to be almost ludicrous. Existing constitutional machinery has arranged that in almost every case of intestacy the male relatives get the lion's share. Thus, if a woman die intestate, all she has, to the exclusion of her children and nearest relatives, goes to her husband. But if a husband die intestate, in no case does his wife inherit all he has. If there are a child or children, two-thirds go to the child or children, and one-third to the wife. If there are no children, but the intestate leaves a wife and a father, they receive half each. If there are a wife and distant relatives, the wife receives half, and the other half is divided amongst the next-of-kin. If there is a wife and absolutely no other relative whatever, the wife still receives only half, and the other half goes to the Crown.

A similar kind of inequality is maintained as regards probate. A widow has to pay duty on every piece of furniture and every article of plate and jewellery in her house. Every item of her and her husband's common property is assumed by the law to be the property of the husband only, and on passing into possession of it the widow has to pay duty to the uttermost farthing. She is thus frequently called upon to pay duty on articles which she may have bought with her own earnings, or which may have been given to her by her own relatives. If she is so unwary as to have had a common banking account with her husband standing in his name, she has to pay probate on her money as well as on his. It is unnecessary to point out that to the whole professional class this necessity of paying probate on what in many cases is the widow's own property, comes at a time when she is impoverished by the death of the chief bread-winner of the family. No such harassing and exacting demands are made upon a man who loses his wife. The assumption of the law is that all their joint property is his only, and he pays no probate on plate, furniture, &c., which they may have worked for and bought together.

It is not, however, denied that some of the most gross of the injustices of the law to women have been remedied during the last ten or twelve years. This has been due in great part to the untiring exertions of the same men and women who are now urging the justice and the expediency of extending the parliamentary suffrage to women. Neither the removal of injustices nor the progress that has been made in the social status of women owe much to the ladies who sign *The Nineteenth Century* protest; but they are kind enough to say that they rejoice in every improvement that has already taken place in the position of women, and they appear to acquiesce in the removal of injustices which have been already removed. But they seem to think improvement may be carried too far. They are like Mr. Brooke in *Middlemarch:* "The fact is human reason may carry you too far— over the hedge, in fact. It carried me a good way at one time; but I saw it would not do. I pulled up. I pulled up in time. But not too hard." In like manner these ladies have no fault to find with the successful efforts which have been made by others to improve the position of women, socially and legally. But the time has come to "pull up." "The emancipating process has now," they declare, "reached the limits fixed by the physical constitution of women." If is not plain why the recording of a vote for a member of Parliament should be beyond the limits fixed by the physical constitution of women. It women may "nurse the sick and take care of the insane," if they may sit on school boards and on boards of guardians, it is not easy to see why their physical constitution stands in the way of their putting a piece of paper in the ballot-box at a parliamentary election. Miss Florence Nightingale, when she went out to the Crimea, had, for several months, ten thousand sick and wounded men under her care. She has been known, in the discharge of her duties, to stand for twenty hours at a stretch. Here was work of which it might, with much plausibility, have been said that it was outside "the limits fixed by the physical constitution of women." And yet it was found that her work was truly womanly, and has had a lasting influence for good on an important department of women's work for all time.

If the extension of the suffrage to duly qualified women is granted, no more will be required of each woman elector in the way of physical or mental effort than is now required of each male elector. In the first place, she will be free to vote or not vote as she chooses. Talk about having the suffrage forced upon her is nonsense. She will not be required to have a complete mastery of finance, or to take the lead and supervision of commerce, or to direct the discipline of the army and navy, or to have mastered the whole of the recent history of British policy in Egypt, South Africa and India. If no men were allowed to vote unless they obtained a pass in all these subjects, the number of electors would be considerably reduced. At the next general election the question which will be most prominently before the electorate will be that of Home Rule. It cannot be that the ladies who sign *The Nineteenth Century* protest think that this is a subject on which the physical constitution of women forbids her forming a rational judgment. For several of the protesting ladies have already expressed their adherence or opposition to Home Rule and are urging other women to do the same. The objections which they urge to women's suffrage on the ground of women's want of knowledge of finance, of the army and navy, of commerce, and foreign policy and so on, would have weight if it were proposed to appoint women to be heads of the departments to which these great national interests are entrusted. They have no weight whatever when applied to the much humbler function of voting for a member of Parliament.

Again the ladies say: "We look for the increasing activity of women in that higher state which rests on thought, conscience, and moral influence; but we protest against their admission to direct power in that State which *does* rest on force—the State in its administrative, military, and financial aspects—where the physical capacity, the accumulated experience and inherited training of men ought to prevail without the harassing interference of those who, though they may be partners with men in debate, can in these matters never be partners with them in action." In the first place it may be pointed out that the distinction sought to be drawn between the State which rests on force, and the State which does not rest on force, is illusory. The ultimate basis of all law is a combination of moral and physical forces. This is as true of the law administered by a school board or a board of guardians as it is of the highest department of the State. Municipal government, in connection with which women have votes, rests on the police force, and ultimately on the power of demanding military support. Women occupy towards the physical force on which all government rests, exactly the same relation as the great majority of men, that is they help to pay for it. If no man were allowed to vote unless he provided in his own person part of the physical force in which governments, whether municipal or imperial, rest, we should go back to the crudest form of Caesarism, or government by an armed force. Every man whose age or physical infirmity unfitted him to bear arms would be disfranchised, and of course deprived of all administrative authority. Two-third of the statesmen who, at present, on both sides of politics, direct the policy of the country, nearly all the journalists who influence the ultimate decision of the nation as to peace and war and other great questions of state, would, if the rule laid down by the ladies were made absolute, be excluded from all interference with politics, because their age, physical infirmities, or physical incapacity precluded them from providing in their own persons the physical force by which the decrees of governments are carried out. Mr. Froude once suggested that when war was impending between two nations, the Secretaries of State for Foreign Affairs should be informed that if they failed to come to an amicable understanding, the first act of the drama of physical conflict should be a personal encounter between the two ministers, armed with revolvers in the back yard of the Foreign Office. He urged that this condition might have a powerful influence in facilitating a settlement of international disputes without recourse to arms. At present, however, the ingenious suggestion has never been seriously considered. One set of men debate, discuss, and decide on a policy that results in war; another, and a totally different set of men, fight and bleed and die. The exigencies of division of labour seem to render it impossible that the men of debate should be identical with the men of action. Journalists sitting comfortably at their desks may, if they wield a waspish pen, goad and sting two nations into war. Stock exchange speculators have been known to precipitate a conflict for the sake of influencing the price of securities. No one talks of disfranchising these men; and yet the enfranchisement of women householders and property owners is objected to because they would vote ay or no in questions of peace and war, without being the partners of men in the actual conflict.

There are many assumptions entirely unsupported by facts and experience in *The Nineteenth Century* protest. One is that women, if they vote, must say farewell to that "womanly influence" which is supposed to be such a powerful factor in politics at the present time. Every woman's influence is just so much, making allowance for the factitious influence of rank, as her character entitles her to. If she is courageous, modest, truthful, diligent, sympathetic, and regardful of the rights and interests of others, she will be a power for good in whatever *entourage* she finds herself. Influence comes from character. Having a vote or not having a vote will not affect "influence," except in so far as it affects character. *The Nineteenth Century* ladies no doubt think that voting in parliamentary elections will lower the character of women, but they by no means prove that this belief is well founded. All experience, as far as it has gone, points in the opposite direction. In those countries in which the course of civilisation has developed and encouraged the independence and emancipation of women, the character of women, and consequently the whole national character, is far higher than in those countries where women have been subjected to more complete political and social subservience. Those who support women's suffrage do so, not in any spirit of vulgar antagonism or rivalry with men; they recognise frankly and fully the differences between men and women; they do not at all wish to see those differences disregarded, least of all do they wish women to cease to be womanly; they do not base the claims of women to representation mainly on the acknowledged injustice of the existing laws to women; but they support it because the experience of other enfranchising acts has shown that the responsibility which goes with the right of voting has a good influence on character; because the exclusion of otherwise qualified citizens from the right of voting on the ground of sex alone, encourages the view that women are not called upon to act or think about the concerns of their country; and because the admission of women to representation is an adjustment of their political status, bringing it into harmony with changes which have already taken place in their social, educational, and industrial status.

ALBERT V. DICEY

lbert Dicey (1835–1922) was a distinguished English jurist and acade-
mic. Educated at Balliol College, Oxford, he held fellowships at
Balliol, Trinity, and All Souls Colleges, and in 1909 became Vinerian
Professor of Law. His many books include *Introduction to the Study of Law of the
Constitution* (1885, and subsequent editions); *A Digest of the Law of England with
Reference to the Conflict of Laws* (1896); and *Letters to a Friend on Votes for Women*
(1909), two chapters of which are presented here.

LETTERS TO A FRIEND ON VOTES FOR WOMEN (SELECTIONS)

In *Letters to a Friend*, Dicey explains how, though for many years a supporter
of woman suffrage, he had become an opponent. As a jurist, he argues primarily on grounds of law and expediency, rather than inquiring into the subject of women's nature or religious truth. He recognizes that woman suffrage
is in accord with liberal principles of equal rights and majority rule. But full
realization of liberal principles would undermine the English regime. For
instance British rule over Ireland is opposed by the wishes of a majority of the
Irish people: "Conservatism may in some instances be an effort to enforce the
supremacy of common justice, and to maintain the unity of a great nation."
    Granting women the vote is in conflict with historical precedent, the
"lessons to be derived from historical experience embodied in the general, if
not universal, customs of mankind."

As a form of government, democracy is plagued by an excess of emotion. Enfranchising women would only exacerbate this problem. Moreover, the results of the contemplated change could include political instability. Because "the basis of all government is force," granting the vote to women, who constitute the majority of the British population, could create a situation in which a weaker class dictates to a stronger. The sorry experience of enfranchised former slaves in the American South "exemplifies the futility of giving to any class, whether of men or of women, political rights in excess of genuine political power."

Reproduced here are Dicey's Introduction and selections from Letter 4, which contains his main arguments against woman suffrage.

LETTERS TO A FRIEND ON VOTES FOR WOMEN

LETTER I

INTRODUCTION

OXFORD.

MY DEAR C.,

You asked how it has happened that, though I was for many years an advocate, I have now become a convinced opponent of the introduction of woman suffrage into England? The question is a natural one. It is the better worth an answer because my own change of opinion has been shared by many of my contemporaries who began to take an interest in politics some fifty or sixty years ago. We were all of us Liberals; we most of us came under the influence of J. S. Mill, and we could not then have found a wiser, a nobler, and, above all, a more public-spirited teacher of the rights and duties of citizens. Under his guidance we favoured every attempt to extend not only the liberty but also the political rights of women. In my own case, my faith in the benefit to be derived from woman suffrage was enhanced by the circumstance, over which I shall always rejoice, that it was my good fortune to take in early manhood a decided though insignificant part in promoting the education of women. In the success of Bedford College, of Newnham College, and of Somerville College, I felt, and I trust I always will feel, the keenest interest. For many years I identified the extension of women's political power with the effort to procure for them every possible opportunity for the development and employment of their natural gifts.

It is never easy to trace the influences which have brought about an honest change in any of one's own beliefs, whether political or religious.

These influences are a quite different thing from the reasons by which a change may be rightly justified. They are not so much arguments as the conditions under which reasons which at one time seemed decisive lose their force, whilst reasoning, which at one time seemed to carry little weight, gains for one's own mind a new power and significance.

The considerations which, independently of specific arguments, have in respect of woman suffrage told upon my own judgment may be summed up under a few new heads:

First, the movement for the maintenance of the union between England and Ireland brought me for the first time into something like active political life. For nearly a quarter of a century I have joined in resistance to every demand for Home Rule. This circumstance told in several respects upon the way in which I gradually came to look upon the movement in favour of woman suffrage.

My Unionism impressed upon me, as did also my keen sympathy with the Northern States of America in their opposition to secession, the thought that Conservatism may in some instances be an effort to enforce the supremacy of common justice, and to maintain the unity of a great nation. It made me feel that the mere desire of a class, however large, for political power or for national independence affords no conclusive reason why the wish should be granted. It raised in my mind the doubt whether the Liberalism of the day, which I had fully accepted, had not exaggerated the wisdom and the justice of yielding, where possible, to every wish entertained by a large number of our fellow-citizens. Since 1885 I have never doubted that a majority of the inhabitants of Ireland are opposed to the Union with Great Britain. I have also never seen the least reason to doubt that the people of the United Kingdom ought to insist upon the maintenance of the Union. Political action, further, under leaders such as the Duke of Devonshire, John Bright, Chamberlain, and Lord James of Hereford, none of whom showed the least sympathy for the movement of woman suffrage, made me begin to question the strength of the arguments, especially the moral arguments, used in its support. At the same time, Gladstone's appeals to the great heart of the people, to the masses against classes, and generally to the sentiment, showed me how easily emotional politics might produce the palliation of gross injustice. Nor could I fail to perceive with new clearness the danger which lurked under the concession of sovereign power to women, who as a body are more readily influenced than men by the emotions of the moment. I neither assert nor hold that political Unionism is logically inconsistent with the belief that English women ought to receive Parliamentary votes. I merely insist upon the simple fact that the grounds on which most Unionists rest their moral right to maintain the Union against the wishes of the majority of the people of Ireland are opposed to some of the reasons and much of the sentiment which tell in favour of the movement for woman suffrage.

Secondly, thought and also experience convinced me that the current maxims of Liberalism (as also Conservatism), though they may contain a large element of important truth, are never absolutely true principles, from which a wise man can safely draw far-reaching logical deductions. As I hope to show you in a future letter, they may be useful watchwords, but they are nothing more. Hence, as years went by, I came to see that democratic maxims, even when endorsed by Mill, possessed nothing like the authority which, in common with most of my contemporaries at Oxford, I used to ascribe to them. I could no longer accept with something like implicit faith every dogma contained in his treatise 'On Liberty.' Later reflection has, indeed, shown me that, whilst his 'Subjection of Women' contains side by side with much noble sentiment, some singularly fallacious reasoning, the treatise 'On Liberty,' so far from supporting the claim of women to political authority, really supplies an argument against the moral claim either of woman or of any other class of the community to share in political power if such participation is opposed to the welfare of the State. It was a great relief, at any rate to myself, to discover that I could reconcile my enthusiasm for everything which promotes the personal freedom and the education of women with the strenuous denial to them of any share in sovereign power.

By degrees, too, the admiration for Mill's extraordinary gift of logical exposition, as well as gratitude for much of his teaching, became in my mind compatible with the admission that with him the reality, though not the form, of logic is often sacrificed to the influence of moral emotion, and that this subordination of his reason to the force of generous passion is nowhere more noticeable than in his 'Subjection of Women.' Mill theoretically grounds all knowledge on experience, but throughout the treatise he minimizes the importance of natural and undisputed facts; he in effect inculcates the neglect of the lessons to be derived from historical experience embodied in the general, if not universal, customs of mankind; he bids his disciples prefer to such teaching conclusions drawn logically enough from some general dogmas which are far from possessing absolute truth. Thus, in favour of some *a priori* assumption as to the essential equality or similarity of human beings, we are counselled to overlook what has curiously been called the 'accident of sex.'

Thirdly, I at last, though slowly, reached the firm conviction that the right to a Parliamentary vote ought not to be considered the private right of the individual who possesses it. It is in reality not a right at all; it is rather a power or function given to a citizen for the benefit not primarily of himself, but of the public. This is assuredly the doctrine of English law, no less than of common sense. It affords the sole, but also the ample, justification for the punishment of both the giving and the receiving of bribes at a Parliamentary election. It justifies the deprivation of whole classes—such, for example, as the Irish forty shilling freeholders—of their votes, and this, too, without giving them any pecuniary or other compensation. My conviction as to the true nature of a Parliamentary vote led inevitably to the conclusion that the expediency, or what in such a matter is the same thing, the justice, of giving Parliamentary votes to English women depends on the answer to the inquiry, not whether a large number of English women, or English women generally, wish for votes, but whether the establishment of woman suffrage will be a benefit to England?

To this question I am unable to return an affirmative answer. I have become, therefore, of necessity an opponent of woman suffrage.

LETTER IV

OBJECTIONS TO WOMAN SUFFRAGE

MY DEAR C.,

One of our friends, to whom you have shown the preceding letters, tells me that I have done nothing except render a service to the suffragists by placing their side of the question at issue in so masterly and conclusive a manner as nearly to convince him that they have the best of the argument. If this is the case, it is certainly time for me to press upon you the objections which lie against any proposal for the admission of English women at the present day to the Parliamentary franchise.

FIRST OBJECTION.—Woman suffrage must ultimately, and probably in no long time, lead to adult suffrage, and will increase all the admitted defects of a so-called universal, or in strictness manhood, suffrage.

The close connection between woman suffrage and adult suffrage, though occasionally denied, is to my mind as clear as day. Every reason and every sentiment which supports the cry of 'Votes for women!' tells, at any rate with nine people out of ten, in favour of adult suffrage. Every citizen of the United Kingdom, for example, pays taxes; how can any man or woman who relies on the dogma that taxation involves representation deny that every citizen of the United Kingdom is entitled to a vote? No one, again who notes the development of popular government throughout the world can doubt the probability that manhood suffrage, which already exists in France, in Germany, in Switzerland, in the United States, and most of our self-governing colonies, will at no distant date be established in the United Kingdom.

Woman suffrage, then, I repeat, assuredly means, if not to-day, yet within a short time, the introduction of adult suffrage, and, independently of the new electors being women, must add to the defects of manhood suffrage. A huge constituency is, just because of its size, a bad electoral body. As the number of electors is increased, the power and the responsibility of each man are diminished. Authority passes into the hands of persons who possess neither the independence due to the possession of property nor the intelligence due to education. Our electorate now consists of some 7,000,000 men. Adult suffrage would create an electorate of, say roundly, at least 20,000,000 individuals, of whom considerably over 10,000,000 would be women. This mere increase in numbers is no slight evil. That more than half the new electors should be absolutely devoid of political training and traditions creates of itself a natural peril; but common sense forbids any fair reasoner to stop at this point. This uneducated majority of the electorate would be women. The very advocates of women suffrage make it part of their case that the civic virtues of women have never as yet been fully developed. Assuredly the most ordinary prudence warns us against admitting to a full share of sovereignty persons who have lacked all experience of its exercise.

Grant, for the sake of argument—though the concession is not justified by our knowledge of human nature—that possession of power invariably teaches its possessors to use it with justice. Still, it remains the height of folly to entrust the guidance of the State, at a time when the country is surrounded by perils of all kinds, to unskilled apprentices who have no experiences in piloting the commonwealth through pressing dangers. The most sagacious advocates of women's rights do not deny that each sex exhibits virtues which are found only in a less degree, or, it may be, not at all, in the other. We hear, as I have pointed out to you, much of the keenness of women's personal sympathies, of their capacity for passionate and often generous emotion; we are told that either nature or training, or both in combination, may lead women to see more readily than men the minute details on which depends the transaction of business. Yet it would not be unfair to say that, while women often perceive more readily than men the actual facts before them, they have a less firm grasp on principles; that a woman, in short, compared with a man of equal ability, may have a better eye for the circumstances around her, but has less of foresight. She has assuredly also less of tenacity.

From differences, upon some of which, in whatever form they ought to be expressed, no man has insisted more strongly than Mill, it follows that the participation of women in sovereign power must introduce into English politics a new and incalculable element which will not work wholly for good. An English democracy, in common with all other democracies, is too emotional. The strong point of popular government is assuredly neither foresight nor firmness of purpose. Now, every student of British history can see that more than once the statesmanlike foresight, and still more certainly the intense tenacity or obstinacy of purpose, which have marked the British aristocracy and the British middle classes, have been the salvation of the country. These qualities defended the independence of England against the despotism of Louis XIV., and, in a later age, against the attacks, first of revolutionary Jacobinism, and next of Napoleonic Imperialism. No one as yet knows whether our democracy can exhibit the unconquerable firmness which once and again has saved England from subjection to foreign power. Who can contemplate without dread a state of things under which democratic passion, intensified by feminine emotion, may deprive the country both of the calmness which foresees and the resolution which repels the onslaught of foreign enemies? There is, we venture to say, no man, and no woman either, who at moments of calm reflection can believe that at a time of threatened invasion, the safety of the country would be increased by the possibility that British policy might be determined by the votes and the influence of the fighting suffragists.

Second Objection.—The grant of votes to women settles nothing. If conceded tomorrow, it must be followed by the cry of 'Seats in Parliament for Women!' 'Places in the Cabinet for women!' 'Judgeships for women!' For the avowed aim of every suffragist, down from John Stuart Mill to Mrs. Pankhurst, is the complete political equality of men and women. The opening of the Parliamentary franchise to women is the encouragement, not the close, of a long agitation.

Third Objection.—The proposed concession of sovereignty to women is in one important respect opposed to every precedent to be found in the constitutional history of England. It has hitherto been with Englishmen a primary and essential condition of the admission of any body of persons to share in sovereign power that the class on whose behalf Parliamentary votes are demanded should be eager and ready to take up Parliamentary responsibilities. In 1832 nobody doubted that the middle classes, or in 1867 that the artisans, desired admission to the full powers of citizenship. But this primary condition of constitutional changes has in the present instance not been fulfilled. Many women, indeed, desire votes; a few women clamour passionately for votes. But a large number of English women protest against the introduction of women suffrage; they deprecate the concession to themselves of rights which they regard as intolerable burdens, and the concession to other women of powers which they believe the recipients cannot exercise with advantage to the country.

This protest must command attention; it reveals an exceptional state of opinion which must, so long as it exists, tell strongly against the introduction of women suffrage into Great Britain....

Nor is there the least lack of public spirit in the protest by freeborn English women against subjection to a sovereignty of women which they neither desire nor revere, and which they believe would be disastrous to the country. One point is past dispute. Every reason which supports the claim of women to votes supports also the right of women to be consulted on the question whether they shall be given votes or not. It is impossible to maintain that women have a right to determine every matter which concerns the interest of England or the British Empire, but have no right to be consulted whether it is well for England and for women themselves that the country should try the new experiment of woman suffrage. No serious reasoner will try to escape this conclusion by the idle retort that a woman who does not desire a vote need not use it. The very essence of her objection is that a vote imposes upon her a duty which may be an intolerable burden, and subjects her to the rule of a class—namely, women—which she deems incompetent to exercise sovereign power.

FOURTH OBJECTION.—The basis of all government is force, which means in the last resort physical strength. But predominant force lies in the hands of men. Now these facts, whether one likes them or not, tell in more ways than people often realize against giving a share in sovereignty to English women. The matter well deserves consideration.

There is, in the first place, a grave danger that the nominally sovereign body may not be in reality able to enforce the law of the land. In this country the legal or constitutional sovereign is Parliament—*i.e.*, the King, the House of Lords, and the House of Commons acting together; but the 'political sovereign' is the electorate, which, being wide enough to share and represent the feelings of the mass of the people, does in general obtain obedience to the laws which it approves. But the reason why laws made with the assent or acquiescence of the electorate are obeyed is that the electors constitute a power to which no single citizen and no class of citizens can offer permanent resistance.

That the employment of physical force is the basis of law and of sovereignty anyone may assure himself by observing the way in which law loses its authority whenever the support whence law derives its power is withdrawn. Why has the law of the land little better than a nominal existence in some parts of Ireland? The answer is that, for reasons of party convenience, the British Government will not in Ireland use the power placed in its hands by Parliament for the enforcement of the law. Let a fighting suffragist in her calmer moments ask herself why it is that her petulance or her cunning is allowed occasionally to interrupt the sittings of the House of Commons, and lower the dignity of Parliament? The answer assuredly is that habitual consideration for the weakness of women makes Englishman for the moment unwilling to use the force needed for the suppression of misbehaviour, which it may any day be necessary to punish with the severity due to serious crime. Meanwhile law is enfeebled unless supported by adequate force. Now the sovereignty of Parliament, or, in other words, the power of the electorate, might easily be imperilled if the majority of the electors were a class which, though more numerous, is weaker than a minority of the nation. But this is exactly the state of things which might arise under a system of adult suffrage, embracing not only men but women. Suppose an Act of Parliament passed which was opposed to the wishes of the decided majority of male electors, but carried practically by the votes of women. In such a case the ominous result would ensue that, whilst the political sovereign—that is, the majority of the electors—supported the law, the body possessed of predominant strength would be strongly opposed to the law. Rarely indeed could it happen that anything like the whole body of female electors would be opposed to anything like the whole body of male electors. It is not necessary for our argument to imagine so portentous a state of affairs. But it is certainly possible under a system of adult suffrage, and in a country where, as in England, women constitute the greater part of the population, that a body composed of a large majority of female electors acting together with a minority of male electors, might force upon the country a law or a policy opposed to the deliberate will and judgment of the majority of Englishmen. Is it certain that in such circumstances Englishmen would obey and enforce a law that punished as a crime conduct in which they in general held ought to be treated as an offence, not against law, but against morality? Can we, again, feel assured that Englishmen might not forbid the making of an ignominious peace, even though the majority of the electorate, consisting for the most part of women, held that the horrors of war must be terminated at all costs by a treaty which, in the eyes of Englishmen, sacrificed the dignity and imperilled the independence of the country?

Add to this a consideration to which little attention has been paid. The army, the police, governors of gaols, every person, in short, by whom the coercive power of the State is directly exercised, must, under any constitution whatever, be men. Whenever, therefore, a large majority of male electors is outvoted by a majority constituted mainly of women, the minority will command that sympathy of the officials by whose hands the State exercises its power. Woman suffrage, therefore, in common with every system which separates nominal sovereignty from the possession of irresistible power, involves the risk that the constitutional sovereign of the country may be rendered powerless by a class, in this instance the majority of the male electors, possessed of predominant physical force....

Full participation, further, not in civil rights, but in sovereignty, depends on capacity to perform all the duties of citizenship; and the defence of his country is at certain periods the main, as at all times it ought to be the essential, duty of a British citizen. But this duty women as a class have not the capacity to perform. No one dreams of the formation of an army of amazons, and, were such a thing a possibility, it would be a step back towards barbarism. Nor is it only in the defence of the country against foreign enemies that women are by nature incapable of taking part. The same is that case with the maintenance of law and order at home. Law is a command; its sanctions are ineffective without force to apply them; and women are unable to share in the forcible maintenance of the laws which, if they had the vote, they would share in making. It is no argument, in this connection, to say that many men are incapable, from age or weakness, of defending the State, but enjoy the franchise all the same. The aged have taken, or been able to take, their share in public duties; the weaklings are exceptions. Of women, the reverse is true. No one dreams that they ought to be constables, officers of police, governors of gaols, or coastguards. No woman is bound, as is a man, to attend the Justices in suppressing a riot upon a pain of fine and imprisonment. All this is no absolute ground for excluding women from a share in sovereign power, but it does afford a ground which is not palpably unjust for their exclusion from political authority.

Distinctions of rights founded upon sex have often given rise to injustice, but they have this in their favour—they rest upon a difference not created by social conventions or by human prejudice and selfishness, or by accidental circumstances (such as riches and poverty), which split society into classes, but upon the nature of things. This difference is as far-reaching as it is natural and immutable. It is one which, just because it is permanent and unchangeable, every honest thinker must take into account. That men are men and women are women is an obvious platitude; but it contains an undeniable truth which, like some other unwelcome facts, rhetoric, even when, as with Mill, it masquerades as strict reasoning cannot conceal. This is a matter worth insisting upon, for there is nothing which hinders the calm discussion of a political problem requiring for its solution something like judicial serenity so much as the difficulty, inseparable from all discussions involving reference to sex, of putting plain facts into plain language. The comparative weakness of women inevitably means loss of power. Nor can it be forgotten not only that women are physically, and probably mentally, weaker than men, but they are inevitably, as a class, burdened with the duties of the utmost national importance, and of an absorbing and exhausting nature, from which men are free. In any case, the close connection between government and force tells against the claim made on behalf of women to the possession of as much political authority as is conceded to men.

HAROLD OWEN

During debates about woman suffrage in Britain, probably the most exhaustive case for the anti-suffrage view was presented by the writer Harold Owen (1872–1930) in *Woman Adrift: A Statement of the Case against Suffragism* (1912). Owen wrote a number of other books in addition to *Woman Adrift*, including *Staffordshire Potter* (1901) and *Disloyalty: The Blight of Pacifism* (1918).

WOMAN ADRIFT (SELECTIONS)

Owen presents a lengthy series of arguments, both theoretical and practical. His primary concern is women's nature and natural sphere, which suffrage would contravene. The argument of proponents of suffrage that granting women the vote is simply an extension of the democratic principle that had led to enfranchising men neglects the crucial fact that this runs against the course of nature. For instance, granting women the vote would masculinize them, imparting to women "a new note of masculine strenuousness and assertiveness." Suffrage is only a single step on the road to equality in other spheres, including women's efforts to gain economic independence, which would run against nature's law and have untoward consequences. For instance, as an outgrowth of the racial attitudes of the time, Owen argues that women would be turned away from their maternal functions, leading to a decrease in the white race in comparison to colored races, for whom woman suffrage was many years away.

According to Owen, natural differences between men and women are "the essential facts of sex." Their different social positions do not stem from human enactments but from nature's order. Owen criticizes the main argument of Mill's *Subjection of Women* for overlooking the claims of nature. Mill argues from a false analogy between relationships between different social classes and between men and women. As the former were imposed by force, the same is true of the latter. But the analogy is false, according to Owen, because it omits the crucial fact that relationships between the sexes are due to natural rather than social forces.

WOMAN ADRIFT*

CHAPTER I.
THE SCOPE OF THE QUESTION.

The fundamental difference of opinion between those who support and those who oppose the extension of the franchise to women is that the former regard that step, with its implications, as one of progress, and the latter look upon it as at best a dangerous experiment and at worst positive retrogression. In one sense of the word—the merely locomotive sense—the supporters are right. To move from any given point to a point beyond is undoubtedly to progress, in the sense of going forward. If A and B are on a cliff, and A remains where he finds himself, fifteen yards from the edge, but B progresses fifteen yards and a bit further than the unprogressive A, he is certainly going forward and leaving A behind. But when B is tumbling over the precipice he might just have time to reflect before he touched bottom that he had not progressed in the beneficent sense of that word.

The modern movement among women has reached a stage when I venture to believe it threatens to become a progression of very much the same kind, and it will be the effort of this book to establish that truth. But to begin with it is not necessary to make that full contention. A preliminary point to be made clear is that, in the development of human political and social institutions, the same law of a false progress may hold good as in the physical world—when illustrated by an example, such as that which I have just given, showing that safety lies in refraining from going forward.

THE "SHORT-CUT" TO SAVE THINKING.

There can, I think, be no denial of the statement that a large proportion of those men who support Women Suffrage do so, not on the particular

*Selections from *Woman Adrift* by Harold Owen are reprinted with permission from J.M. Dent and Sons, Ltd.

ground that they believe the extension, in and of itself, to be desirable, or because they have sufficient enthusiasm for it to overcome their misgivings, but because they regard it as part of a general political progress. To satisfy their minds on this ground they do not need to carry them beyond the Reform Bill of 1832. Then the lower middle classes were enfranchised; in 1867 and 1884 the Franchise was further extended; Manhood Suffrage is now almost as good as an accomplished fact; and the extension of the franchise to women thus seems to them to be merely the completion of the movement of political enfranchisement and the last stage in the realization of a perfect democracy—or, I should say, of a perfect democratic form of government.

This is a short cut to an approval of the creed, and undoubtedly accounts for the majority of conversions among men. But this view obviously ignores altogether the consideration that permeates the entire case against the creed—the consideration that man and woman are as different in their social functions as they are in their physical structure. The short cut which allows for no foot to be put upon this widely disputed territory of sexual difference is clearly an entirely untrustworthy path to take. It is as though two persons, debating whether they should each take part in a walk to Brighton, took notice only of the fact that other men had performed the same pedestrian feat, and ignored altogether their own particular and relative fitness for the ordeal—their age, training and physical efficiency. And to the man who does not allow himself to think of what is involved in the assertion that woman is entitled to the franchise because man has secured it, that short-cut is the obvious and easy way to a whole-hearted support of the case....

THE "DEMOCRATIC" ARGUMENT

But the argument that the extension of political power to women is now the next step in the march of democratic progress has to be met. It might be met in one direct way (if a man could now be found with the courage of anti-democratic sentiments) by denying the necessary virtue of democratic forms of government at all. But this is not an age in which such a denial could be profitably made in controversy, for the man who made it would put himself out of court. An oblique answer, however, might be made by the man who, though faithful to the democratic principles of government so far as his experience of its operation enabled him to approve of it, nevertheless put forward this reservation: that a democratic principle which involved the admission, and the eventual predominance, of woman in the control of the State would be a worse evil than a form of government which fell short of the democratic principle. Or, to put it in another way: If the democratic principle, carried to its logical human conclusion, is to land us into a state of society which, whether it be on a democratic basis or not, would not be a good state of society, then the democratic principle had better not be carried to its logical conclusion....

MAN AND THE RACE.

Of course, it is really a question of Free Will and Predestination all over again, but in the secular sphere. Is it given to man in the political community to have the same responsibility of choice in his political actions as is given him as an individual? We know that the individual man may make false steps that ruin his individual career or character. Is it not possible that political man may take false steps that will injure and even ruin his race?

I see no reason to doubt the possibility; or to doubt that the false step may be taken even in the name of progress. It is in fact much more likely that such a step would be taken from good motives united to bad judgment than in any other way. Indeed, one cannot imagine man, considered as society, hastening the doom or decay of the race by any conscious and deliberate intention. But the question is whether he may have it in his power to affect adversely the course of the human race by adopting some rash and heedless experiment such as is involved in changing the position of woman by giving her political power and encouraging her to gain economic independence and to take an equal part with him, on equal terms, in the "struggle for life."

One ultimate consequence of this "liberation," would be the evolution of another type of woman than that of to-day. For it is impossible to suppose that woman is going to follow man's pursuits and take her part in the rough and tumble of the world—not only the world of politics, as we shall see—without approximating herself to his characteristics. Even to-day there is a new note of masculine strenuousness and assertiveness in woman as the result of her freer movement in the world, and it is only reasonable to suppose that after, say, three centuries of "equality" with man she would have developed masculine traits up to the point where Nature bars the way by the final and essential fact of sex. And side by side with this approximation to masculine characteristics there would be a corresponding decline of those traits which now we speak of as "womanly." We may go even further, and say that it is highly probable that there would be a corresponding variation in the characteristics of man. A race of men born of several generations of mothers competing with men and each other in the struggle for life (which even an optimist may expect to be still in progress three hundred years hence) and a race of men, moreover, who are no longer the protectors of women, but their rivals and "equals," is not likely to be a race of men that has altered for the better, judged by our standard of the qualities that constitute masculinity. We may therefore arrive at the production of a race of men and women who are utterly unlike the men and women of our conception and experience to-day.

Several answers may be made to this exercise in forecasting the possibilities of a modification of men and women by the operation of all that is implied in Woman Suffrage and that lies beyond it. There is, first, that of the man who regards the modern woman's movement as a "superficial" issue, a mere matter of franchise; of marking a ballot paper; of reading the political leaders in the newspapers; of making occasional speeches; and of joining one or two of the thousand and one societies and leagues that will spring into existence, as the first organised step in the general and political regeneration of society that is to follow woman's advent into the political sphere. But that answer need not detain us. The mind that does not grasp the possibilities of the forces that would be liberated by a wholesale change in the status of woman is too shallow to be considered—though it is really a dangerous type of mind—in any serious argument....

THE LONG VIEW...

Economic independence is as much the objective of the movement as political equality and power. But it is certain that the economic independence, and still more the struggle to attain it, will diminish enormously both the opportunities and capacity for the exercise of woman's maternal functions and duties. Let us assume that the woman's movement in England makes headway and succeeds in all its aims. Inspired by such an example, feminism in other countries will assert itself to the same degree, and it will only be a question of time for the movement to prevail among all the white races, that is amongst the most progressive and civilised portion of mankind. The result of this widespread independence of woman would be, with absolute certainty, the numerical decrease of the white races; and this would coincide with the increasing efficiency of coloured races all over the world, brought about by the adoption of the industrial and scientific methods of the white man. These methods, however, are more easily adopted and put into practice than the new ethical and political principles of the white races, and many generations of coloured people would live and die before any change took place in their own social and racial characteristics and customs. To copy the design of a battleship or an aeroplane is an easier thing than to copy either the political genius or the social institutions of another race; and material efficiency is more easily imitable than moral or political principles. Hence it might well be that just when the white races were numerically declining rapidly, through the operation of the white woman's economic independence, the coloured races were gaining a predominant position on the strength of the white man's—and not the white woman's—inventive and mechanical genius....

CHAPTER IV.
"AS IT WAS IN THE BEGINNING."

A chapter dealing with some of the essential differences between men and women is a convenient place for uttering a certain warning and a certain protest. The protest is against the indignation which plain language concerning the sexes incites among Suffragists. The warning is that if it be necessary to use plain language about the essential facts of sex, plain language must be used. It is indeed an odd thing that although women are now the most audacious breakers of convention, and although women novelists are the greatest offenders in the production of erotic fiction, a man is rebuked for calling attention to some of the plain facts about the phenomenon of sex even in a serious discussion by which they themselves have raised the whole question of the difference between one sex and another. I have known cases in which men, dealing straightforwardly and reverently with some of the fundamental truths about the sexes, have been rebuked by Suffragists for being "coarse-minded." It may or may not have been that the modesty of the protestants was shocked. But what chiefly concerned them was that it is an extremely easy thing to cover a man with ignominy by pretending or asserting that he has shocked sensitive female ears, and so that prudery was, in some cases coming within my own knowledge, merely a characteristically mean way of taking advantage of one aspect of that difference in sex which they deny....

Nature's Fiat.

The simple truth is that woman started the race (if the idea of rivalry is to be allowed at all) horribly handicapped by the fact that Nature assigned to her the function of giving birth to children; and Nature, moreover, inconsiderately ordained that the human gestatory period should be nine months—probably a very senseless arrangement, but there it is—and so the race could only be perpetuated by woman being *hors de combat*, so far as any violent physical struggle for life was concerned, for a considerable portion of each year during the effective use of her fecund period— that is to say , during the most active period of her life. Moreover, Nature ordained that even when a woman was not engaged in the work of perpetuating the race, she should be subject to physical phenomena during those same years, which amounted to physical disabilities when considered in relation to man's freedom from anything of the kind, and so impaired her physical efficiency compared with his. These inalienable features of her sex may not be desirable, but as they are there, and are naturally incidental to the perpetuation of the race, and exist even apart from it, they must be accepted.

MAN THE WORKER.

But man was placed under no such disabilities. The act which put woman out of the combat for at least three months of the year did not lay him under any such prolonged physical disability. If it had done, how would men and women have lived, seeing that there is no human neuter to look after them? And so Nature herself, and not man, doomed woman to an unequal physical relation with man, and it is an inequality from which she cannot escape, except to some extent by the evasion of Nature's intention concerning her, in avoiding maternity altogether—which is the direction in which the extremer doctrines of modern feminism are tending. But even by that deliberate evasion of her duty—an evasion which contracts woman, as will shortly be shown, out of the only sphere in which she is biologically or socially essential— she cannot wholly escape from the ban of physical inferiority. For woman's physical structure, confirmed by the ages during which she has discharged her maternal duties as a matter of course, has become unsuited to such violent physical exertion as a man can sustain, and Nature has decreed that even if she avoids maternity, her physical constitution is subject to ravages and changes which have no physiological counterpart in man.

And so, although we know really nothing historically of our very earliest ancestors, we know that even their relations to each other, as primitive man and woman, must have been determined for them. The first woman on earth was no doubt a stalwart, sinewy, hairy and uncouth creature—very different from the refined product of our civilisation and of the long process of female differentiation in social function which began even then. But we can see how the differentiation must have begun. When the first man discovered that his mate was with child, he saw that he was born into a scheme of things in which he would have to do the hardest work, and that his mate would have to remain behind in whatever was their dwelling whilst he adventured forth in quest of their common elemental wants; or, if they were nomads, that he would have to bear the heavier burdens and shield his mate from whatever physical fatigue he could spare her. One cannot suppose that the primitive animalistic man carried his tenderness and care to the same pitch as that which he exhibits to-day, but he must have learnt the elements of a crude chivalry even then, or the race would hardly have got a start at all. And the arrival of the offspring , and then its successors, would naturally confirm her domestic status. The offspring had to be nursed and nurtured during its helpless years (and the human child takes longer than any other young animal to arrive at maturity), the slain birds and animals brought home by man had to be prepared for food and their skins prepared for clothing; and so without any inherited experience or traditional knowledge, the first man and the first woman found their spheres delimited for them—mapped out by Nature herself. In short, the beginning of the difference between the social functions of man and woman *was* in the beginning.

All this, of course (and a little more to follow), is very elementary truth, but the point is that it *is* the truth. And though it is elementary it is all-important. Or rather, because it is elementary it is all-important. The elemental facts are what should guide us in dealing with so general and broad and deep a question as that of sex, the prime and elemental facts of which will always remain defiantly true. And so it is more important that we should consider the inalienable, coherent, and elemental facts of sex than such abnormal or accidental modifications of them as may be furnished here and there by ancient or modern examples.

Having now seen how and when woman's social relation to man was determined; how and when the natural spheres of man and woman were delimited; and why it comes about that woman is man's physical inferior, and at a disadvantage with man in confronting the external world, we may now begin to consider whither this physical inferiority of woman has led, and how far it governs her aptitude, not only as a human being in her personal and domestic relations with man, but in her relation to all those activities which build up and maintain the State.

CHAPTER V
THE FALSE ANALOGY.

Mill's work is extremely logical—*but he laid his own foundations.* He saw in the relations between man and woman only an extension and a survival of other forms of tyranny or the denial of liberty. Looking back upon history, he saw that all the struggles of men, except those made against Nature herself, were struggles of one class against the bondage in which another class held them—of slaves against their owners, of the feudal serf against the over-lord, of the pleb against the patrician, of nobles against kings, and the common people against everybody but themselves. And in considering the political development of nations, he saw that it had depended and arisen from the emancipation of one class after another, and the overthrowing of one social dominion after another. And then looking at these things, he saw in the political unenfranchisement of women the old tyranny of class, and almost the last remaining subjection of one class to another, the last denial of political freedom: "By degrees the slavery of the male sex has been at length abolished, and that of the female sex has been gradually changed to a milder dependence. But this dependence ... is the primitive state of slavery lasting on.... It has not lost the taint of its brutal origin."

And so we come to the false analogy which, I venture to think, entirely vitiates Mill's work. The analogy is between men and women (considered as masters and slaves) and the artificial divisions among mankind in which one class has been held in subjection by another. But Mill was too good a logician to overlook the weakness—a weakness at the very core of his argument. He recognised that it might be detected, then met it obliquely, and then proceeded on his way as though he had disposed of the objection that the analogy was false. And he performed this feat partly by the use he made of the word "natural," using it in two senses, and then confusing the whole point by the ambiguity of the word. He recognises the objection to the falseness of the analogy in these words, taken from the earliest pages of the book:

> "Some will object that comparison cannot fairly be made between the government of the male sex and the forms of unjust power which I have adduced in illustration of it, since these are arbitrary, and the effect of mere usurpation, while it, on the contrary, is natural. But was there ever a domination which did not appear natural to those who possessed it?"

Now, that evades the point altogether. Recognising the weakness of the comparison, he meets it by what is really a juggle on the word "natural" (though the juggle comes out more clearly in a long passage in continuance of that which I have quoted). But those who "object to the comparison" are still right, for the simple reason that whatever confusion other ages and peoples may have made in the use of the word "natural," the subjections of the classes he has instanced *are* "arbitrary" and *are* the effect of "mere usurpation," while "on the contrary" the division between men and women has no counterpart whatever in the artificial and arbitrary and *mutable* divisions between different classes of men. Mill does get round the objection to his comparison, but he gets round it by making a wide detour and ignoring the really natural division of the sexes, and by assuming the difference between them—and consequently the difference in their political status—to be no more "natural" than the division between the different classes of men was rightly or wrongly supposed by them to be. The difference between a peer and a commoner is *not* natural—the difference between a peer and a peeress *is* natural.

And so we can leave out of account altogether the question of whether dead and gone people were right or wrong in their idea of what was natural, or whether Mill himself used the term in an ambiguous or equivocal sense. But taking things as they are and as we ourselves interpret them, we say that whilst the gulf between serfs and seigneurs may have appeared "natural" to them whereas it was only customary, the gulf between men and women *is* natural in the true and proper sense of the word, as meaning that it belongs inherently to created beings. So it is not because we defend the subjection of women as "natural" that we can say his analogy is false, but we say that his analogy is false because it is made between two totally different entities—made, that is to say, between (1) serfs and seigneurs, whose differences *are* arbitrary, and "natural" only in the loose sense of the word, and (2) men and women, whose differences are not arbitrary at all, but are *natural* in the right and proper sense of the word.

And the false analogy is constantly appearing; as for instance, in the following passage: "The social subordination of women thus stands out an isolated fact in modern institutions.... This entire discrepancy between the social fact and all those which accompany it ... should at least suffice to make this, like the choice between republicanism and royalty, a balanced question." But there is no choice between being a man and being a woman. Men and women, moreover, may exist in the same state, but republicanism and royalty cannot. Men and women together make the human race, but republicanism and royalty together make nothing—except, perhaps, the happy compromise of our own constitutional monarchy. But they are in their essence opposed things, and mutually exclusive, and men and women are complementary things, mutually interdependent.

THE UNIQUENESS OF THE HUMAN SEX.

But if you regard women as one class and men as another, each struggling against the other in the political and social world, with diverging interests and not common interests, rivals and competitors and equals in the struggle for life, interchangeable parts in the social mechanism, so that a woman may become a man just as easily as a monarchy can become a republic, or a serf become a freeman, then it is not a difficult task in logic to establish the case that there should be, in justice, the same precise and actual equality between the two "classes" of men and women as had been obtained in the other classes. But men and women are *not* classes—they are sexes, the two halves of a whole, and the logic that might be invincible when applied to class breaks down altogether when you apply it to sex, for there is no analogy possible between them. The relations between man and woman are not political or even social—they are personal in the highest degree and in a kind that exists in no other relation of life whatever....

A RIVAL ANALOGY.

And it is just because Mill ignored that entirely fundamental fact of the uniqueness of the thing he compares with all sorts of unlike things, that his magnificent logic and his sometimes beautiful but often pedantic English and his wonderful learning, and his passion for justice for justice's sake, are all useless. If you compare man with aristocracy, and woman with democracy, or reverse the process, you can so something of what Mill did—making the proper allowance for differences in talents. But you will have been arguing vainly. How can the relations between woman and man be adjusted on any lines or principles applicable to any other sphere or relation of life? How can a man argue from the relations between master and slave or king and subject what principle of conduct should govern his relations to a being who fills such a place in his life as woman does—to a being who fills the dreams of his youth, and inspires his manhood, and shares his bed, and at whose side he wishes to lie when both come to their eternal sleep?—or who, on the other hand, fills his life with the torments of the damned because she drinks like a fish and pawns his clothes?

We can see clearly enough why and where Mill's analogy was false if we only consider that he omitted one other and very important and human relationship, that of employer and employed. You cannot say that the relations of employer and employed are analogous to those of a government and the governed, or are to be decided by any analogies drawn from the political relations of men. For a totally different set of considerations arises when you are dealing with employers in relation to employed than when you are dealing with the relation of a man to the State, or of a slave to his owner. We should think it absurd to say that because a monarchical State was transformed by the people into a republic that therefore an industry should be transformed by the employed into a cooperative society. It might or might not be the right thing to do, but the republic and monarchy would have nothing to do with it. But if we can see the falseness of the analogy there, how much greater is the fallacy in deciding that the relations between man and woman should be guided by any evidence or experience drawn from the political warfare or changes made in the artificially distinguished classes of men, or the industrial relations of employers and employed? It may be right or wrong that there should be no employed or employers at all—it may be right or wrong that the relations between employers and employed should be so transformed that the employed should become the employers, or something in between, and neither the one thing nor the other. But you cannot talk of man and woman in terms of government and people, class and class, slave and slave-owner, any more than of employer and employed. The employer may become an employee, and the employed employ him; or the serf may become a seigneur, or a plebian become a patrician and buy his former patron up. But a woman cannot become a man, and the sexes cannot so transform themselves that they become neither the one thing nor the other—at any rate one sincerely hopes not, though we shall see later that something like that is going to be attempted. And so when analogies are drawn from any source whatever to fix the relations between man and woman, they must be false analogies; and any logic or noble pleading based upon a false analogy must lead to a false conclusion. And that is exactly what Mill's "Subjection of Women" leads to. It is vitiated at its very source by an imperfect and false notion of what men and women really are, and it is a masterpiece of self delusion.

CONCLUSION

A fter attaining the vote, women continued to struggle for equal treatment under the law. With achievement of its central goal, the women's movement became less focused on a single animating principle. Its agenda became more diffuse, as suggested by the evolution of the National American Woman Suffrage Association into the League of Women Voters, in 1920.

The performance of women in the public sphere has largely refuted old claims about their inability to assume a place in society alongside men. Women have participated in democratic politics much as men have. The vote did not irreparably damage women's nature or bring on the catastrophic consequences opponents of suffrage had forecast. As Elizabeth Cady Stanton predicted, woman suffrage was a first step. Since the ratification of the Nineteenth Amendment, women have progressed from voting to being elected to political office. Although no woman has been elected to a national political office in the United States, Margaret Thatcher became Prime Minister of Great Britain in 1979 and was a dominant political figure through the 1980s. In the United States, women have been elected governors, and to the House of Representatives and United States Senate. In 1984, Geraldine Ferraro received the nomination for Vice-President from one of the major American political parties. Women have attained seats on the Supreme Court, beginning with Sandra Day O'Connor in 1981, and high Cabinet positions, most notably when Madeline Albright became Secretary of State.

On the other hand, women's participation in politics has not dramatically changed the political system. There is room for disagreement about specific aspects of political evolution, but clearly, female political leaders have shown themselves to have the same strengths and shortcomings as their male counterparts. They are as politically adroit, as nationalistic, as careerist. Mrs. Thatcher is a case in point, as are the late Indira Gandhi in India, and the late Golda Meir in Israel.

In certain ways, women have behaved in political affairs somewhat differently from men. Notably, in the United States, they have supported the Democratic Party more strongly than men. For instance, in the elections of 1996, Bill Clinton received the support of 59.7 percent of female voters, as compared to 45.2 percent of males.[1] 45.9 percent of males voted for Bob Dole, but only 34 percent of females did. In Congressional races, 51.6 percent of women voted for Democratic candidates for the House of Representatives and 57.6 percent for Democratic candidates for the Senate. 42.5 percent of men supported Democratic House candidates and 43.4 percent Democratic Senate candidates. But it is unlikely that this reflects a demonstrably "feminine" nature. More important is the fact that the Democrats are perceived as supporting issues—social welfare and education policies, family and medical leave, and so forth—that are of deep concern to many women.

In areas outside the political sphere, women have been approaching parity with men. Consider, for instance, women's educational opportunities. As noted in the Introduction, before Oberlin College began admitting women, in 1834, no college in the United States did so. This situation changed markedly in subsequent decades. Mt. Holyoke College, the oldest higher education institution for women, was founded in 1836 as a "female seminary" before evolving into one of the leading colleges in the United States. After the Civil War, a number of celebrated colleges for women opened. These include Vassar in 1865, Wellesley in 1870, and Smith in 1871. Radcliffe College was founded in 1875, Bryn Mawr in 1885, and Barnard in 1889. Formerly male colleges, including Cornell and Wesleyan, began admitting women soon after the Civil War. The movement toward coeducation has continued until recent times. Both Yale and Princeton Universities began admitting women in 1969. The formerly all-male University of Virginia began admitting women in 1972 after a Federal District Court found against its single-sex policy. At the present time, women have largely, though not entirely, closed the gap with men in terms of educational opportunities. In 1995, similar percentages of men and women had completed high school (81.7 percent and 81.6 percent , respectively), but 26 percent of men had completed college, as compared to 20.2 percent of women. This is a significant percentage gain for women since 1960, when 9.7 percent of men and 5.8 percent of women had completed college.[2]

Principles guaranteeing women equal educational opportunities are firmly established in American law. In the important 1982 Supreme Court case *Mississippi University for Women* v. *Hogan,* a number of important principles were affirmed.[3] This case is particularly interesting for our purposes because it concerned the 1974 attempt by a man, Joe Hogan, to gain entrance to the formerly all-female Mississippi University for Women, to attain a degree in nursing. In part, the University's Charter had read:

> The purpose and aim of the Mississippi State College for Women is the moral and intellectual advancement of the girls of the state by the maintenance of a first-class institution for their education in the arts and sciences, for their training in normal school methods and kindergarten, for their instruction in bookkeeping, photography, stenography, telegraphy, and typewriting, and in designing, drawing, engraving, and painting, and their industrial application, and for their instruction in fancy, general and practical needlework, and in such other industrial branches as experience, from time to time, shall suggest as necessary or proper to fit them for the practical affairs of life.

The Court responded favorably to Hogan's suit, arguing that people of one sex could not be excluded from public educational institutions without strong justification. Writing for the majority, Justice Sandra Day O'Connor stated that the fact that, in this case, exclusionary policies were directed against males rather than females did not affect this requirement. Moreover, determinations in this regard "must be applied free of fixed notions concerning the roles and abilities of males and females." Justice O'Connor continued:

> Care must be taken in ascertaining whether the statutory objective itself reflects archaic and stereotypic notions. Thus, if the statutory objective is to exclude or "protect" members of one gender because they are presumed to suffer from an inherent handicap or to be innately inferior, the objective itself is illegitimate.

Careful analysis of the reasons for excluding members of one sex is necessary to ensure that public policy is "determined through reasoned analysis rather than through the mechanical application of traditional, often inaccurate, assumptions about the proper roles of men and women."

Similar arguments were presented by the second woman appointed to the Court, Ruth Bader Ginsburg, in the 1996 case, *United States* v. *Virginia et al.*[4] The decision in this case struck down the single-sex policy at Virginia Military Institute, a state-supported military school. Writing for the majority, Justice Ginsburg affirmed what has become a fundamental principle of

American law: "Neither federal nor state government acts compatibly with equal protection when a law or official policy denies to women, simply because they are women, full citizenship" or equal ability to achieve and contribute to society, "based on their individual talents and capacities."

Although in many areas of the law traditional notions of women's nature and limited potential have been largely overcome, in other areas strong disagreements continue. Consider debates about abortion rights, one of the most contentious issues in contemporary American politics. Recent scholars have argued that the debate about abortion is largely waged between proponents of competing world views, between competing notions of what people see as "sacred and important."[5] Competing conceptions of women's nature are central to these views. For prochoice activists, control over abortion symbolizes a women's control over her reproductive life, which in turn signals "that a women is no longer on unequal biological footing with a man; ... and thus can achieve the same level of social and economic autonomy and power as a man." For prolife activists, in contrast, "abortion symbolizes an affront to the high and holy calling of motherhood. Since only women can have children, motherhood is viewed as a responsibility dictated by nature for the perpetuation of the human race."[6]

According to Kristin Luker, an important recent scholar, representative statements of the prolife view contain the following assessments of women's nature:[7]

[Men and women] were created differently and we're meant to complement each other, and when you get away from our [proper] roles as such, you start obscuring them.

I think I like men enough to know that men still want women to be a little bit feminine and all the rest of it, and I think [pro-choice] people have helped destroy that, I think they've made women into something like the same as men, and we're not. I think we're totally different. I don't think that means that we can't do some jobs they do, but I think we're totally different.

Luker describes the views put forth by opposing camps in the abortion debate as follows:[8]

[W]hereas pro-life people believe that men and women are inherently different and therefore have different "natural" roles in life, prochoice people believe that men and women are substantially equal, by which they mean substantially similar. As a result, they see women's reproductive and family roles not as a "natural" niche but as potential barriers to full equality.

In spheres outside woman suffrage and abortion, claims concerning women's essential nature were long used to restrict women's rights. Arguments like those traced throughout this volume were used to prevent women's entry into important economic spheres. In 1873, the United States Supreme Court upheld a decision by the Illinois Supreme Court which had supported state law denying women the right to practice law. In part, the Illinois Court argued as follows:[9]

[T]he civil law, as well as nature herself, has always recognized a wide difference in the respective spheres and destinies of man and woman. Man is, or should be, woman's protector and defender. The natural and proper timidity and delicacy which belongs to the female sex evidently unfits it for many of the occupations of civil life. The constitution of the family organization, which is founded in the divine ordinance, as well as in the nature of things, indicates the domestic sphere as that which properly belongs to the domain and functions of womanhood. The harmony, not to say identity, of interest and views which belong, or should belong, to the family institution is repugnant to the idea of a woman adopting a distinct and independent career from that of her husband. So firmly fixed was this sentiment in the founders of the common law that it became a maxim of that system of jurisprudence that a woman had no legal existence separate from her husband, who was regarded as her head and representative in the social state....

Needless to say, with large-scale changes throughout society, women have achieved opportunities long denied them, including of course, the right to practice law. According to U.S. Census data, in 1983, 15.3 percent of lawyers in the United States, were women. By 1995, this figure had risen sharply to 26.2 percent .[10] In other fields as well, women continue to lag behind men, although the gap is narrowing. In 1983, 20.5 percent of natural scientists were women; in 1995 the figure was 27.3 percent . In 1983, 36.3 percent of college and university teachers were women; in 1995, this figure had risen to 45.2 percent . But in many fields traditionally dominated by women, there has been little change. In 1983, 83.3 percent of elementary school teachers were women; in 1995, this figure had actually increased to 84.1 percent. In 1983, 85.8 percent of registered nurses were women; this percentage was unchanged in 1995.

Even with the progress that has occurred in many fields, women still lag behind men in important respects. For instance, in 1994, average annual earnings for a man were $41,118, as compared to $27,162 for a woman.[11]

Attempts to amend the United States Constitution to include an Equal Rights Amendment (ERA) have been unsuccessful for more than 75 years. In 1923, the National Women's Party, the militant breakaway wing of the

National American Woman Suffrage Association, held a convention at Seneca Falls. There Alice Paul, leader of the party, presented a draft of the Equal Rights Amendment to the membership, and it was unanimously accepted. The amendment read:[12]

> Men and Women shall have equal rights throughout the United States and every place subject to its jurisdiction.

The amendment was first introduced in both the Senate and the House of Representatives in 1923. It failed to achieve congressional approval in 1923 and in every succeeding term until 1972, when both houses finally approved it. However, the ERA was not subsequently ratified by three-fourths of the states. Although supporters of the ERA (especially the National Organization of Women) lobbied state legislatures for ten years, in 1982 they were forced to admit defeat.

The mixed results of the struggle on this front illustrate the fact that, at the present time, the struggle for women's rights continues.

NOTES

1. These and the following figures are from 1996 National Election Studies, conducted by the Center for Political Studies at the University of Michigan. The figures for the presidential election do not add up to 100% because of the campaign of Ross Perot, who was supported by 8.9% of males and 6.3% of females.
2. U.S. Department of Commerce, *Statistical Abstract of the United States* (Washington, D.C., 1996), Table 242.
3. *Mississippi University for Women* v. *Hogan*, 458 U.S. 718 (1982), from which all quotations in this paragraph are drawn.
4. *United States* v. *Virginia et al.*, 518 U.S. 515 (1996).
5. K. Luker, *Abortion and the Politics of Motherhood* (Berkeley, 1984), p. 7.
6. J. Hunter, *Before the Shooting Begins* (New York, 1994), p. 15.
7. Luker, *Abortion*, pp. 160, 162 (brackets in Luker).
8. Ibid., pp. 175–76.
9. *Bradwell* v. *State of Illinois*, 83 US 130 (1873).
10. Figures in this paragraph from 1996 *Statistical Abstract of the United States*, Table 637.
11. Ibid., Table 728.
12. W. Langley and V. Fox, eds., *Women's Rights in the United States: A Documentary History* (Westport, Conn., 1994), p. 236.

SOURCES

For reasons of space, we have removed footnotes from all selections.

A Member of the Women's Liberal Federation. "A Reply to Mr. Gladstone's Letter on Woman Suffrage." London: R. Forder, 1892.

"An Appeal against Female Suffrage." *The Nineteenth Century,* Vol. 148 (June 1889), pp. 781–5.

Addams, Jane. "Why Women Should Vote." *Ladies' Home Journal,* Vol. 27 (January 1910), pp. 21–2.

Anthony, Susan B. Trial of Susan B. Anthony. In I. H. Harper, *The Life and Work of Susan B. Anthony,* Vol I. Indianapolis, Ind.: Hollenbeck Press, 1898, pp. 437–441.

———. "Woman Wants Bread, Not the Ballot!" In I. H. Harper, *The Life and Work of Susan B. Anthony,* Vol I. Indianapolis, Ind.: Hollenbeck Press, 1898, pp. 996–1003.

Blackwell, Henry. "A Solution of the Southern Question." *Woman's Journal,* Vol. 21, No. 39 (September 27, 1890), pp. 305–6.

Bodichon, Barbara. "Reasons for and against the Enfranchisement of Women." London: National Society for Women's Suffrage, 1872.

Bushnell, Horace. *Women's Suffrage: The Reform against Nature.* New York: C. Scribner and Company, 1869.

Catt, Carrie Chapman. "Need for Organization Rather Than Education." In HWS, IV, 248–9.

————. "Speech to Iowa Convention, 1894." *Woman's Journal,* Vol. 25, No. 50 (Dec. 15, 1894), p. 394.

————. "A League of Women Voters." In *HWS,* V, p. 684.

Cleveland, Grover. "Would Woman Suffrage Be Unwise?" *Ladies' Home Journal,* Vol. 22 (October, 1905), pp. 7–8

Declaration of Sentiments and Resolutions, Seneca Falls, N.Y., 1848. In *HWS,* I, pp. 70–73.

Dicey, Albert V. *Letters to a Friend on Votes for Women.* London: J. Murray, 1909.

Douglass, Frederick. Editorial in *The North Star.* In *HWS,* I, p. 74.

Fawcett, Millicent. "A Reply to the Letter of Mr. Samuel Smith, M.P., on Women's Suffrage." Westminster, 1892.

Fordyce, James. *Sermons to Young Women,* 6th ed. Dublin: J. Williams, 1767.

Gilman, Charlotte Perkins. "The Ballot as an Improver of Motherhood." In *HWS,* IV, pp. 266–67

Gladstone, William Ewart. "Female Suffrage: A letter to Samuel Smith [dated April 11, 1892, on the bill extending the parliamentary suffrage to women]. London: J. Murray, 1892.

Gregory, John. *A Father's Legacy to His Daughters.* 1774; rpt. London: Pickering & Chotto, 1996.

Grimké, Angelina. *Letters to Catherine E. Beecher in Reply to an Essay on Slavery and Abolitionism. Addressed to A.E. Grimké.* Boston: I. Knapp, 1838.

Grimké, Sarah. *Letters on the Equality of the Sexes and the Condition of Woman. Addressed to Mary S. Parker, President of the Boston Female Anti-slavery Society.* Boston: I. Knapp, 1838.

Kearney, Belle. "The South and Woman Suffrage." *Woman's Journal,* Vol. 34, No. 14 (April 4, 1903), pp. 106–7.

Macaulay, Thomas. "Mill on Government." In *The Complete Works of Lord Macaulay,* 12 vols. London: Longmans Green & Co., 1898. Vol. 7, pp. 327–71.

Meyer, Annie Nathan. "Woman's Assumption of Sex Superiority." *North American Review,* Vol. 128 (January 1904), pp. 103–9.

Mill, James. "Essay on Government." In *Essays on Government, Jurisprudence [Etc.].* London: J. Innes, 1825; rpt. 1828.

Mill, John Stuart. "Suffrage for Women." New York: National-American Woman Suffrage Association, 1895.

————. *The Subjection of Women.* New York: National-American Woman Suffrage Association, 1895.

Owen, Harold. *Woman Adrift: A Statement of the Case against Suffragism.* New York: E. P. Dutton, 1912.

Pankhurst, Emmeline. *My Own Story.* New York: Hearst's International Library Co., 1914.

Parkman, Francis. "Some of the Reasons against Woman Suffrage." New York, 1896[?].

Rousseau, Jean-Jacques. *Emile.* Barbara Foxley, trans. London: Dent, 1948.

Stanton, Elizabeth Cady. "The Solitude of Self." In *HWS*, IV, pp. 189–91.

———. "Arguments in Favor of a Sixteenth Amendment." In *HWS*, II, pp. 348–55.

——— and others. Introduction. In *The Woman's Bible*, Two Parts. New York: European Publishing Co., 1895, 1898.

Stanton, Elizabeth Cady, et al., eds. *History of Woman Suffrage*, 6 vols. (New York and Rochester, 1881–1922). Abbreviated *HWS*.

Taylor, Harriet. "Enfranchisement of Women." Syracuse, N.Y., 1853.

Truth, Sojourner. "Aint I a Woman." In *HWS*, I, pp. 115–7.

———. "Keep the Thing Going While Things Are Stirring." In *HWS*, I, pp. 193–4.

Wollstonecraft, Mary. *A Vindication of the Rights of Women*, new ed., with an introduction by Mrs. Henry Fawcett. New York: Humboldt Publishing Co., 1891.

"Women's Suffrage: A Reply." *Fortnightly Review* (July 1889), pp. 123–31.

Woodhull, Victoria. "Address before Judiciary Committee of U.S. House of Representatives." In *HWS*, II, pp. 444–8.

INDEX